Insist That They Love You

Insist That They Love You

Craig Rodwell and the Fight for Gay Pride

John Van Hoesen

Aevo UTP
An imprint of University of Toronto Press
Toronto Buffalo London
utppublishing.com

© John Van Hoesen 2025

All rights reserved. No part of this publication may be reproduced, stored in or introduced into a retrieval system, or transmitted in any form or by any means (electronic, mechanical, photocopying, recording, or otherwise) without the prior written permission of both the copyright owner and the above publisher of this book.

Library and Archives Canada Cataloguing in Publication

Title: Insist that they love you : Craig Rodwell and the fight for gay pride / John Van Hoesen.
Other titles: Craig Rodwell and the fight for gay pride
Names: Van Hoesen, John, author.
Description: Includes bibliographical references and index.
Identifiers: Canadiana (print) 20250167352 | Canadiana (ebook) 20250167409 | ISBN 9781487562908 (cloth) | ISBN 9781487562922 (EPUB) | ISBN 9781487562915 (PDF)
Subjects: LCSH: Rodwell, Craig L. | LCSH: Gay activists – United States – Biography. | LCSH: Gay liberation movement – United States – History – 20th century. | LCSH: Gay rights – United States – History – 20th century. | LCGFT: Biographies.
Classification: LCC HQ75.8.R63 V36 2025 | DDC 306.76/62092 – dc23

ISBN 978-1-4875-6290-8 (cloth)   ISBN 978-1-4875-6292-2 (EPUB)
                                  ISBN 978-1-4875-6291-5 (PDF)

Printed in Canada

Cover design: Val Cooke
Cover image: Craig Rodwell speaking out against the portrayal of gay men in the film *Cruising* in New York in July 1979. © Bettye Lane/Manuscripts and Archives Division, The New York Public Library

We wish to acknowledge the land on which the University of Toronto Press operates. This land is the traditional territory of the Wendat, the Anishnaabeg, the Haudenosaunee, the Métis, and the Mississaugas of the Credit First Nation.

University of Toronto Press acknowledges the financial support of the Government of Canada, the Canada Council for the Arts, and the Ontario Arts Council, an agency of the Government of Ontario, for its publishing activities.

  Canada Council   Conseil des Arts
                      for the Arts   du Canada

Funded by the   Financé par le
Government   gouvernement
of Canada   du Canada

In memory of my own Marian

Contents

Introduction 1

1 Early Out 7

2 New York I – Harvey Milk, Light and Dark Days 27

3 New York II – Militants in Mattachine 39

4 Inside the Oscar Wilde – Mercer Street 57

5 *The New York Hymnal* 83

6 Stonewall and Gay Power 99

7 Dear Craig 117

8 Let's March 125

9 *QQ Magazine* 151

10 Christian Science 179

11 Inside the Oscar Wilde – Christopher Street 197

12 Monuments, Myths, and Memorials   235

13 Transitions   253

Epilogue   257

Acknowledgments   271

Appendix A: The New York Hymnal, *1968*   277

Appendix B: QQ Magazine, *1970–1971*   287

Appendix C: QQ Magazine, *1972*   313

Appendix D: QQ Magazine, *1973*   339

Notes   361

Bibliography   387

Index   395

Illustrations appear at the end of chapters 5, 6, 8, and 9 and after page 184.

Introduction

On November 12, 1969, Craig Rodwell, Ellen Broidy, and Fred Sargeant were picketing the Time-Life Building in New York. I was a teenager growing up on a dairy farm in rural Vermont, and their world was as far from mine as one could imagine. Most of the time when we weren't in school, we were feeding cows, fixing fences, or storing the hay crop. But even though we were far away from the skyscrapers and urban life, there was something we had in common that fall – the October 31 issue of *Time* magazine. It hit the newsstands in New York and the activists took to the streets; it landed next to the butter dish on our kitchen table, and I read every word.

After examining six unflattering stereotypes and including a sidebar on whether homosexuals were sick, *Time's* cover story concluded in its next-to-last sentence that "homosexuality is a serious and sometimes crippling maladjustment...." Just four months after the Stonewall riots, where Craig Rodwell's rallying cry of "Gay Power" gave voice to a growing outrage against oppression, New Yorkers were incensed. It's fair to say that most gay American teenagers had little awareness that this fight was occurring on their behalf. It was hard to fathom; in those years, the words *queer* and *faggot* were daggers thrust from behind that would stiffen the backs of uncertain teenage boys.

Rodwell had already opened his ground-breaking Oscar Wilde Memorial Bookshop in New York, the first bookstore dedicated solely to gay and lesbian literature. Ellen Broidy was a friend and volunteer. Fred Sargeant was Rodwell's lover, manager of the shop, and vice chair of Rodwell's Homophile Youth Movement in Neighborhoods. The three of them, along with Broidy's partner, Linda Rhodes, would develop the concept and proposal for the first Pride march in 1970, one year after Stonewall.

Rodwell was one of the most militant activists of this shining moment in the 1960s and '70s. He worked to obliterate what he called "heterosexism" and to fulfill his purpose: that gay men and women could be themselves, stand up for themselves, and live a proud life. His contribution to the movement for gay rights was wide and deep, organizational and individual. He could be tender, warm, and focused, or stubborn and angry.

His life was a struggle. The drama started early as he was cast into foster homes, reform school, and the precocious life of a teenager plying the streets of Chicago. He knew before most of us that he had a calling, and he headed for New York and the Mattachine Society. He fell in love and then into despair, but the movement kept him going until what was something of a bittersweet end.

By chance, I came to know of Rodwell more than twenty years after he had opened the Oscar Wilde Memorial Bookshop, after I met Fred Sargeant, who would become my own life partner. I never met Craig; he had become ill by the time I was learning the magnitude of his contribution. But he left behind a half-dozen oral histories and recorded interviews and a trove of papers at the New York Public Library that became central to the research for this book.

From 1970 to 1973, Rodwell wrote twenty-one articles and editorials for *QQ Magazine*, which had a national readership in the tens of thousands. There's no way to measure the influence Rodwell exercised, as he walked readers through a growing consciousness of gay freedom, but it had to have been enormous. The *QQ* articles are included at the end of this biography because they articulate in Craig's own words the arc of gay liberation for the movement and for himself.

I have for the most part used the language of the times. It's an imperfect transposition to substitute different words for *homophile* and *homosexual*, which had a certain meaning in the '50s, '60s, and '70s. When *gay* and *lesbian* are used, they are not meant to be exclusionary, but rather an accurate depiction of how people thought and spoke at the time. Rodwell himself always capitalized the words *Gay* and *Lesbian*, and if he used the word *Gay* by itself he intended it to be an umbrella for women and men. His colleagues and friends knew him as a fierce feminist and inclusive employer long before diversity, equity, and inclusion became a part of professional vocabulary. Some of the language in Rodwell's own articles is jarring today, but it reflects the culture and vocabulary of more than fifty years ago. I have also tried to reconcile various published discrepancies in the timeline of Rodwell's life through research of primary source documents, newspaper accounts, public records, interviews, and the published record.

Rodwell never saw himself as a leader, yet his activism broke ground for thousands to lead an open and respected gay life. Today there are millions of marchers across the globe who stand up for themselves every year in parades that were first launched on June 28, 1970. Rodwell showed that it takes fortitude and courage to be open, to use your real name, and to insist on respect for your community.

Many people were responsible for important advances in gay liberation, but no one bridged the phases of the movement quite like Rodwell. As Ellen Broidy reflected in my interview with her in 2022, "Craig was not a reformist in the Mattachine mold; then again, he was not a revolutionary. He was revolutionary, but not in the GLF [Gay Liberation Front] mold. He would have stood there by himself; he was fearless." And Toby Marotta, in his 1981 book, *The Politics of Homosexuality*, called Rodwell "the first eastern homophile leader to act like a gay liberationist."

When one examines Rodwell's impact on gay liberation across his life, it's hard to conclude that there was someone who did more to holistically draw the movement together. Where other pioneers of the time may have focused on institutional reforms, Rodwell focused on cultural inequities. He pushed the limits of the old guard at the Mattachine Society of New York, he drew in younger members, he walked the first picket lines, and he put his name and his face out in the public eye. In the fight for freedom, he took action into his own hands, and he wanted to make it easier for others to do the same. Through the Oscar Wilde Memorial Bookshop, he hoped to open minds, realize possibilities, and establish dignity for the community. His daring move to open a street-front location with a plate-glass window, complete with a *Gay Is Good* sign, was an example of his insistent belief that one had to take on prejudice openly.

At the Stonewall riots, when he shouted out a call for "Gay Power," the first response was quiet and tentative giddiness. So he shouted again.

When we look back on the main events of gay liberation, Rodwell was not only present, but his fingerprints were all over the cause. This book is not an effort to position him as the sole leader of the movement or to displace the recognition of others. It is meant to establish the fact that Rodwell's life is a missing link in our history – and perhaps more than others, with his fearless determination, he was a unique conscience of gay liberation. Freedoms are never fully secured, as history shows. The commitment and sacrifices that early leaders like Rodwell made are enduring examples of the fortitude it takes for those freedoms to be attained.

1

Early Out

I tell gay people, "Be firm with your family; insist that they come to an understanding of you, that they read certain things, that they meet your friends, insist that they love you as their son or daughter – which means they know you."

– Craig Rodwell[1]

After a tumultuous childhood and a decade of militancy, and at just thirty years old, this was the life lesson Craig Rodwell wanted to impart to the world.

The long road to that lesson began on October 31, 1940, when Craig Louis Rodwell (eight pounds, five ounces) was born in Chicago to Louis Alfred and Marion "Sally" Dunlop Rodwell.[2] The Rodwells were married in 1935 in New York City. Louis Rodwell was a traveling salesman for Eastman Kodak. Marion Rodwell grew up on the family farm near Rochester, NY. She was the first in her family to leave the farm for higher education, attending business school and gaining secretarial skills. The couple met in Rochester and moved to New York and then to Chicago, where Louis Rodwell had been transferred before Craig was born.

Within ten months, the Rodwells had separated. This was Louis Rodwell's second of several marriages in his lifetime, and by 1945 the couple had divorced.

"My father went off to the war, and came back from the war, but not back to my mother."[3]

Thus began an unsettled and scrappy early life of a child largely left to his own resources with a single, working mother.[4]

Craig recalled a childhood story often told to him that foreshadowed his independent spirit. One day his mother had pulled to the curb on her way to work. She had tucked some cash into Craig's pocket to pay for his foster care and then scooted him out of the car. No more than four years old, he padded down the street. Not keen on his foster care, he captured the eyes of a young couple approaching him. They looked like a trustworthy alternative, so he asked: If he gave them his money, would they take care of him?

"I lived in foster homes till I was about six. I would spend weekends with her [Marion], but during the week I would live in these other homes."[5]

When Craig was five and in day care, one woman told Marion that for a fee Craig could stay in her own home, which would offer more stability. But it turned out that Craig was going to be the woman's helper. She was taking in laundry, and Craig was going to help her work sheets and towels through the wringers of a mangle. Then, the woman and her husband said they wanted to adopt Craig. With the threat of a proposed adoption looming, Marion was able to place Craig in a boarding school, which would – for better or worse – have a bearing on the rest of his life.

"When I was six, she sent me out to an institution, where I actually grew up, where I lived until I was fourteen."[6]

The school was the Chicago Junior School in Elgin, IL, a boarding school for forty-five problem boys – boys with health or disciplinary issues, or boys with no other family willing to take them in. Administration was strict and the school was run by Christian Scientists.

Chicago Junior was described by the *Chicago Tribune* as a school for boys from broken homes. "Those who can pay their tuition do so. The others receive scholarships provided by 12 groups in various sections of the Chicago area...."

The paper described the campus buildings as having an English design, built with stone, wood and brick. The coloring was generally gray. These are the buildings Craig would navigate – a dining hall, dormitories, administration and classroom buildings, and a gymnasium. There was also a pool.

George Kilburn was the superintendent of the school.[7] Kilburn had graduated from the University of Maine and had a master's degree from the University of California. When Craig arrived, Kilburn had been superintendent for well over a decade.[8]

When the taillights of Marion's car disappeared, her six-year-old son, probably dazed, was in the hands of the house mothers. But Craig quickly became acquainted with his new life: no calls from parents and visits just once a month, up at 5 a.m., breakfast in silence, and a half-hour Bible study. Religion was going to be morning, noon, and night. Christian Science was everywhere. Sports were encouraged, and here Craig would develop the beginnings of a lifelong love of baseball and the Chicago Cubs.

Marion documented Craig's early life during her visits to Chicago Junior in a carefully kept photo album. In a 1948 snapshot, seven third-grade boys huddle around an elderly woman and a library table. They are listening to a story; Craig appears vaguely interested.[9] But he did have a favorite story that would foreshadow a turning point in his life twenty years later. *The Happy Prince*, by Oscar Wilde, was a children's fairy tale about a statue prince who gives away the jewels he is embellished with to help people in need. The prince invokes the help of a sparrow to distribute the jewels to the poor until there are no more jewels to give, and the statue and the sparrow die. Craig never forgot the moral of the story.

Craig would be at odds with George Kilburn for the duration of his time at Chicago Junior School. The boys had a television set in a common room, and they would watch programs with actors Sid Caesar and Imogene Coca. This exposure to the entertainment world inspired an interest in movie stars, so at ten years old, Craig began sending out letters with requests for signed photos. That often meant that pictures came back with the stars photographed in their bathing suits. The collection expanded and word got to Kilburn, who determined it was improperly sexual, and it was taken away.

The television era also provided an entry into the world of politics and presidential election results. By 1952, Craig had his own presidential candidate – Democrat and Illinois Governor Adlai Stevenson – who would be defeated by Republican Dwight D. Eisenhower. At age thirteen, Craig was already reading the Democratic National Committee magazine.

Chicago Junior School would be the crucible for emotional and sexual discovery. Craig recalled that he was introduced to his own sexuality by an older classmate, who took him into the woods on the school grounds for the discovery. Afterward, Craig remembered that he felt no shame.

By the time he reached seventh grade, Craig had a steady boyfriend. The two of them established what Craig felt was his first real emotional affair.

"Just as heterosexual youngsters start to develop their sexual and emotional feelings towards the opposite sex, I and many of the other boys were developing our feelings toward the same sex. And we had much the same kind of crushes."[10]

The two boys spent lots of time together and even held hands on the way to the dining hall. One day they slipped away to catch a double-header Chicago Cubs game at Wrigley Field. Returning from their escapade much too late, the boys walked along the railroad tracks to get back to the school, where they were immediately punished by George Kilburn.

The relationships among the boys at Chicago Junior did not escape Superintendent Kilburn, who called an assembly to scold all the boys for rumors of sexual activity.

In 1954, with the arrival of eighth grade, it was time for graduation. The original fifteen boys had been reduced to ten. Two years after their graduation, George Kilburn would die, at the age of sixty. He would be buried in Elgin.

The trials and tribulations of life in foster homes and boarding school were not the story of Marion's family photo album. Her record of Craig's early years and her visits with him was a happy one. On the black paper pages of her album, a Mother's Day photo from 1945 is held in place with the stick-on corner tabs – Craig is in a sailor shirt, sitting on a stone wall with his mother standing at his side. A 1947 Christmas card features a snapshot of Craig. In the fifth grade, Marion documents "a day of golf" in a sequence of three photos together, as Craig is becoming a little lanky. Marion saved the photo from the Elgin *Daily Courier News* from a class visit in 1951 – including two of Craig's friends, Tony and Harry. At the top of the clipping, Craig wrote "Me" with an arrow pointing to his spot in the group photo. In photos from 1952 and 1953, Craig was often photographed in jacket and slacks, confidence written all over his face, and a smile – he resembled his mother.[11]

After spending his formative years under the watchful eyes of people who were not his parents, Craig returned home to live with his mother in Chicago's Rogers Park for his high school years. Rogers Park is the northernmost community of Chicago, which saw a rise in the construction of large apartment buildings during the early 1900s to accommodate population growth that would continue past World War II. Home was just a mile from Rogers Park beach on Lake Michigan, and nine miles from downtown. Craig and his mother and his new stepfather lived at 7353 North Damen Avenue in a large U-shaped, 1920s yellow-brick apartment complex.[12]

The fenced-in world of forty-five boys and their house mothers in Elgin was nothing like Craig's new surroundings – a sea of unknown classmates at school, and a new freedom to roam, all to be navigated with the unflinching determination of a thirteen-year-old well beyond his years.

Craig's memories of his four years in public school at Chicago's Sullivan High had less to do with classes or friends or extracurricular activities and everything to do with his life outside of school. He felt largely anonymous among 600 boys and 600 girls at Sullivan. By his own account, he was a poor student who never did his homework. His social contacts were narrow – he had a good friend, Jerry, and he remembered taking Nicki to the prom. But unlike Chicago Junior School, where boys could be together, it seemed there was no way in 1954 to have a relationship with another boy in a public high school.

In 1957, he took a typing class to gain some skills for an eventual work life. He wanted to take shorthand, but boys at the time were not allowed to sign up for shorthand, which was considered a girl's skill. Sullivan graded students with five letter grades – Superior, Excellent, Good, Fair, and D for failure. Rodwell's "superior" typing skills were among his highest grades of his high school years.[13]

He excelled in US history, public speaking, and geometry and struggled in English and Latin. One of his English teachers noted in the report that Craig didn't complete required homework. Instead of physical education classes, he joined the Junior Reserve Officer Training Corps, where he excelled again. Army JROTC had been established by the National Defense Act in 1916 and was created to promote good citizenship and character in its young cadets. In the 1955 Navillus school yearbook (Sullivan spelled backward), Craig was photographed with the Crack Drill Platoon. Marion Rodwell's family photo album captured Craig in his well-fitting and well-pressed JROTC uniform in 1957. In a photo of a Corps marching unit, she had marked Craig's position with an arrow.[14]

But it was the streets of Chicago that called out to Craig – and they would be the scene of several dramatic events.

In September 1954, the Chicago Cubs would finish seventh in the National League with a record of 64–90.[15] A heatwave had marked summer in the Midwest, but by the third week in September there had been some rain. Craig, who had developed an early interest in newspapers, was out to get the evening paper to check on the box score from the day before. It was raining again, and as he was walking home, a man caught up to him, remarking that "it's even too wet for the ducks." Craig was being cruised, maybe for the first time, and he never forgot those words. So he told the man to call him at his mother's apartment the next day.[16]

The next night, Craig offered up one of his many excuses to his mother to be out after dark, and the rendezvous was on.

The imprint of the experience lasted a lifetime – a young man in his twenties, a sportscar, Craig climbing in, speeding off to the countryside, where, behind a billboard in a harvested cornfield, they had sex. Because of the rain, the fields were soaked. When the man put the car in gear, the rear wheels just spun up mud and corn stalks. At 11 p.m., they walked to a gas station to get help and a tow truck, with a made-up story about how and why they were there to begin with.

"Anyway, that was sort of the beginning of my – that's where I first learned the word gay. I didn't know the word gay even up until then. I had no label. To me, everybody was like me."[17]

Nothing seemed wrong with this scenario to Craig, or with several other encounters with adult men who would have sex with an underage teenager. Still, Craig always told people he was older than his true age. As he patrolled the streets of Chicago in his leather jacket and engineer boots, he was seventeen in his mind, and that was his story. Now he knew there were places he could go to find others like him. Several nights a week and on weekends, Craig would cruise the streets – Clark and Division streets, among other areas – sometimes until 2 a.m. He always had a wild story for Marion to cover his nightly jaunts, but she disapproved and was perpetually annoyed. He, however, was thrilled.

Another interaction, though, was about to occur that would not end with what Craig thought was the humorous romp of a bold teenager.

In his new unbridled life, Craig, only a few months into his freshman year at Sullivan High, made his way to Clark and Division streets on the night of January 3, 1955. He was fourteen now, but as he said, with his look and with a cigarette in his hand, he felt he could be a convincing seventeen-year-old. He was exploding with his new freedom and the prospect that he might find the love of his life around the next corner. In truth, he was a precocious teenager in a dangerous adult world.

That night, as he cruised Division Street, he met Frank, a thirty-eight-year-old assistant counter worker and cook at Walgreen's, where he had worked for about six weeks. It was one of several jobs he'd held in Chicago over the previous five years.[18]

Frank was Francis Bucalo, who had grown up in Springfield, MA. It was nine years since Frank had been honorably discharged from the US Army Air Force, where he had enlisted and served for four years, from 1942 to 1946. He had served in the European Theater for thirty months. He had bounced around the country after his discharge and had at least two run-ins with the law. He was arrested for three counts of breaking-and-entering and theft in Hartford, CT, in 1949, and two years later he was a suspect in a child molestation case in Los Angeles.

He had a place, he told Craig, and they could walk to it – the fifty-room Dearborn Manor Hotel, where Frank had rented a single room, probably for about $10 a week, with a bathroom down the hall. After the encounter came to a close, Craig was remarking about the scented soap in the sink – Frank gave him a bar – and they left for the walk back to the subway so Craig could get home.

Soon after 10 p.m., as they neared the corner of Clark and Schiller streets, police converged upon them. Craig and

Frank were immediately separated on the sidewalk and taken into custody.

Craig tried out a story that lasted only briefly – he was really seventeen, and Frank was a friend of the family. But placed in a room with an officer banging his fist on the table, he was told to get on with the truth and that the police had already called his mother and new stepfather.[19]

"I'd always been brought up that the best thing to do was to tell the truth essentially. So, I told the absolute truth. I mean, everything, thinking that everything would be fine. But, of course, it wasn't."[20]

Police asked Craig if he had been paid by Frank; it is likely they were watching the street for hustlers, but Craig had only a vague understanding of what a prostitute was, and it wasn't him. He had not been paid, but it didn't matter.

The judicial process kicked in. By January 20, the sheriff's office had served summonses on five police officers of the 36th District, and Craig and Marion Rodwell were to appear before a grand jury on January 25. The indictment that was handed up charged Frank Bucalo with a crime against nature for immoral, improper, and indecent liberties with a child under the age of fifteen and for rendering a child guilty of indecent and lascivious conduct, all of which was too obscene to be "spread upon the record of the court." Bail was set at $5,000.[21]

Criminal subpoenas were then issued; Frank pleaded not guilty at the arraignment and agreed to a bench trial. The Probation Department for Cook County did an investigation of Frank's background. Frank, having no money or assets, was assigned representation by the public defender. The trial was set for February 9 with Judge Richard Austin.

Marion, angry and silent, would drive Craig to court hearings in the courthouse on the south side.

At the trial, Craig, Marion, and the police officers were all listed as witnesses for the prosecution. The public defender had listed one witness on Frank's behalf, the clerk of the Dearborn Manor. After another attempt by the district attorney's office to get Craig to say that he had been paid for the encounter with Frank, the trial concluded. Judge Austin found Frank Bucalo guilty as charged in the indictment. An application for probation was approved, and Frank was placed on probation for two years, with the first sixty days to be served in the Cook County Jail. The case for Frank from start to finish lasted just over a month.

Meanwhile, Craig faced a juvenile proceeding himself, where it was concluded that he should be sentenced to the state reformatory.

Again, Marion faced overwhelming circumstances with her precociously gay and defiant son. She had already had a close call with the threat of adoption when Craig was in day care, and Craig had been away for much of his childhood at the Chicago Junior School. Marion was distraught at the prospect of losing her son once again. And she was in another unlucky marriage, this time to printer and former prize fighter Henry "Hank" Kastman, whom she had married in 1951.

The marriage would last just a few years. A violent glass-breaking incident between Marion and Hank in the kitchen caused Craig to pull a knife on Hank. One night during the court crisis, Kastman let Craig know what he thought about him, telling him that when he was young, he and his friends would beat up the queers for sport.

After her short marriage to Louis Rodwell and her second marriage to Hank Kastman, Marion would not marry a third time. But in her way, she would stand by her son until the end.

Ultimately, Marion asked the hearing officer for an alternative to sending Craig away.

"I can remember my mother just breaking down and crying, getting down on her knees and begging this woman that she would do anything if they wouldn't send me away."

The hearing officer acquiesced, and the result was two years' probation for Craig, but Marion would have to put him under the care of a psychiatrist twice a week with a report to the probation officer every Saturday.

The required psychiatry sessions only resulted in papering over the truth, with Craig making up stories about dates and dances with girls. The psychiatrist acknowledged to Craig that he was – as he already knew – a gay person.

Craig hadn't even heard of the word *pedophilia* and didn't know what a pederast was; he felt he had the emotional capacity to handle himself. But the adults had the power. Had Frank decided against taking Rodwell to his room, Craig wouldn't have gone through a courtroom drama or spent years on probation or had sessions with a psychiatrist.

Back at Sullivan that semester, Craig's circumstances showed up in his report card. He had failed Latin, struggled with English, and his teachers noted that he was inattentive or indifferent.

The court drama faded, but another crisis was around the corner. Craig struck up a relationship with a former student at Loyola University. The man would arrive at the North Damen Street apartment around 3 p.m. and leave before Marion arrived home from work at 6 p.m. But one time, the connection didn't go well. The sex turned bad, Craig resisted, and he was assaulted. He remembered that there was "blood all over." But he never told anyone. Later, in March 1957, the man, who was now twenty-five and assistant to the dean, was accused of taking nude photographs of a sixteen-year-old boy. According to the *Chicago Tribune* report, when police took him home to get photos that were to prove his innocence, he shot himself in the room upstairs while the detective talked with his mother downstairs. Craig clipped the article from the paper so that his mother wouldn't see it.[22]

Frank Bucalo disappeared into the city forever, as far as Craig knew, but the vivid details of the court case lived in Craig's mind for the rest of his life. In fact, he had hoped to see him again, perhaps to share regrets, but he never did. All his life, he believed that Frank had been sent away for five years, when in fact it was just sixty days. Craig never knew about Frank's previous problems with the law. And Frank never apologized.

Frank successfully completed his probation in February 1957, the month before the Loyola assistant took his own life. Whether Frank had any further run-ins with the law is not known. At some point, he took a job with the Chicago Lottery Commission and later retired from that position. He died in Chicago in 1988 at the age of seventy-two at the

Northwestern Veterans Administration Hospital. His obituary in the *Transcript-Telegram* in Massachusetts said that memorial contributions could be made to Father Flanagan's Boys Home in Boys Town, Nebraska.[23]

The imprint of these crises lasted a lifetime for the fourteen-year-old, who could not conceive of their potential catastrophic outcome. In today's terms, Craig was a teenager at risk. Not only did he endure an early-life criminal experience, but he carried the guilt about what happened to Frank Bucalo for decades. In his later years, Craig speculated that some of these experiences affected his emotional state and most likely contributed to a higher level of internal strife.

Meanwhile, Craig's father seems to have been all but absent from his son's life. In December 1954, shortly before the January disaster in the Cook County Court, he sent a letter to North Damen Street, addressed to Craig, in which he commented on his long absence. "It's been a long time since your dad took the time to write to you and he doesn't feel good about it," Rodwell wrote, referring to himself in the third person. He went on to say that he wanted to take Craig to his cabin in Canada to get it ready for sale now that he had been transferred to Milwaukee with the Recordak division of Eastman Kodak. He regretted that a Christmas gift of a vest the year before had been the wrong size and enclosed a check for twenty dollars (a little over $200 in 2024) for Craig to purchase something "real sharp" for himself.[24]

It's unknown what "a long time" had been, but there was no reference in this letter of Craig's recent graduation from Chicago Junior School or his entrance into Sullivan High.

Craig's father signed off with best wishes for Christmas to "you and mother" – "Affectionately, Dad."

◆◆◆◆

Some of the pieces to the puzzle of gay life for Craig began to fall into place. At fifteen, still underage, Craig had other travels around the city on warm days after school, including one to the Oak Street beach on Lake Michigan. There, Harry – older and forty-something – would introduce Craig to the wider gay world in *ONE* magazine and the *Mattachine Review*.[25]

This new information piqued his enthusiasm, and he was determined to get involved. He found a downtown Chicago address in the *Mattachine Review* and promptly headed to it. But as he studied the building directory, there was nothing listed for Mattachine. He had expected to walk into a professional office and announce that he was there to fight for the rights of people like him. He was ready to go to work, but the address was just a mailbox – there were no offices, no people.

Disappointed but undeterred, if he would not find Mattachine in Chicago, he would go where Mattachine was – New York. That's where he knew he had to go. He had heard about Greenwich Village. In the Midwest, the word was out that that was where the "queers" lived.

"That was what you heard in the Midwest at the time. So as soon as I heard that, I started saving all my money."

The Mattachine Society, founded by Henry (Harry) Hay in Los Angeles as an informal discussion group in 1950, articulated its mission in Spring 1951 – to unify homosexuals, educate homosexuals and heterosexuals, and lead. They would assist homosexuals victimized by oppression. They would use the name *Mattachine*, from the medieval French society known as Societé Mattachine, which was a secret society of unmarried men who would wear masks during various rituals. Anonymously, the masked entertainers could voice complaints against oppression and deflect any punishment.[26] The Mattachine Society of New York was founded in 1955, and Chicago Mattachine got underway with early formations in the late 1950s and early '60s, ultimately taking hold as Midwest Mattachine in 1965.

But in the meantime, Craig still had to get through high school. Outside of school, his life was packed with cruising the streets, dodging his mother, afternoons at the beach, Cubs games, and whatever summer job he could pick up to support his primary goal – to raise money to get to New York. In the summers, he took mailroom and office jobs at Kaiser Aluminum and at a law firm, and he asked for cash for birthdays and Christmas, accumulating about $500.

While working at the law firm, with his consciousness now starting to simmer, Craig created a flyer; he would take some action of his own. The flyer demanded: "Homosexuals Unite – Tear Off Your Masks" and was accompanied by Rodwell's hand drawing of a mask. He produced a few hundred copies and took them to his Rogers Park neighborhood, where he slid them into mailboxes. Later he learned that the neighbors believed the campaign was the work of two gay hairdressers, who were evicted for their brazenness. It was his first militant action.

On June 27, 1958, Craig Rodwell graduated from Sullivan High School. He had "satisfactorily completed the educational program of this four-year high school and (was) awarded this diploma by authority of the Board of Education, City of Chicago."[27]

Meanwhile, Marion was not so sure about the New York idea. Her son had always been interested in ballet, so she would take him to Boston instead to study at the Boston Conservatory of Music, a college for music, drama, and dance, where he had been accepted in March. In her mind, it was a safer bet than New York. Off they went, with Marion in the driver's seat. She would set up her untetherable son, now truly seventeen years old, in a rooming house with six elderly women, who would all share one bathroom and a payphone. She enrolled him in Boston and returned to Chicago.

It wasn't going to work out. Within weeks, Craig had his own apartment and was cruising the Boston Public Gardens and gay areas. In Boston, he went inside his first bar – the Punch Bowl. Still underage for the bar scene, he would find ways in and stay in the back. Surprisingly, his first semester was not a total failure – he received good grades in theory and solfège, English and French, and no grades in piano and kinesiology.[28]

But Craig had no intention of staying in Boston, and by Christmas he told his mother that a career in ballet would only happen in New York. And Marion relented.

✦✦✦✦✦

In January 1959, Craig arrived in New York City, where he imagined his gay life and work would flourish. He found a room at the YMCA on 34th Street, where he could stay for something like $3 a night. He knew no one, but not for long. At the Y, he met Collin from Helena, AK, another young man with dance ambitions, who would later play a key role on the darkest day of Craig's life. Collin wanted to be a chorus boy in musical theater. Within months, Craig, Collin, and Jack, from the Chicago Junior School days, found an apartment on 16th Street off Seventh Avenue.

The typing class at Sullivan High School came in handy – it helped Craig to get a job at a plastic flower factory at 16th Street and Union Square, where he could do office work.

But he couldn't throw himself into activism as he had hoped when he arrived in New York. When he located the Mattachine office at 1133 Broadway, they told him he was still too young to be a member. Now eighteen, he felt like membership was always just out of reach. But he could attend the Mattachine's West Side Discussion Group meetings at the Freedom House on 40th Street, where speakers talked about the causes of homosexuality and occasionally about civil rights issues to an audience of business-suited men in their fifties and sixties.

Meanwhile, Craig was able to continue his interest in ballet with a scholarship at the American School of Ballet. While it would not become his life's passion, the role of male ballet dancers and the attitudes of George Balanchine himself would make it into Craig's articles and editorials in years to come. Gay male ballet dancers did not have a place unless they could be seen as straight and athletic, a practice Craig saw as unfair and homophobic.[29]

With no money and being too young to go to gay bars or enter gay society, Craig developed a group of friends who would find their entertainment on the streets of his new city. A diverse group, the street queens, as they called themselves, moved about as a band of a dozen, being outrageous, heckling the heterosexuals, and trying to stay ahead of the cops where there was sure to be harassment.[30]

They would head for Eighth Street and Greenwich Avenue, cruising areas near the gay bars. But the police were always watching.

"The cops would come up and they'd hit you with their billy clubs. They'd say, 'keep moving, faggot,' and they'd poke you."

2

New York I – Harvey Milk, Light and Dark Days

One September night in 1959, Craig had been cruising Washington Square Park an hour after the park had closed. Two plainclothes policemen had their eye on him, and they approached his bench. What was the "faggot" doing here, they wanted to know. Craig had a question of his own – he wanted to know why they were harassing gay people. Things moved quickly after that – Craig was arrested and hauled off to the Sixth Precinct, the cops belittling him all the way. Pushed around and thrown to the floor, he was locked up. One of the cops looked in: "What's the matter, lose your purse?" Craig's retort: "What's the matter, never seen a faggot before?"[1]

His lawyer tried a calm approach. Attorney Samuel Smoleff prepared a polite memo to the magistrate, asking for better treatment. Attorney Smoleff described what had happened:

> Craig Rodwell is a young man, approaching 19. He is studying dancing at the Ballet Russe de Monte Carlo.
>
> On the evening of Sunday, September 20, he visited Greenwich Village. He started for home about 1 A.M., Monday, September 21.
>
> At Washington Square, he sat down on one of the benches just inside the park. Two plainclothesmen arrested him for being in the park after midnight and took him to the 6th Precinct Station....[2]

Once Craig's residence was confirmed, Smoleff's memo said that Craig was released with an appearance scheduled in front of the magistrate seven days later. Craig had been told by the police that he would be fined $2, but when he got to court, the fine was $5, which he didn't have. After a few requests, he was allowed to phone a friend (his roommate, Collin) who came to the rescue with the extra $3. Until Collin arrived, Craig was placed in a cell "with three derelicts."

Smoleff's complaint received a quick response from the chief city magistrate, acknowledging that "in this instance it would have been better wisdom not to detain him in the interim."[3]

The scrappy street life of Craig's late teens was almost a continuation of his late nights on the streets of Chicago.

Then, in 1961, his cruising brought him to Central Park West at 88th Street, and Craig, now twenty, looked into the eyes of thirty-one-year-old Harvey Milk. They were taken with each other.⁴

By this time, Craig's radical temperature was on the rise. He had been volunteering with New York Mattachine, realizing the goal he had sought since high school. His occasional volunteer work had grown significantly, and he became more involved with the *New York Mattachine Newsletter*, where his typing skills and enthusiasm made him a welcome asset. Working there, he learned how to lay out and paste up newsletter pages, skills he would use in the years to come.

Harvey, though, was closeted; it would be years before he would move to San Francisco and open Castro Camera from the inspiration he would gain at the Oscar Wilde Memorial Bookshop, and long before he would run for the Board of Supervisors there as an openly gay candidate.

For Craig, it was the first time, after the cruising and crises of his teenage and young adult years, that he had met someone he imagined that he could spend the rest of his life with. The first mature romance, it seemed as though it would all fit together. Craig could dedicate his life to the homophile movement, and he would gain the emotional connectedness he sought in a relationship – a thing he'd valued since the days at Chicago Junior School. Craig was buoyed by Harvey's gregarious personality and the two of them clicked.⁵

Unlike Craig's fractured younger years in Chicago, Harvey had been raised in Woodmere and Bayshore, NY. His grandparents had opened a dry goods store in Woodmere – Milk's Dry Goods – which later became the largest department store on Long Island. His grandfather had established the first synagogue in the Woodmere area. His parents opened a furrier when they moved to Bayshore.

Harvey had graduated from Bayshore High School in 1947, a decade before Craig would graduate from Sullivan High in Chicago. Where Craig spent his high school years exploring his sexuality and the street scene, Harvey had joined the basketball and football teams. He had developed an early affinity for opera and used his allowance to attend performances at the old Metropolitan Opera House.

Where Craig wore his sexuality on his sleeve from the start, Harvey had kept his a secret.

It wasn't that Harvey didn't act on his feelings – shortly after graduating from high school, he was rounded up with a group of other shirtless men cruising an area of Central Park. Going shirtless was considered indecent exposure, and fortunately for him that day, the police were satisfied enough with striking fear into the hearts of the men they placed in the paddy wagon.[6]

Having recently broken up with his lover, Joe Campbell, in the last months of 1961, Harvey was reluctantly moving on.

The new romance was sparkling for Craig. Harvey, who had a good job on Wall Street, would give Craig a wake-up call every morning so he would be up for his ballet classes. He was funny and made Craig laugh. Several nights a week, Harvey would take Craig to different ethnic restaurants to experience the fabric of the city. At Christmas, Harvey walked the eight short blocks from his apartment to Craig's laden with packages of sentimental gifts. One gift for Craig was a small porcelain vase with a paper flower that Craig could take with him for a civilized table setting when he was having his lunches in Central Park. They went to the Ice Capades, museums, and the opera, but they were also on different paths.

First, Harvey was annoyed that Craig and Collin had distributed pamphlets promoting the West Side Discussion Group meetings to potential gay residents in the neighborhood. The West Side group was a more conservative spinoff of the Mattachine Society of New York and sponsored regular get-togethers to discuss topics related to the issues of homosexuals. But Harvey thought Craig was being reckless by endangering others with potential exposure.

Then there was Craig's still thriving sexual freedom.

A turning point came one night when they were out for supper. Harvey raised an unpleasant subject – he had contracted gonorrhea. However, he knew that he had been faithful to Craig. So the conversation went in one direction – Craig was also infected. Despite his devotion to Harvey, Craig had not been monogamous, and now things would never be the same.[7]

Then, not a full year into their relationship, on Labor Day weekend, Craig would fatefully take in the last days of summer at the gay section of Riis Park.[8]

Jacob Riis Park in Queens was named for the photojournalist and social reformer who had once lived in Queens. The eastern section of the public beach was popular with gay men and women as early as the 1940s and was an established haven for the gay community by the 1960s.[9]

By this time, after the court fiasco in Chicago, the incident in Washington Square Park, and the poking and shoving of the cops from his street queen days, Craig had accumulated a hot resentment toward police.

Officers had their eyes on Riis Park, especially the gay area, where they could hand out dozens of tickets to men for wearing inappropriate bathing suits. An old park regulation gave them the authority to issue a ticket if the suit didn't cover the body from above the navel to below the thigh. The bikini style of the 1960s, especially popular with gay men, did not comply.

Most beachgoers would cover themselves with a towel to avoid getting a ticket if they were spotted by police, who were stationed near the bathhouse. But not Craig. As he neared the bathhouse and the concession, the cops began writing him up for his illegal suit. He wasn't having it and began calling them out for harassment. A crowd started to gather as Craig was grabbed up by the cops and marched away to a police room.

The moment-by-moment of the next hours and days was seared into Craig's brain – he was thrown to the floor, heard "the usual faggot and that kind of stuff," and was taken to the precinct, where he was locked in a cell and taunted. After some verbal harassment, he was asked to state his name and address, as he remembered, over and over again. Finally, he went silent, refusing to speak at all.

Sometime around midnight, handcuffed together with various criminal elements, he was taken to night court – no shoes, just a shirt, shorts, and his beach bag, standing in front of the judge. Still silent, Craig was taken into the judge's chambers, where the judge asked him what the matter was.

He seemed friendly and trustworthy, and Craig spilled out the whole story. It seemed like it was going to be okay.

Back in the courtroom, the judge told Craig he was going to let him go but that he would have to return to the Queens County Court in two weeks to pay a fine of $10.

When it came time for the court appearance two weeks later, Craig arrived with no lawyer, thinking he was there to pay a fine. When they called his name to answer the charges, though, it was nothing like he expected. The charges were read: violation of park regulations, resisting arrest, and inciting a riot. Again, he was face to face with a judge on the witness stand, and he began to relate his story. The judge dismissed the inciting-to-riot charge right away, but the bathing suit violation was another matter. Craig began to tell his whole truth – that homosexual men were being harassed by the police with this regulation.

"And I was looking right in his eyes, and I saw the very split second that he realized that I was one of those fucking queers."[10]

The judge's attitude shifted. Now that he realized Craig was a homosexual, it was over. He reached for his gavel and pounded out the sentence – a $25 fine or three days in jail.

But Craig had come with $10 in his pocket and the court wouldn't take his watch to settle the difference.[11] Off he went to the House of Detention in Brooklyn.

The guard there was unimpressed by Craig's continued silence. He shoved Craig's head into the cell bars, ordered him to hand over his wallet, and threw it on the floor for the "faggot" to pick up as the meager contents emptied out. This time, his bravery and determination disintegrated into tears.

He was locked up in what was called the "queens' tank," with thirty or forty other men – some street queens in jail for wearing drag, some hustlers. There were no privileges, except for the use of a recreation room. Craig made the best of it and taught a few ballet lessons for the gays in the tank.

During this disappearance, Harvey began to wonder what had happened to Craig. Even though the gonorrhea incident had put him off, he was still concerned and asked Collin when Craig was going to be back.[12]

When he did return, Craig explained what had happened at Riis Park and the House of Detention. But to see him this way – Craig's thick, boyish chestnut hair, parted on the side with the wave over his forehead, was gone, as they had shaved his head in detention – Harvey was taken aback, and the prospect of publicity was alarming.

The conservative Harvey Milk and militant Craig Rodwell would not mesh. Harvey began to withdraw. There were fewer and fewer phone calls until there were none. Craig recalled that Harvey was terrified that his carefully constructed life would be upended by his relationship with Craig.[13]

As Harvey pulled away, Craig despaired over losing him. The losses were mounting. Harvey was gone, Craig was giving up on the ballet classes, he had not developed a career, and the whole Riis Park incident had shaken him. For the second time in his life, Craig Rodwell felt he could not go on. He got his hands on a bottle of Tuinal barbiturates.[14]

Collin Oswalt had moved to New York City from Memphis, where he had spent a year after leaving home in Helena, AK. When he and Craig first became friends at the YMCA in 1959 (Collin was nineteen; Craig was eighteen), they had something in common – they both aspired to be dancers. And while Craig involved him in some of his early activism, Collin's passion was in the arts, the movies, and the theater. Tall, at 6 foot 2 inches, and lean, he would get close to auditioning for parts, but he never felt he was ready to make the leap. One of four sons, he was the funniest one, and valued for his friendship and loyalty, although he was an intensely private person.[15]

A few times a week, Collin would leave their 16th Street apartment to take in old movies on 42nd Street, double features that would keep him out for hours. It was on one of these nights that Craig would take the pills.

Craig gave notice at his job, and he arranged for a new home for their two cats. He wrote a note for Collin; he wanted him to call Craig's aunt, who would then call Craig's mother, informing her of his death. He didn't want his mother to hear it from the police.

At some point, between taking the pills and arranging the note, it seems that Craig fell, possibly hitting his head on the fireplace. However it happened, he passed out on the floor.

By coincidence, this night Collin skipped the second feature and decided to come home, where he found Craig collapsed. But there was a pulse, and Collin called for help. Craig was rushed to Harlem Hospital, where his stomach was emptied and he was revived with adrenaline. He had not died; his loyal friend Collin had come to the rescue.

But it was going to be a long road back.

Next would be a month-long sentence at Bellevue Hospital, during the time that Bellevue was associated with mental illness treatment. Craig found no treatment there, no therapy, and he quickly learned how to ditch the medications.

The way out of Bellevue would be to get into a private institution, which would mean someone would have to pay for the care. His mostly absent father, Louis Rodwell, and his devoted mother, Marion, both arrived in New York, and Craig was transferred to St. Luke's psychiatric ward. Throughout the episode, Craig felt lucky to have avoided shock therapy.

Recovery would continue at the home of his half-brother and sister-in-law – Jack and Joanne Rodwell – in Pleasantville, NY, but there was a relapse, a dependency on prescription drugs, a return to the hospital, and ultimately a return to Manhattan. He got a job at a steamship line, until a contract with the US Navy meant security clearances were needed, and Craig would not be able to get one.

The life he had expected to lead in New York had not gone as he had hoped, and he returned to his mother's apartment in Chicago, where he found a factory job. But a friend encouraged him, through numerous letters and pleas, to move to Hollywood in the fall of 1963, all based on a brief encounter in New York. Craig, coming out of his most vulnerable time, agreed. But arriving in Los Angeles, he knew immediately that it was the wrong move.

Harvey Milk was having his own troubles. Having lost his long-term relationship with Joe Campbell, the relationship with Craig, and unhappy with his job at the Great

American Insurance Co., he had left New York for Puerto Rico, and then headed to Miami Beach to find new work. Nothing materialized and he had returned to Manhattan, where, in the summer of 1963, he secured a position as a securities research analyst at Bache and Company.[16]

Harvey had visited Craig just once during his recovery at St. Luke's. They wouldn't connect again until the Oscar Wilde opened years later.

3

New York II – Militants in Mattachine

After the disasters of 1962 and 1963, Craig would try again in New York, dedicating himself to the work of the homophile movement. January 1964 was going to be a fresh start.

He resumed his commitment to New York Mattachine, working on the monthly newsletter, where he set the type for Randy Wicker's what's-happening column, "The Wicker Report," painstakingly justifying every line for a professional look. By February, he was named assistant editor, and he was asked what pseudonym he planned to use in the masthead. When he said he would use his own name, Mattachine convinced him otherwise and for three issues, Craig was Craig Philips, assistant editor. By May, uncomfortable with the façade, Craig reverted to using his real name.[1]

Craig was the youngest member of New York Mattachine.[2] Most of the members were older, in their fifties and sixties. He was okay with whatever disparities there might be at first, because it was a thrill to distribute flyers about Mattachine meetings and just to know that there were people like him, gathering to think and talk about the lives of gay people.

The 1964 Mattachine newsletters often promoted speakers who would provide psychological analysis of homosexuality. Expert speakers essentially told the members why they were like they were. Many of the older conservative members saw their sexuality as something to be tolerated but not normal by a heterosexual society's definition. And there were speakers on religion and homosexuality. Mattachine couldn't do political activity – they feared job losses if they were exposed – and they were fearful of what a young militant like Craig might cause with his radical ideas.

"But at the beginning, when I first started there, the self-hatred was – it wasn't even called self-hatred.... They couldn't conceive of the idea of fighting for one's right to be homosexual."[3]

Amid his return to New York that winter, one night while cruising in the Village, Craig caught the eye of a former schoolteacher from Kentucky. It was the start of a tense personal and professional relationship with Dick Leitsch.[4]

Leitsch had heard of Mattachine but was not involved. As a brief affair got underway, Leitsch realized that Craig was spending most nights at Mattachine meetings or staffing the office. Encouraged by Craig, Leitsch joined up himself. There, Leitsch became friends (and later roommates) with another Mattachine member whom Craig had also brought in, Julian Hodges. The three of them – Leitsch, Hodges, and Rodwell – would set out to change the agenda.

In May, Julian succeeded Paul Speier as president of New York Mattachine and actively sought publicity for the organization under his own name.[5] He was one of the younger, more militant members and promised a new approach.

Meanwhile, Craig's personal relationship with Leitsch went sour very quickly. Craig had just returned to New York that winter from his year-long "hiatus." While he was at first charmed by Leitsch's personality, he increasingly found him to be too critical and too controlling.

"We weren't lovers; Dick thought we were lovers."

By Memorial Day, he had told Leitsch that it just wasn't there. Leitsch then laid out the problems of their relationship in a three-page, single-spaced typewritten letter. While declaring his enduring love for Craig, he also blamed him.[6]

The two were a mismatch personally and professionally, a dynamic that would play out in their correspondence. As their short affair collapsed, Leitsch found Craig to be narcissistic and having a "big affair with himself." He thought that Craig lacked trust and the characteristics that would bring him happiness throughout his years. He predicted that Craig would lead a plodding and miserable life. The resentments ran deep. While Craig in later years did not hesitate to criticize his former friend, especially for the demise of the Mattachine Society of New York, he often tried to take the high road and seemed to have an easier time of it.

Craig had apparently suggested that the two put the bitterness aside, and in July, writing from Fire Island, Leitsch agreed that they should try. He half-apologized for his previous psychoanalysis but concluded with some suggestions for how Craig could learn to truly love someone else. Meanwhile, Leitsch would be back in New York for the Mattachine board meeting later that month. He would see Craig there.[7]

The work at Mattachine provided a way for both men to put their testy words behind them, and they managed to negotiate a working relationship for the good of the cause. In fact, Craig promoted the team of Julian Hodges and Leitsch for president and vice president in the May 1965 Mattachine elections. Hodges had held the presidency in 1964, with the trust of the more conservative members of the organization. But times were changing, and the new militant team was voted in. Craig adopted a new slogan: "Let's Get Mattachine Moving."[8]

In an appeal for contributions to the cause, Julian wrote in the Eastern Mattachine Magazine that "it is our function to overcome this hostility through active and positive efforts to gain full civil and social rights for members." He said that Mattachine would protest unfair employment practices and unfair treatment by police and government, that the organization would protect homosexuals in trouble legally and educate the public to stamp out prejudice.[9]

But his efforts were short-lived. By fall, concern over finances caused Hodges to resign abruptly and move to Miami. Dick Leitsch ascended and would serve until 1971.[10]

♦♦♦♦♦

Saturday, September 19, 1964, broke as a gray, drizzly day in New York with the afternoon temperature peaking in the

60s. In the park on Broadway near the Customs House, a small group was gathering to do something no one else had done before – a homosexual picket. They didn't know how their plan would play out, and while committed, they were anxious.

This date falls squarely in what the Selective Service calls the "Vietnam War Period." Men ages eighteen to twenty-six were required to register for the draft. And when they did, they would be classified based on a pre-induction medical questionnaire. 1-A meant you were healthy and ready to serve. And 4-F meant you were "unfit for military service," on physical, mental, or moral grounds.

Someone would be designated 4-F if, during their induction examination, they checked the box indicating homosexual tendencies or if the military determined they had homosexual tendencies. The military policy in the 1960s, in effect since 1943, stated that homosexuals were to be banned from any military service. The fallout from a 4-F classification could be life-changing – draft paper codes were well known, so it was quite clear why someone was not admitted or why they were discharged. For gay people who did want to serve, they were denied a future in the military. Then, for them and for others who didn't want to serve but were doing their duty by registering, their job futures were in jeopardy, as prospective employers could ask about someone's draft status and rule them out of a job.[11]

Craig had been here before. The previous summer he received his order to come to the station for his physical examination into the armed forces. There's no question that he would have checked the box.

On this Saturday, the small band of ten homosexual and heterosexual picketers headed to Lower Manhattan and 39 Whitehall Street, the Armed Forces Whitehall Street Induction Center. Dressed in professional attire and fortified with picket signs, they marched in a circle in front of the center for a couple of hours.[12]

Leading the charge was Randy Wicker, an early and ground-breaking gay militant in Mattachine and founder of the Homosexual League of New York, who would later provide buttons for the Oscar Wilde Memorial Bookshop. The confidentiality of draft records was being breached, and he hoisted his sign with the accusation: "Army Invades Sexual Privacy." Right behind him was Craig with his sign, "Keep Draft Records Private."

No one really noticed. Rodwell remembered that "one sergeant" in the doorway gave them a disinterested look. There was no media coverage, in part because the group had yet to learn its media skills. As Renée Cafiero, fourth in the picket line and a lesbian member of Mattachine, remembered: "We had no spectators, actually, there was nobody there! It was a Saturday!"[13]

While there was no immediate effect, the door was cracked open; a few brave protesters had put themselves on the line in the first-ever picket for homosexual rights.[14] And it was a catharsis. Cafiero felt that the brave picketers had successfully tested the waters and were ready for much bigger ideas in the coming year.[15]

Those much bigger ideas turned into a ground-breaking set of pickets in 1965 in Washington, New York, Philadelphia, and San Francisco.[16] Wicker had already advocated protest actions, and Frank Kameny was encouraged by Jack Nichols and his partner Lige Clarke to initiate a White House picket under the auspices of the Mattachine Society of Washington. The protests had the support and participation of Barbara Gittings, editor of the lesbian journal *The Ladder*. Craig Rodwell would join in with his own proposal.

While Craig respected Kameny, their relationship was an uneasy one. Kameny, fifteen years older than Craig, was co-founder of Mattachine Washington and the East Coast Homophile Organizations (ECHO), an umbrella group that formed in 1962 to improve communication and cooperation. His background was completely different from Craig's. He was an astronomer with a doctorate from Harvard, had worked for and been fired by the US Army Map Service, and might have hoped to be an astronaut. He had an intense focus on homosexuals' rights under the law and in government. Known for his fairly stiff and demanding personality, he and Craig could get on each other's nerves.

By 1965, Kameny was aggressively arguing against the homosexuality-is-a-sickness theory, and in March, Mattachine Washington adopted a policy promoted by Kameny, Jack Nichols, and Lilli Vincenz:

> The Mattachine Society of Washington takes the position that in the absence of valid evidence to the contrary, homosexuality is not a sickness, disturbance, or other pathology in any sense, but is merely a preference, orientation, or propensity, on par with, and not different in kind from, heterosexuality.[17]

That policy was drafted shortly before the New York Mattachine election in May, when the young militants took charge.

Meanwhile, on April 15, 1965, Fidel Castro's government newspaper reported that homosexuals were not considered to be part of the Cuban movement, which was interpreted to mean that homosexuals would be rounded up and sent to detention or labor camps.[18] The news was the spark for activists Jack Nichols in Washington and Wicker and Rodwell in New York to initiate pickets in both cities. Kameny had been considering pickets, and after adjusting the message to focus on homosexual discrimination in this country, the pickets were on. The Washington picket would occur on Saturday, April 17, in front of the White House late in the afternoon, when ten picketers made history with the first protest for gay rights in the nation's capital.

The next day, Wicker and Rodwell led twenty-nine protesters on an Easter Sunday picket at the United Nations to protest the imprisonment of homosexuals in Cuba. As Kameny had suggested, the message was combined: "15,000,000 US Homosexuals Protest Federal Treatment" and "Cuba's Government Persecutes Homosexuals," the picket signs shouted.[19]

There were nine pickets in all that year, and it would change the course for gay rights.[20]

The second picket at the White House was staged on May 29, with thirteen protesting prejudice against homosexuals. Unlike the first picket, this one received press from more than a half-dozen mainstream organizations.

The next picket was a protest against employment discrimination on June 26 at the Civil Service Commission with twenty-five picketers.

But it was the picket at the White House in May that had been the "most wonderful day" of Craig's life – to be out in the open and calling on official Washington to change. On the way back to New York, he couldn't fathom that it might end there, and in a booth at a "greasy spoon" restaurant with Leitsch, Kameny, and Nichols, Rodwell pitched an idea. The militants should stage a protest every year on July 4 at Independence Hall in Philadelphia to remind people that there was a minority group that still did not have the basic rights of life, liberty, and the pursuit of happiness as set forth in the 1776 Declaration of Independence. It would be called the "Annual Reminder."[21]

Kameny was convinced, and with quick organization, on July 4, outside of Independence Hall, forty-four picketers marched in a circle in 80-degree heat. The first Annual Reminder was a success.[22]

A two-sentence mention in the July 4 holiday roundup on page one of the *Philadelphia Inquirer* the next day read: "Across the street from the national shrine, a group of 30 neatly dressed men and women picketed in a circle. Their signs asked for equal rights for homosexuals." The paper's lead story of the day was a B-52 bombing out of Guam on a North Vietnamese communications and staging area.[23]

Organized by Kameny, Barbara Gittings, and Rodwell, and under the auspices of Kameny's East Coast Homophile Organizations, the picket had followed the rules laid down by Kameny. The idea was that to gain the attention of the heterosexual majorities, picketers would need to look "employable" and as Rodwell said, "ordinary." Kameny had described the look after the White House picket: "well-groomed, and well-dressed – suits, white shirts, and ties, for men; dresses for women...."[24]

In the *New York Mattachine Newsletter* that summer, the "next demonstration" mentioned was the July 31 picket at the Pentagon. All members were encouraged to attend: "You have the right to protest the policy that, in effect, states you may not serve your country in the armed forces if you so choose, and that makes it difficult to for you to remain in the service and be discharged honorably if you are drafted."[25]

After the sixteen-person protest at the Pentagon came the picket on August 28 at the State Department, where fourteen protesters raised signs about employment and security clearances; then September 26 at the Grace Cathedral in San Francisco, where thirty protested discrimination against a minister who was an ally of the community; and another picket at the White House in October with forty-five demonstrators. Craig organized the chartered buses to take the New York contingent to the demonstrations. He remembered that the bus driver was fascinated by the men and women in business attire who "looked like a church group."[26]

The idea for the Annual Reminder would stick, with Kameny as "spokesman" and with the rules for picketing that he had administered the previous year. For the second Annual Reminder, he wrote to Craig about signage – all signs should be twenty-eight inches by twenty-two inches, and people shouldn't be assembling them at the last minute on the bus. Also, all the edges should be bound with masking tape.[27] The reminders occurred after the main Fourth of July events, and videos of the event included the patriotic music that would still be playing amid the picket.

Meanwhile, Craig wrote in a letter to John Marshall, president of the Mattachine Society of Washington, that the reminders would be "self-perpetuating." The Annual Reminder Committee itself would have no formal structure, "other than each sponsoring organization having one person serve as Co-Chairman with an equal voice in the preparations." A number of modifications were requested after the first reminder: Kameny was asked to shorten a densely worded leaflet that would be passed out, and the issue of business attire was chafing – Craig told Marshall that they would try to be as reasonable as possible, and he suggested that if a couple of co-sponsors wanted change, it might be possible to relax the rules.[28]

With forty-eight donations, the Annual Reminder Committee raised more than $300. Craig reserved a forty-two-passenger bus through the Allied Bus Corp., for $135. The picketers would board the bus for the two-hour trip at 11 a.m. on July 4 at 1133 Broadway, with the return from Philadelphia at 6:30 p.m.[29]

There would be a third Annual Reminder in 1967, and the demonstration at Independence Hall would draw the attention of the Associated Press, which put out a neutral, four-paragraph story about the neatly dressed, placard-carrying demonstrators. It would be carried in newspapers around the country.

In 1968, the bus would roll up in front of the newly opened Oscar Wilde Memorial Bookshop at 291 Mercer Street. More than forty people would sign up for what would later be known as the next-to-last reminder at Independence Hall. Again, the demonstration would be sponsored by the Eastern Regional Conference of Homophile Organizations [ERCHO, successor to ECHO] and would now be backed by eleven member groups.

The concept of a perpetual demonstration each July 4 would end with the fifth reminder, which would take place the week after the 1969 Stonewall riots. By then it would be clear to Craig that the time for solemn, polite pickets was over.

The pickets were not occurring in isolation for Craig. The summer of the nine pickets, Craig had announced in the *New York Mattachine Newsletter* the formation of Mattachine Young Adults. The purpose of the group was "to develop leadership and initiative, to act as an 'action' group in promoting the program of the Society, and to perform various tasks assigned to it by the Board of Directors." All "young homosexuals (and sympathetic heterosexuals, for that matter) between the ages of 18–35 are invited to participate."

Craig summarized the purpose of Mattachine Young Adults when he spoke to Midwest Mattachine the following year: "(O)ne of the devices that dominant groups in various cultures have used to oppress certain minorities is to instill in the young people of that minority a feeling of inferiority and unworthiness." He compared the struggle of young homosexuals with the civil rights struggle of African American youth. "Through economic sanctions and social pressures both have been made to feel this sense of inferiority. It is primarily for combatting these negative and erroneous beliefs that Mattachine Young Adults was formed."[30]

Mattachine would help new members gain a sense of usefulness and self-respect: "The way we try to accomplish this at MSNY is not through a social program but a social action program. It is the function of the Young Adults Group to run the literature table at all public meetings, to act as hosts on various occasions – such as last Fall's ECHO Conference, and the forthcoming chartered buses to Philadelphia on July Fourth."

Mattachine Young Adults passed out 50,000 leaflets in just one year.

Meanwhile, in the mid-1960s, while the militants were finding their voices at protests and refining their picketing strategy, social repression was all around, especially in the bars: "They would send a plainclothes officer into a gay bar, usually wearing a fuzzy sweater and sneakers, which was the uniform of the day. And they would strike up a conversation with you and invite you home with them. As soon as you left the bar with them and got out in the street, they'd arrest you."[31]

It was also still considered "disorderly" to serve homosexuals in New York bars under State Liquor Authority regulations. A bar could lose its license if it knowingly served homosexuals, so some bars had signs in their windows telling gays to stay clear.[32]

Since social spaces were not safe, the militants decided they were going to challenge that, too. The "sit-in" had already been established by the mid-1960s, after Black Americans in many locations took their seats at whites-only lunch counters. Their sit-ins had become an established form of nonviolent protest.[33] Under the Mattachine banner, and in what would become a gay milestone, Dick Leitsch approached Rodwell and John Timmons with a plan. They would stage a "sip-in."[34]

On April 21, 1966, they telegrammed *The New York Times*, the *New York Post*, and *The Village Voice* to let reporters know they would be challenging the liquor regulation against homosexuals. They were going to make their stand at the Ukrainian-American Village Restaurant in St. Mark's Place. The sign outside said: "If You're Gay, Please Go Away."

When they arrived at the restaurant, though, it had closed; one of the reporters had tipped them off that the confrontation was coming, and the establishment decided it wanted nothing to do with it.

The troop moved on to the Howard Johnson's at Sixth Avenue and Eighth Street, which was patronized by gays. Inside, they had their speech ready. They recited the State Liquor Authority prohibition on serving homosexuals, they announced themselves as homosexuals, and they each ordered a Scotch and soda. The manager came over and, not wanting to get into the situation, had a canny response – he would serve them free drinks. He called for three bourbons and introduced a new rebuttal – how was it really possible to know if someone was a homosexual anyway?

A little way up Sixth Avenue at the Waikiki, the same course of events played out as at Howard Johnson's.

Their plan dashed in the first three tries, they headed for Julius' Bar on West 10th Street, which was adapting to the changing social clientele of its neighborhood. There, they got their case. As they proclaimed their sexuality and their intent to be served, the manager put his hand over Leitsch's glass, saying "I think it's in the law."[35]

In a now-famous photograph by Fred McDarrah, Leitsch is in the center of the photo looking directly across the bar at the manager, with Timmons to his right and Rodwell to his left. Randy Wicker had also joined the group, and all of them were in jackets and ties and white shirts. The manager has his hand over Leitsch's empty glass.[36]

Meanwhile, *New York Times* reporter Thomas A. Johnson filed his story. The headline the next day read: "Three Deviates Invite Exclusion By Bars." The lead of the one-column story at the top-center of page forty-three focused on the difficulty the group had in finding a restaurant that would participate in the action to deny them service.

Johnson also wrote in his story that the State Liquor Authority, when reached for a comment, said that service was up to individual restaurants and bars, and that the Authority was not responsible for discrimination.

The next day, on behalf of the Mattachine Society of New York, Craig issued a press release. Mattachine had deemed the action a success. First, they had proved that there was confusion over the State Liquor Authority regulations, since two of the restaurants served openly homosexual customers alcohol, which would have made the restaurant a "disorderly house." Second, the press release pointed out another contradiction – that previous court cases had determined that "disorderly" applied to homosexuals who had been convicted of solicitation. This was the first time the Liquor Authority was asked to clarify the presence of homosexuals in bars when there were no disorderly convictions. Finally, the press release said that Mattachine wasn't going to report the two restaurants that did serve them to the Liquor Authority, but they would report Julius' for discrimination based on sexual orientation. Even so, Mattachine said it "bears no ill will against Julius'" and they offered to pay the bar's legal fees. The press contact was Craig Rodwell.[37]

A political response followed a week later, as the State Liquor Authority reaffirmed to *The New York Times* – in a story deep inside the newspaper and below the fold on page fifty-five – that they did not encourage bars to refuse service to homosexuals, that it could be a matter for the Commission on Human Rights. The Commission said it would seek to end discrimination by bars if it came to their attention.[38]

Less than a month later, the *Times* reported, at the bottom of page thirty-six, that the police commissioner ordered that officers were not to entrap homosexuals in gay bars.[39]

Not only had the militants gained traction within New York politics and inside the bars, they had gained some footing in the press.

"I realized then and I realize now that in terms of changing gay people's perceptions of themselves – who we are and what we should be and where we should be going ... you have to have media coverage that portrays you in a positive, forthright manner," Rodwell said twenty years later. "And that ultimately has that effect of making other gay people more open."[40]

Like others around the country, Mattachine Midwest had heard of the sip-in at Julius' and they were seeking inspiration themselves. Rodwell was making a trip back to Chicago to see his mother, and he was invited to speak to the group at their May meeting for a pep talk.

There he met David Stienecker, who had never encountered anyone like Craig before. There was an energy about him that was inspiring – his message that gay people had a right to be who they were and to be respected for it.[41]

The two of them hit it off, and for six weeks in the summer of 1966, Stienecker shared Craig's Horatio Street fourth-floor walkup, cooling off in the summer heat by putting an ice block in front of a fan. But it was obvious a long-term affair wasn't in the cards. Perhaps, Stienecker later speculated, because of a residual guilt over the encounter with Frank Bucalo in Craig's teenage years.

By the late 1960s, Stienecker had moved back to Chicago where, like Craig, he became involved in the Mattachine newsletter. He returned to his position as newsletter editor in 1969, where he reported that a Chicago police officer was entrapping gay men after having sex with them. His reporting led to a knock on his own apartment door one Saturday morning in February 1970, and he was face to face with the police officer, who was in plainclothes – he was being arrested on criminal defamation misdemeanor charges. Stienecker insisted on calling his attorney, and the officer called for the paddy wagon. Stienecker stood his ground and took his case to court. After three appearances, the police paperwork had gone missing and the judge dismissed the case. But this was not without cost – he ultimately lost his job as a researcher for the World Book Encyclopedia. Stienecker's story was carried in the March 1970 issue of the *New York Mattachine Newsletter*.

After living in Chicago and Florida for a time, Stienecker moved back to New York in 1979 and remained friends with Craig, following his work. Like many others, he was moved by Craig's activism and his personal appeal for people to stand up for themselves. Stienecker took part in the Pride march every year. From a distance, he maintained an emotional bond with Craig for many years to come.

4

Inside the Oscar Wilde – Mercer Street

Craig had long imagined that something much bigger could come from his literature table at the Mattachine meetings and their upstairs and out-of-sight headquarters.

"We were in a little office on Broadway and 26th Street, and I wanted Mattachine to open up a storefront somewhere. You know, to be out in the community, down here in the Village. And [I] actually got them to let us look around at a few storefronts, the board of directors, but they chickened out."[1]

One of those locations was a ground floor space on Hudson and 10th, which he got Dick Leitsch to visit. But Craig was not sure that Dick had even delivered the proposal. Dick told him that the board just wasn't ready for that kind of visibility.

The friction between the two of them had not abated after their short affair, despite Craig's efforts. He would sometimes hear from someone that Dick feared he was plotting against him, and Craig would try to assure Dick that it was not so.

"I meant what I said, Dick," he wrote, "about 'wiping the slate clean' at the Special Board meeting a couple of weeks ago. I'm not going to try and convince you here that I am not after your job – only time will prove that."[2]

But with Julian Hodges now gone as president and with other roadblocks at Mattachine, the exhilaration and enthusiasm for the organization that Craig felt when he came to New York in 1959 had worn out. He announced his resignation in December 1966 and delivered his confirmation letter in January 1967.[3]

If Mattachine wouldn't invest in a storefront, Craig would.

He had anticipated this day, so, in the summer of 1966, he began to raise money. He headed to John Whyte's Fire Island Pines Botel, where he took a summer job on the staff as a "house boy" and later "assistant manager" at the gay resort. For two summers, six days a week (off on Tuesdays), he cleaned toilets, made beds, worked in the bar, and did whatever needed to be done for $125 a week, including room and board.[4]

On the dance floor, men were still required to face a woman while dancing, so when asked, Craig reluctantly climbed a ladder, where he had to monitor the dance area for violators by shining a flashlight around the room. The "ladder" was so well known that it even made it into John Whyte's obituary in *The New York Times*.[5]

Meanwhile, the Suffolk County, Long Island, police were coming over to Fire Island and raiding the "meat rack," where hundreds of gay men gathered to find sexual partners. The police would arrest them, chain them to each other or to a pole, and take them to a court set up in the back room of a drug store, where fines were levied and collected.

Craig spent his two summers on Fire Island at the peak of the arrests, which would result in a series of trials in 1968 (a year before the Stonewall riots) in which juries put an end to the gay raids, declaring the men innocent of morals charges.[6]

Craig's determination to soldier through whatever jobs needed to be done on Fire Island resulted in more than $1,000 that he could put toward starting his own bookshop. It also resulted in another run-in with drug culture, when, during his second summer of long hours, he was introduced to speed (which he later kicked in favor of periodic use of marijuana).

Space was available at 291 Mercer Street, a classic New York side street address. Near Eighth Street, Cooper Union, and New York University, there was foot traffic, a deli on the corner, a high-rise across the street, an art gallery a few doors down, and a pet grooming shop. The space was a small, one-room, brick-fronted shop with a plate glass window that rented for $115 a month. Craig would take it.[7]

The landlord asked him what he intended to do with the space, and Craig told him he was going to open a bookshop. He wanted to know the name of the shop and Craig told him it would be "The Oscar Wilde Memorial Bookshop."

The landlord had heard of Oscar Wilde, but he didn't ask Rodwell to elaborate further, and the deal was done.[8]

The day before the opening, Marion Rodwell Kastman flew to New York from Chicago. After all that mother and son had been through, this had to be a happy day. Craig brought his mother directly to the shop from the airport and they worked all night to set up a modest ten shelves and twenty-five titles of three copies each, along with various literature and buttons promoting the movement.

The previous week, a teaser had appeared in *The Village Voice* for the Oscar Wilde, asking: "Curious? You Should Be." It was followed up with a one-column advertisement on Thursday, November 16, 1967, which announced the "Grand Opening Weekend." It included the address, telephone number, and Craig's name.[9]

On Saturday, Craig unlocked the door at 11 a.m.; he would close up at 7. On Sunday, the shop would welcome visitors from noon to 5. There would be free coffee and pastries, a free copy of the ACLU statement on homosexual law reform, and a 10 percent discount for students and members of homophile organizations.[10]

The press release for the opening led with a political tone:

> At a time when a major contender for the 1968 GOP presidential nomination is being accused of tolerating homosexuals on his staff and for not firing them immediately, it is indeed timely that the OSCAR WILDE MEMORIAL BOOKSHOP should open.[11]

Why Oscar Wilde? The release explained:

Oscar Wilde, the first homosexual in modern times to defend publicly the homosexual way of life, is a martyr to what has recently become known as the "homophile movement." The example of his life was a moving force in the recent passage by the English Parliament of the Wolfenden proposals which, in effect, legalized homosexuality in England.[12]

There would be books (non-fiction and fiction), pamphlets and periodicals, cards, buttons, and other items pertaining to the homophile movement. There would be a community bulletin board, a clearing house for homosexual law reform, and a monthly magazine. And there would be no porn.[13]

Signs in the window proclaimed, "Gay Is Good," and "A Bookshop for the Homophile Movement."

That weekend, sitting at a small table in the new shop was Foster Gunnison Jr., of Hartford, CT, who was there to sign his new pamphlet, "An Introduction to the Homophile Movement."[14] Foster, who was in his early forties when the shop opened, had met Craig at the Mattachine Society and would be a lifelong friend and defender. He would play a trusted role in the months before the first Pride march.

With master's degrees in psychology and philosophy, Foster had just published his thirty-seven-page paper in September, and it was presented to the Committee on Religion and Psychiatry of the American Psychiatric Association in October. Here, "amid a claimed abundance of myths, half-truths, and cynical speculations on the subject of homosexuality," he would lay out the history of the homophile movement and "call attention" to the movement's difficulties in connecting with professional organizations, particularly psychiatry.[15]

As to the use of the term *homophile*, Foster explained that "it places the emphasis on 'love' ('phile') rather than 'sex,'" and it could be "applied to organizations which include heterosexual members or supporters without implying that they are themselves homosexual." There was another reason: The word could be used as a euphemism for homosexual when circumstances were otherwise constricting.[16]

Foster would certainly have drawn from his friendship with Craig when he wrote in his concluding paragraphs that "the organized homosexual is coming more and more to regard himself as in no way inferior because of his homosexuality, or homosexuality as in no way inferior to its counterpart as a valid mode of human self-expression; and he is expecting that society will eventually come around to a similar view."[17]

With the shoestring grand opening, America's first bookshop dedicated solely to gay and lesbian literature had made history.[18]

"My general policy was to have a shop where gay people didn't feel they were being exploited either sexually or economically," Craig said three years after opening. "People call me a puritan, and in a sense I have to agree with them. I don't mean I'm a puritan sexually – far from it. But the reason I'm against most of the highly sexual magazines, for example, is not the content particularly – although it's done rather leeringly – but the whole sexploitation angle. A ten-dollar price on something that makes sex look dirty and furtive."[19]

By the end of November, Craig's weekly advertisement in the *Voice* was now identifying the shop as "A Bookshop for the Homophile Movement."

While the opening was a big success and Craig quickly sold out of what he considered to be the better titles, the shop's landlord was not pleased. Not knowing that the bookshop was going to be a bookshop for gays and lesbians, he wanted to challenge the lease, but it was rock solid and too late for him to do anything about it. By 1973, when he moved the shop to Christopher Street, the landlord told him he had learned from the experience and had respect for Craig and the bookshop's customers.[20]

The name of the shop became an emblem of the gay liberation movement, and as Craig had hoped, it drew customers. Oscar Wilde was so widely known for his literary contributions and his homosexuality that people would know what the shop was about. It was indeed prophetic that Wilde's *The Happy Prince* was Craig's favorite book as a child at Chicago Junior School, even though he didn't realize the connection when he was thinking of the public face of the bookshop.[21]

Wilde, who was tried, convicted, and jailed for his homosexuality, was widely praised for his artistic and literary depth and creativity. In 1882, his four-month lecture tour of the United States stretched into an entire year, ending with a stay in Greenwich Village.[22]

Oscar Wilde would show up in Craig's life in different ways. It's likely that when Craig was assistant editor at the *New York Mattachine Newsletter*, he typeset a review of a new biography of Wilde's lover, Lord Alfred Douglas.[23]

The bookshop always stocked at least one title by Wilde.[24] There were three titles in the mail-order catalog from 1968: *The Riddle of Shakespeare's Sonnets*, by Stephen Spender and others, with complete texts of Shakespeare's sonnets and Wilde's novella *Portrait of Mr. W.H.*; *De Profundis*, the text of Wilde's letter to Lord Alfred Douglas during Wilde's imprisonment; and *Five Plays by Oscar Wilde*. The catalog quotes from *The Picture of Dorian Gray*: "There is no such thing as a moral or an immoral book. Books are well written or badly written. That is all."[25] It was Douglas, Wilde's young lover, who wrote the now famous words (sometimes misattributed to Wilde), "I am the love that dare not speak its name" in his poem "The Two Loves."[26]

But here, in the Oscar Wilde, homosexual love would be spoken, promoted, and thought of positively. People would be inspired to be open. And others, including Harvey Milk, would be inspired to follow in Craig's footsteps.

Not everyone thought he would succeed with a serious bookshop. Clark Polak was the founder of *DRUM* magazine in 1964, published by the Janus Society in Philadelphia. The magazine featured the male physique and promoted sexually positive attitudes. He also operated Trojan Book Service out of Philadelphia, which distributed gay porn. Polak wrote to Craig when the shop was opening and told him he would never make it on literature alone:

> The mass of those persons who will be your customers want photographs and strong fiction. They do not want Mary Renault. If you continue to specialize in this way, you won't make it.[27]

◆◆◆◆◆

Soon after the Oscar Wilde opened, the small, carefully worded *Village Voice* advertisement announcing its arrival caught the eye of a young man from Connecticut who had been hopping on the train to New York since he was sixteen years old.

Fred Sargeant, just nineteen, was working a data processing job in a brokerage house on Wall Street. The *Voice* advertisement had gotten his attention – this was an actual bookshop, not a porn store. He stopped in, met Craig, and purchased one of the homophile periodicals from the still-modest inventory; the two of them had an immediate connection, and Sargeant returned a week later.

After the closing bell on Wall Street, he would regularly stop by the shop to see Craig, and they would share a light supper before Fred returned to his apartment on 59th Street.[28]

As the short days of the winter of 1967–8 lengthened, Craig invited Fred to move in. To save money, Craig had rented a second-floor, cold-water apartment at Eighth Avenue and 15th Street. It was freezing, and after staying there a matter of days Fred convinced Craig that with his own limited income they could and had to do better. As Fred walked by 350 Bleecker on the way to the Oscar Wilde, he saw a for-rent sign in the window. Third floor, apartment 3V, for $200 a month – they would take it. The Bleecker Street apartment would turn out be a nerve center of the gay movement for the next few years and home to Craig for the rest of his life.

Physically, the Oscar Wilde Memorial Bookshop was small – one room with a tiny bathroom that was used to store what inventory they could afford. To increase the stock, Craig and Fred would make regular trips to Bookazine on West 10th Street near the Hudson River, walking back as many titles as they could pay for and carry. If they bought ten books it could have an impact on what they would eat for supper. On a lean day, that meal might be an English muffin.

Randy Wicker had opened his button shop – the Underground Uplift Unlimited at 28 St. Mark's Place in 1966.[29] Craig had known Randy through New York Mattachine, the Induction Center demonstration, the sip-in at Julius', and other protests. Randy supported the bookshop and helped with the button inventory. Among the buttons in the display were "Gay Is Good" and "Buy Gay," which was a slogan the shop adopted. You could also buy the interlocking male or female biological symbols buttons, or "Homosexuals for Peace." All buttons were twenty-five cents.[30] Matchbooks, bumper stickers, and other small items helped to keep the store going in its early months.

When Craig and Fred moved to Bleecker Street, the Oscar Wilde moved to a more consistent operation with regular hours. Fred would open the shop in the morning and Craig would come in later so that Fred could get to his job at Carlisle & Jacquelin. Later that winter, business was picking up, so Fred quit his job on Wall Street to work in the bookshop full-time, becoming its first manager. For Craig, what he had once just imagined was now taking real shape. The militant protests were getting noticed, his storefront, with its plate-glass window and positive displays of gay literature, was open. Some days when they closed up, Craig would be off to bingo at the Catholic church and Fred would head back to Bleecker Street. Craig had a committed relationship; his life with Fred was stable. In this moment, everything seemed to be working.

The Oscar Wilde had opened at a junction of historical events. The US involvement in the Vietnam War was in its peak years, college campus protests and demonstrations were everywhere, the struggle for civil rights was boiling over, hippies had declared a "generation gap," and political assassinations stunned the nation.

Even in that climate, young homosexuals across America would not dare to tell their families, their employers, or even their closest friends about their true lives. Even in Greenwich Village, the gay mecca, potential customers would pace back and forth outside the Oscar Wilde, working up the courage to take the plunge. Once inside, they would try at first to hide their faces.

Craig and Fred looked for even the smallest steps to make life easier. Every customer who walked through the door was greeted warmly. They set out to assure patrons that they were welcome here, they were respected here, and they were valued in society. The mail-order catalog explained:

> It is a bookshop with a purpose – namely, to provide young Homosexual men and women with literature and counseling to help them gain a sense of pride and dignity as young Homosexuals. In our first year, we counseled more than 1,000 young people along these lines.[31]

The first year also saw the number of books, periodicals, and pamphlets triple, much of it still coming one armload at a time from Bookazine.

Instead of secretly searching the library shelves for any book that might mention homosexuality, usually in the psychiatry section, gay men and women now had a resource. Titles in the catalog included *The Gay World*, the playscript of *The Boys in the Band*, Donald Webster Cory's *The Homosexual in America* and *The Lesbian in America*, *Billy Budd*, and *The Alice B. Toklas Cookbook*. A collection of pamphlets included "Homosexuality & the Armed Services," a guide for draft-age homosexual men and women, and "The Church & the Homosexual." A sample packet of eight different homophile publications offered a window into the gay world around the country.[32]

Fred sent a copy of Dr. Martin Hoffman's *The Gay World* to his mother in Connecticut, hoping it would break the ice about his new life in New York. After receiving it, his mother didn't speak to him for a year.

Craig wanted the Oscar Wilde to have a coffee-shop feel, so coffee and donuts were available.

Music was also part of the shop's atmosphere from the beginning. Terry Rohnke, who later went on to be technical director for *Saturday Night Live* and the *David Letterman Show*, was another early friend of the shop. Rohnke had his own studio and produced reel-to-reel tapes for the shop. Fred was the deejay for the shop radio station – WGAY – and Rohnke would distribute a three-hour taped program to subscribers.

Later, in 1969, when actor and singer Zebedy Colt produced arrangements of classic torch songs for the vinyl LP *I'll Sing for You*, the 33-rpm record flew off the shelves – it was the first time most people heard a man seriously singing love songs about another man. And the music, recorded with the London Philharmonic, was good – although it could become a little tiresome if you worked at the Oscar Wilde and heard the songs over and over.

The warm welcome of the Oscar Wilde was extended to customers by "Michael" and "Albert," two schnauzers – brothers – who were featured in advertisements for the shop. The dogs had the effect of releasing the anxiety a customer might feel in an openly gay place.

Advertisements in *The Village Voice* gradually became more direct. Craig had sought to use the word *gay* in the publication's bulletin board section, but in the winter of 1968, he was told that *gay* could not be used to advertise the *New York Hymnal* as "New York's Gay Monthly." Craig protested with a letter to publisher (and one of the *Village Voice* founders) Ed Fancher.

"This afternoon, I was informed ... that our ad could no longer use the word 'gay' in it," Craig wrote. He said when he talked to the clerk, she told him she objected to the word, that she considered it "morose," and that she thought homosexuals were "sick."[33]

Later that year, though, the words "Buy Gay" appeared in the Oscar Wilde's Christmas advertising in the same publication.

Then, on September 12, 1969, the Gay Liberation Front staged a protest in front of *The Village Voice* because the paper would not allow the word *gay* in the GLF classified advertisement seeking writers and in advertising for their dances. About a hundred picketers showed up in front of the corner office at Christopher Street and Seventh Avenue, and by the end of the day three of them were allowed to meet with Fancher, who ultimately backed down and said that the words *gay* and *homosexual* would be acceptable in the classified copy.[34]

As the tide turned, Craig's weekly advertising shifted from the "bookshop of the homophile movement," to his "Buy Gay" slogan, and then to "gay and proud." Week after week, *Voice* readers would see the reinforcing phrase "Gay and Proud" in the shop's advertising.

In *QQ Magazine,* some of the "gay and proud" ads included a photo of Craig and Fred, pictured with "Albert" and "Michael" in front of them on the counter. The ads said, "gay guides," "homophile periodicals," "fiction & nonfiction," and "stop by or send 25¢ for catalog."

The Oscar Wilde was advertised as a shop for homosexual men and women, but titles for women were less available in the late 1960s. The 1968 mail-order catalog listed some lesbian-related books, including *Sex Variant Women in Literature* by Jeannette Foster, *The Lesbian in America* by Donald Webster Cory, *Olivia,* an English novel, and *The Mesh* by Lucie Marshal. Pamphlets included "The Lesbian in Literature" and "Homosexuality & the Armed Services," for men and women. Periodicals included *The Ladder* (the lesbian review) and the newsletter from the New York Daughters of Bilitis.[35]

While Craig was an early bridge between the gay and lesbian communities, correspondence in June 1970 between Craig and the Daughters of Bilitis raised the issue of titles available for women at the shop. Craig had heard criticisms of the Oscar Wilde's stock in the lesbian community and that a picket was being considered. He responded to the DOB in New York, stating that the shop carried items for both men and women and said so in its advertising. About 25 percent of the customers were homosexual women, and the shop shelves reflected the available published works for women, which were outnumbered by publications for men. Craig wrote that it was also difficult to get copies of *The Ladder* to sell and that at the New York DOB office he was told they didn't talk to "gentlemen." Barbara Grier, editor of *The Ladder* from Kansas City, wrote back immediately to calm things down and to assure Craig that she supported him, the Oscar Wilde, and that she knew of no efforts to picket the shop and would not endorse them if they occurred. Craig had also noted in his correspondence that he paid women and men employees at the same rate.[36]

Craig had respect for the lesbian community, and by the end of his life, some of his friends would refer to him as a fierce feminist. At an ECHO conference in Washington, he remembered being moved to tears as he watched Barbara Gittings and Kay Tobin Lahusen set up recording equipment for the panelists. They were working together with "love and intensity," and it was "the same thing I felt."[37] Moved by the "genuine devotion showed through simple actions" was how Craig put it, reflecting what he wanted to attain in his own relationships.

Without the restrictions of Mattachine, Craig could forge his own community movement through the Oscar Wilde. His idea was to pair the bookshop business with a movement organization. He named it the Homophile Youth

Movement in Neighborhoods. HYMN would do some of its most important work as the Stonewall riots broke in 1969.

HYMN operated very loosely to bring people together to take action where it was needed. There were no *Roberts' Rules of Order* and no membership fees. If you wanted to be a member, you were a member. Fred Sargeant became the vice chair of HYMN. The "in Neighborhoods" suffix was added because Craig did not want the acronym to be perceived as male-only and sexist, which he thought would be the case with three letters (HYM). He was ahead of his time, as the term *sexist* wasn't part of the vernacular in 1967. But his goal was visibility for both men and women.

With the Oscar Wilde's shelves stocked and HYMN established, Craig began a publication of his own: *The New York Hymnal*. *The Hymnal* debuted in February 1968; it was six pages on eight-and-a-half by eleven-inch stock, with Rodwell's own graphics, using his typewriter for body type and the Bodoni font for headline and display typography.[38]

With HYMN formed, Craig used the organization's weight to further address his complaints with the newspapers. He wrote to the editor of the *New York Post* to protest "giving so much space and credence to such blatantly prejudiced individuals regarding homosexuals." He begged them to rethink "the harm that such articles, unchallenged, can do to reinforce the climate of hatred and fear of the homosexual."[39]

He wrote letters to the editor. One to the *Post* pointed the finger at columnist Harriet Van Horne for a piece in which she warned that overcrowded cities would harbor "violence, homosexuality, mental illness and untended babies left to die." In another she listed the Oscar Wilde among the "objectional institutions in today's world."

Craig had much kinder words for Abigail Van Buren, "Dear Abby," whose column he read regularly. "You mentioned at the end of your 2/9 column that people had written you to blast you for your refusal to put down the Homosexual," he wrote. "So I thought you might like to receive a letter from someone commending you for your humanness in your attitudes toward Gay people."

◆◆◆◆◆

Kay Tobin Lahusen, who had known Rodwell through previous demonstrations and included him as one of the fifteen profiles in her 1972 book *The Gay Crusaders*, remembered the early days in the bookshop as lean but exhilarating. She told one interviewer that Craig certainly "wasn't about to publish books about psychiatrists saying we were sick."

"He would sit there on cold winter nights with his little dog at his side, his little Schnauzer, and he would have the coffee pot on and some donuts, maybe, if it was a cold night. And he would talk to the people who wandered in. Many of them were gay people who just desperately needed somebody to talk to and needed to see a book that was halfway positive, at least. He was doing, I think, a very good service in the movement."[40]

Lahusen had insight into Rodwell's personality: "Craig often said, I'm not a very gregarious person, but he realized so many people needed somebody to talk to, so it was really wonderful. He really wanted it as a service to the gay movement and a way to help the gay minority, and never mind the older, stodgy New York Mattachine."

While Rodwell devoted his life as a facilitator of change, he did not relish the role of leader, yet he gravitated to positions of leadership in the movement and as a personal advisor, providing solace and hope for countless homosexuals across the country.

◆◆◆◆◆

Ora McCreary graduated from Dartmouth College in 1967 and then from Rutgers University in 1969. His lover was living in New York and McCreary moved to the city to be with him the week before the Stonewall riots. The year before, McCreary, then twenty-two, had visited the Oscar Wilde. It took courage just to walk through the door:

> On my first visit I approached it from the opposite side of the street, glancing into the shop with pretended nonchalance, my nervousness barely hidden. I walked back and forth probably ten times before I went in. (An onlooker might have said "he was acting suspiciously.") Fred was behind the counter. He later talked about how often he saw people across the street doing the same thing I had done before they got up the nerve to walk through the door.[41]

McCreary and his lover Charles became good friends with Craig and Fred. It was at their apartment in Washington Square Village that Rodwell and Sargeant had spent the evening having dinner and playing cards before walking home and encountering the start of the Stonewall riots.

McCreary was also one of the participants in the recordings for "WGAY" by Terry Rohnke. He recalled that the circle of friends and acquaintances from the bookshop who would gather for the sessions would include Craig, Fred, Barbara Gittings, Kay Tobin Lahusen, and Frank Kameny.

♦♦♦♦♦

Craig, Fred, and the Oscar Wilde's close family of volunteers were befriended by Bernard Koten, a Russian language instructor at New York University. He was a gay, died-in-the-wool Communist, and someone the FBI had their eyes on. Koten lived in an uptown commune and supported the young activists' work. He was a regular and an anchor of sorts to these young radicals.

Knowing how little money Craig and Fred lived on, Koten would often bring food. When it came time to move into 350 Bleecker, the rotund, fifty-something Koten helped them walk their belongings to the new apartment. When they settled in, their possessions consisted of a convertible sofa-bed, a burgundy dresser Fred had found in a secondhand shop, a black-and-white television on a stool, Craig's manual typewriter, and their prized possession – a glass-top coffee table.

In the spring of 1968, Koten returned to Eastern Europe and Prague to visit friends, but it was during the Prague Spring of government reforms and mass protests. Concerned that Koten might not be able to get out of the country in the turmoil, Craig and Fred contacted the State Department in Prague to try to reach him. Koten was able to leave, and on his way home, he picked up gifts. He knew about

Fred's French heritage (he was born in Fontainebleau), so he brought back a poster from the May riots in Paris ("Frontiére Repression") and a hand-carved bread board.

Someone else touched by Bernard's steady influence at the shop was Ellen Broidy, who would later play a key role in the 1970 Pride march.

Ellen was a student at NYU in 1967, and Mercer Street was on the route she took home from the main campus. One day she noticed that the storefront at 291 Mercer was getting a new tenant, and she wandered in. She was immediately taken by the openness of the bookshop with its large window that, unlike the bars and clubs, was "not going to be painted black." The message she got was "come in, come home."[42]

After the shop opened, Ellen offered to take volunteer shifts behind the checkout desk. Over time, the Oscar Wilde became a second home for her and members of the NYU Student Homophile League. They would meet on campus, but they would gravitate to the bookshop.

It was a brave act just to walk into an openly gay bookshop, and Ellen remembered that many people would enter the Oscar Wilde and announce that they were working on "a paper on sociology," which was often true for both students and faculty.

Ellen and her then-partner Linda Rhodes had long talks with Craig about books that would appeal to women, especially books in which the lesbian characters didn't die in the plot sequence. The late sixties were an inflection point for lesbians in literature, when positive lesbian characters were starting to appear. Craig responded, trying to find books that were affirming.

What still stands out in Ellen's mind is the day that Craig invited her to paint a heart on the bathroom wall and to paint her and Linda's names in it. The heart was photographed and made it, as Ellen remembered, into an article in *Time* magazine.

For Ellen, Craig's view of gay pride had shaped her own consciousness as an out lesbian: "not only being who you are but being damn proud of who you are." Craig had an "absolute passion to uncover things that reflected our experience back to us in ways that were not mediated by the church, the medical profession, or the criminal law establishment."[43]

Two years later, it would be Ellen who would stand up at the Eastern Regional Conference of Homophile Organizations (formerly ECHO) to present the resolution that resulted in the first Pride march.

They had their differences. Ellen was nonplussed with Craig's name for the Homophile Youth Movement in Neighborhoods. HYMN didn't exactly sound welcoming to lesbians, but she overlooked it. But after the Stonewall riots, they would split over the direction of the movement, with Ellen leaning into the work of the Gay Liberation Front.

◆◆◆◆◆

In 1970, Jonathan Ned Katz, who had grown up in New York, was tentatively becoming aware of the gay movement. The Oscar Wilde was just a mile away from his childhood home on Jane Street. That year, he was entering his thirties, closeted, and he found himself in front of the bookshop. Twice he walked around the block, thankful that 291 Mercer was a quiet location, not on the main streets. His impression, accurately, was that here was this tiny place and if he could just get through the door, "[i]t was like a statement; it was scary to go into a gay bookstore. What does that say about conditioning to be made so anxious.... It made you gay if you walked into a gay place."[44]

Jonathan soon found other doors to walk through – he became involved in the Gay Activists Alliance meetings in 1971. Then in 1972, he participated in his first Christopher Street Liberation Day march. And he would have more interactions with the Oscar Wilde later when he published his ground-breaking work *Gay American History: Lesbians & Gay Men in the USA*.

◆◆◆◆

The relationship between Craig and Fred came at a critical time. They were among the new arrivals in New York in their twenties who shared a sense of outrage at the injustices toward homosexuals across the country. Part of that outrage was toward the misperception that if you were gay, you were only entitled to live the life of a broken person. That was seen as the mantle of Mattachine. But they were not going to be broken spirits; in fact, this was a basis for their relationship.[45]

That the two men were together made it possible to keep the shop open, functioning, and successful. Fred could open in the morning, Craig could process mail orders from Bleecker Street, and they could scrimp and save to make ends meet. Every penny counted. They had installed a two-button rotary phone at home and at the shop, with one button for the apartment and one button for the Oscar Wilde. To save money on message units charged by New York Telephone, they would use the button lights and the "flash" that would occur when you picked up the receiver to communicate so that they could talk over the line without charges – a 1960s intercom.

Fred, with some financial background and years working in his own family's business as a teenager, kept the business side on sure footing, so Craig could devote more time to activism – the Annual Reminders, *The Hymnal*, and a slew of letters and communications about the movement.

There was not only financial risk in opening the Oscar Wilde, but there was also personal risk. In the first years, threats over the phone were common. Craig remembered one person calling many times over the course of a day, with threats such as "I'm going to burn you down [and] stick knives in you."[46]

Over the course of a day, they kept the receipts from sales in a cash box, and every so often Fred would move the cash to a spot under a cushion in the event of an attempted theft. In the early days, the loss of a day's receipts would have been a significant setback.

When they came to open the shop, they sometimes found threats scrawled on the outside, such as a swastika or phrases like "kill fags." One day the window to the shop door had been broken. Just days before, the beat cop had come in looking for the shop to go "on the pad" for $5 a week, but they refused to pay for protection. Anonymous threatening letters also came in the mail, handwritten, with epithets about the "fucking queers." In one case, Craig had alerted the FBI in New York to the threats and provided them with two of the letters. One had been addressed to Fred, promising a phone call the next week, "and if you hang up, expect the worst." The FBI returned the letters, saying the office "would take no active investigation in this matter."[47]

As public awareness of the Oscar Wilde grew, especially after the Stonewall riots and the Pride march the following year, threatening calls, profanities, and hang-ups were common. Vandals broke in one night and tossed the shop, strewing books everywhere.

In 1969, bombs were going off in New York and around the country. *The New York Times* reported eight bombings in just four months.[48] While most of the bombs were targeted at large institutions, not all radicals supported the new visibility of the homophile movement, and Rodwell and Sargeant were advised to avoid drawing attention to themselves by making public statements about the bombs.

By the time the Stonewall riots were about to erupt, they had established the personal and professional partnership that gave the Oscar Wilde its stability. The division of labor also made it possible for Craig to write the now-famous "Mafia and Cops" leaflet that he, Fred, and HYMN members distributed during the riots that helped to define and raise the profile of the resistance. The bookshop also functioned as a communication center after the Stonewall riots, during a time when there was no social media, no cell phones, no texting, and no widespread use of computers.

This cohesive partnership would play out many times in these months, and again when Craig called for an end to the Annual Reminders after Stonewall, realizing that something more than a quiet picket in front of Independence Hall needed to happen. The bookshop again was a community node, and the apartment was the meeting place. It was there that Craig, Fred, Ellen Broidy, and her girlfriend, Linda Rhodes, developed the resolution that they would take to the Eastern Regional Conference of Homophile Organizations to gain the support that would result in the historic march up Sixth Avenue from Greenwich Village to Sheep Meadow in Central Park on June 28, 1970.

Would the Oscar Wilde survive all of this? Or would it fail as Clark Polak predicted? In one of the most widely read columns of the time – "The Homosexual Citizen" in *SCREW* magazine – authors Jack Nichols and Lige Clarke unabashedly praised and promoted Craig for investing his personal savings and putting himself out front to create an unofficial community center and bookshop that wasn't a porn store.[49]

Before Craig moved the bookshop to Christopher Street in 1973, he took stock of the progress of the movement since the shop opened in 1967. In a draft letter to "Gay Brothers & Gay Sisters," he acknowledged that friends had told him that a "legitimate" bookshop wouldn't survive. But it had. "While the past 4½ years haven't been financially spectacular for me (the bookshop is a day-to-day operation), the personal satisfaction and joy in seeing our people begin to stir and throw off the chains that have bound us for centuries, is reward enough."[50]

5

The New York Hymnal

Volume I, No. 1 of *The New York Hymnal*[1] was published in February 1968, just three months after Craig opened the Oscar Wilde and a year and a half before the Stonewall riots. Its pages came to life on one of his prized possessions – the portable light table, squeezed into the kitchen-dining space at 350 Bleecker. He would stare into its white glare for hours at a time, composing and designing and straightening the pre-press pages of *The Hymnal*. They would have proper margins and typography; his Bodoni style headlines would be straight and (mostly) centered. He could set type with his trusty typewriter. And with a variety of border tapes, dry-transfer lettering, and a blade, he was in the publishing business.[2]

Craig had soaked up the press since he was a kid. He had composed and distributed his take-off-your-masks flyer as a teenager in Chicago and the flyers in New York that were so alarming to Harvey Milk. His high school typing class and temporary office jobs later on sharpened his editing skills. He was influenced by his mother, who had spent her life working in office and secretarial positions. His literature table at the Mattachine meetings exposed him to various pamphlets and possibilities, and he learned about graphic design and paste-up through his work on the Mattachine newsletter. He had created signs with countless slogans to be hoisted in pickets in New York, Washington, and Philadelphia. Now, with his own public-facing bookshop, he could create a center for the gay and lesbian community and a publication to promote the movement.

The Hymnal was an extension of HYMN, the sponsor of the Oscar Wilde's outreach and activism. Above the nameplate for the first editions of *The Hymnal* was its slogan "a publication of the homophile movement." The publication would be available for thirty cents or $4 for a year's subscription by mail.

The community was starved for information in the mid-1960s, and Craig strived to fill the need. By the time the Stonewall riots exploded, it is estimated that altogether the circulations of gay and lesbian publications were no more than 55,000.[3] Some had circulations in the hundreds or low thousands. Craig carried a number of these as current or back issues at the Oscar Wilde. Listed in the catalog for 1968 were six periodicals, mostly the "latest issue" in each case, but the shop also purchased back issues of publications. The shop carried *The Ladder*, the *Los Angeles Advocate*, which had begun only six months prior and was also a monthly newspaper, the San Francisco *Vector*, *DRUM* from Philadelphia,

The Albatross out of Houston, *Tangents*, and *ONE* (which had ceased publication in 1967) from Los Angeles. They were stocked in the Oscar Wilde as available, and a sample packet of all of them was listed in the catalog. Free newsletters from the West Side Discussion Group and the Daughters of Bilitis in New York were also in the shop.

The Hymnal would be part of the ground-breaking change in the lesbian and gay press. Its publication followed the rise (and fall) of the early *ONE* and *Mattachine Review* magazines, and it was part of the wave of more activist periodicals like *Vector* from the Society for Individual Rights in San Franciso and from an updated approach at *The Ladder* by the Daughters of Bilitis. The inchoate mission of the gay and lesbian counterculture would coalesce in the pages of these publications.

Without formal training, Craig jumped in. He would do advocacy journalism, he would report on politics from a gay perspective, and he would build community through the pages of *The Hymnal*. He carved out a niche. With its letter-sized format, it didn't look like the smaller journals of previous years, such as *The Homosexual Citizen*, which was published by the Mattachine Society of Washington. It did not feature the frontal nudity of the popular *DRUM* magazine, nor was it a sounding board in the way *The Ladder* billed its contents. Its mission was more aggressive than *Vector's* "dedicated to the education of all people."

In the first issue, Craig announced the purpose of the publication under the headline "HYMNAL Makes Bow." He said that *The Hymnal* would be directed toward the homosexual community – he wasn't publishing to gain acceptance from a general audience. He said *The Hymnal* would be both informational and motivational: News articles, reviews, and nightlife would be covered, along with voter registration campaigns, promotion of events like the Annual Reminders (three of which had occurred so far), and the idea of getting people to join the movement. While rudimentary, it would be one of the early homegrown news publications of the liberation movement.

Why "hymnal"?

"Because HYMNAL will have a 'religious' fervor and crusading spirit in its treatment of the homosexual way of life and the homophile movement. We will make no pretense of speaking to the heterosexual in trying to persuade him to 'accept' homosexuals."[4]

More than a year before Craig shouted his now famous call for "Gay Power" outside the Stonewall Inn in June 1969, he said when introducing his new publication that "In a sense, HYMNAL is bringing Gay Power to New York."

The lead story in the first issue was headlined "Mafia on the Spot" with the subhead "Mafia Control of Gay Bars Comes to Public's Attention." In his investigative reporter persona, Craig singled out the Stonewall on Christopher Street as representative, with its poor conditions and Mafia ownership, foreshadowing its place in history a year and four months later. He cited from a reliable source that the Health Department was looking into hepatitis cases that may have originated at the Stonewall due to unsanitary conditions. Unintimidated by bureaucracy, he got on the phone to the Sanitary Inspection Office and the Liquor Authority, with no luck. Undeterred, he pressed on. Here, he said, was how you could identify whether a gay bar was controlled by the Mafia:

1. When you walk in, there will be at least one or two "gray goons" sitting near the door checking out everyone as they enter. If it's a Mafia "private club" like the Stone Wall [sic] or the Bon Soir, and you are wearing a jacket and tie and don't fit the Mafia's stereotype of a "fairy," the goons at the door will refuse to let you in.
2. The bar will be dark – to hide the filth and to give the place an atmosphere of "anything goes."
3. On Friday and Saturday nights, it will cost you $3 or $4 to get in and they will give you 2 tickets for drinks.
4. There will very likely be dancing in a back room hidden from view when you enter the bar.
5. Policemen will make periodic and mysterious appearances to talk with the goons at the door.
6. The general atmosphere will be one of licentiousness and gloom.[5]

Craig went on to list ten other bars in Greenwich Village that could be identified with the aforementioned checklist. He concluded that there was going to be little government help to fight the Mafia monopoly, so he urged people to stop patronizing the bars. He promised much more reporting ahead, and he came through in later issues.[6]

Craig's activism was often expressed in two ways. First, he would shout down a system of oppression, and then he would calmly support and guide the gay community on a more personal level – they could overcome the oppression to live a better and more open life. He would bang out an in-your-face protest leaflet in one moment, and in the next write a kind letter to a Midwest teenager, struggling to come to terms with his homosexuality.

"Mafia on the Spot" nailed them both. Craig insisted on accountability from the government, and then he went directly to the almost brotherly advice to the gay community: Here's how you can identify a Mafia controlled bar; understand this and protect yourself.

Having insisted as a child and teenager on the right to be open about his own homosexuality, he would spend his adult years pulling back the curtain of secrecy that made oppression possible and showing how life for gays and lesbians could be normal.

Craig followed up his first issue's "Mafia on the Spot" by comparing the gay cultures of New York and San Francisco in the second issue of *The Hymnal*.

Why Mafia ownership of the bars was a main issue may not be obvious more than fifty years later, with decades of Pride marches, same-sex marriage, and people from the community in all walks of life.

Dating back to Prohibition, the Mafia found the distribution of alcohol to be profitable, so they were well positioned to capitalize on the (mis)fortunes of society. When gay bars run by legitimate businesses were shut down in a wave of societal "cleanups" in New York, the field was wide open for the Mafia to capitalize on the outsiders of society, which in the 1960s included the gay community, "deviants" often lumped together with prostitutes and the homeless as undesirable. Prior to the 1966 "sip-in" at Julius', which challenged the regulation, it had been deemed illegal to serve alcohol to homosexuals. It was illegal for gays and lesbians to dance together, and to dress any way other than in the male or female attire that matched one's sex. It was all seen as disorderly conduct. But the culture was evolving, and people were congregating. With nowhere else to go, they were gathering at Mafia-run bars like the Stonewall Inn on Christopher Street. But the Mafia was no friend to the gay clientele. Customers were gouged, treated to watered-down drinks, unsanitary conditions, and even blackmail in the dim light and sordid conditions of this Mafia cave. And by paying off the police, the bars could largely go about their business.[7]

When the Stonewall riots came along, while it was no longer illegal to serve alcohol to gay people, a bar still needed a liquor license, and politicians still had the means to force the undesirable segments of society out of sight by closing their gathering places.

The Stonewall got a mention in the first edition of *The Hymnal*, which introduced a column by "Carl Lee," called "It's What's Happening." Craig allowed for some creative use of pseudonyms to boost the content in his pages, and Lee was likely one of them.[8] The column, a digest and promotion of the bar and dating scene, mentioned repeated rumors that the Stonewall was closing, and that a computerized dating service – Man-to-Man – was being introduced.

By June 1968, Lee was still on the Stonewall's case: "still in operation, unfortunately. Hoping to save their declining business, the Mafia management instituted 'go-go boys' on platforms…. This 'new look' along with the filthy john, the high prices and the goons assure that the Stone wall [sic] remains the tackiest joint in town...."

The Hymnal also sought to bring a national and world context to the liberation movement with a digest of news items called "Signs of the Times," which was similar to other news clippings in the lesbian and gay press. In one issue, among the nine items in the digest was a notice that the New York Court of Appeals had ruled the previous December that "close dancing to slow music between members of the same sex is not illegal." Another item quoted an article in *The New York Times* reporting on the Canadian House of Commons' approval of a measure permitting homosexual acts between consenting adults. Still another announced the quarterly meeting of the Eastern Regional Conference of Homophile Organizations, which would include planning for the fourth Annual Reminder. And another reported that membership at the Corduroy Club on West 38th Street – one club in New York that was not Mafia run – had grown to 1,000.[9]

"Signs of the Times" in *The Hymnal* was a cornucopia of political, social, and economic items that revealed much about gay life in the late 1960s. The column reported that while the New York appeals judge allowed close dancing among same-sex couples, the Roseland Dance Palace "banned dancing between people of the same sex." Another item reported on the East German Parliament voting a new penal code that "remove[d] criminal sanctions against private homosexual acts." And another picked up on "the new Prime Minister of Canada, Pierre Elliott Trudeau," who said that "[t]here is no place for the state in the bedrooms of the nation."

In another issue, "Signs of the Times" news clips reported that "Canada has become the first country to elect a Chief Executive who had as a major campaign theme the reform and liberalization of the laws governing homosexuality." And about popular newspaper columnist Dear Abby: "[A] homosexual sought Abby's advice on whether he should leave his lover of eight years and marry in order to 'have a wife to introduce to my associates.' Abby's advice: 'Don't "use" a woman to try to fool the public.'"

Upon the death of Martin Luther King Jr. in April 1968, Craig editorialized on King's contributions and said that homosexuals should follow the lessons and example of his life. Craig told his readers that their cause was a case of civil rights too, and that dignity and self-respect were the roots of the homophile movement as well as the civil liberties movement.

In the third issue (the same issue dedicated to the memory of Martin Luther King Jr.), Craig carried a statement from the Committee to Fight Exclusion of Homosexuals from the Armed Forces as his lead story, which called out that less obvious homosexuals were being drafted to boost the number of people serving in Vietnam. The Committee was demanding uniform national standards instead of the independent judgments by induction centers. At the end, Craig added that HYMN was counseling draft-age homosexuals on their "rights and options."

Craig was not going to leave coverage of government and politics to the heterosexuals. With a presidential election coming, he would do his own political poll of 263 homosexual voters in New York City – the Homophile Opinion

Poll, a project of HYMN – to encourage the community to get involved in politics and register to vote. Senator Eugene McCarthy was the top vote-getter in the poll; Senator Robert Kennedy was second.

He sent a complimentary subscription and received a thank you from the office of Mayor John Lindsay.[10]

The Hymnal debuted in one of the most tumultuous years in US history, with the unpopular Vietnam War, political assassinations, the civil rights movement, student unrest on campuses, and the election of Richard Nixon. After the assassination of Robert F. Kennedy, Craig decided it was time to focus on society's sickness. He placed his editorial in the lead position in the June–July issue:

> We live in an era where nothing is more needed as a commitment by millions of people to stand up for what they believe in; yet up to now have been either afraid or too timid to act on that belief. We contend that society's psychosis regarding sexuality, and particularly homosexuality, is one of the factors contributing to the general "sickness" of society.

Converting his point into direct action, he encouraged people to step forward and get to Philadelphia for the July 4 Annual Reminder to demand their rights under the Constitution.

By fall 1968, Rodwell marked the progress of the homophile movement with the lead piece, "Gay Power Gains." He purposefully promoted the use of the "gay power concept" and "Gay Is Good," which was Frank Kameny's slogan that had just been approved for the North American

Conference of Homophile Organizations. Craig's list of accomplishments by the movement began with the example of a front-page story in the *Wall Street Journal* on the growing militancy of homosexuals. He also cited the WBAI radio program *The New Symposium*, which addressed homosexual topics and issues. Charles Pitts from *The New Symposium II* would come to the Oscar Wilde shortly after the Stonewall riots to interview and record Fred Sargeant for a first-hand account of the riot. Craig cited a civil lawsuit against the Bureau of Social Services demanding an end to discrimination against homosexual case workers, the founding of a Council on Religion and the Homosexual, conciliatory statements from New York Governor Nelson Rockefeller, and – what Craig considered most important – "a trend among our homosexual youth not to settle for a 'double life.'"

On the cultural side, *The Hymnal* reviewed the theater scene, mentioning in the April 1968 edition's unbylined column (not believed to be written by Craig): "A new play by Matt Crowley, 'The Boys in the Band,' opened at Theater Four on April 14, Easter Sunday. It is about homosexuals at a party and has received wide acclaim from prevue audiences." In the next issue: "Rudolf Nureyev took in 'The Boys in the Band' and caused quite a stir in the audience."

The play continued to make news in *The Hymnal's* On Stage column as it passed its 150th performance in August 1968. The movie *The Fox*, based loosely on D.H. Lawrence's novel about the relationship between two women, was stirring up controversy. And *Time* magazine, which would be protested for its overview of the homosexual in America the following year, published a feature on the history of homosexuality in the movies from 1929 to 1968.

Craig also allowed for an astrology column – "Gaystrology" – that viewed the alignment of the stars through gay eyes.[11]

Craig was a fan of the Society for Individual Rights in San Francisco, reporting that they had the right approach toward keeping the Mafia out of gay bars. He devoted a full page to SIR's "Homosexual Bill of Rights" – that "private consensual sex acts between persons over the age of consent shall not be offenses"; that "solicitation for any sexual act shall not be an offense except upon the filing of a complaint by the aggrieved party, not a police officer or agent"; that "a person's sexual orientation or practice shall not be a factor in the granting of or renewing of Federal security clearance, visas, and the granting of citizenship"; that "Service in and discharge from the armed forces and eligibility to VA [veterans'] benefits shall be without reference to homosexuality"; and that "A person's sexual orientation or practice shall not affect his eligibility for employment with federal, state, or local governments." SIR's bill of rights went on to include ten areas of immediate reform.

"Buy Gay" was promoted in the first edition. With purchasing power could come social power. Craig wrote, "One way that everyone can actively support the homophile movement is by supporting those who support the movement. This is the essence of Gay Power."

By mid-1968, Craig had brought in advertising revenue for close to a third of the space in his twelve-page double issue for August–September.

His own half-page advertisement for the Oscar Wilde is a window into what the community was reading in the late 1960s. Some of the titles listed:

- *Numbers*, by John Rechy, in paperback for $1.25
- *Myra Breckinridge*, by Gore Vidal, in paperback for $1.25
- *Giovanni's Room*, by James Baldwin, in paperback for $.75
- *Last Exit to Brooklyn*, by Hubert Selby, in paperback for $1.25
- *The Heart in Exile*, by Rodney Garland, in paperback for $.75
- *Staircase*, by Charles Dyer, the playscript for $1.95
- *The Lesbian in America*, by Donald Webster Cory, in paperback for $.75
- *The Grapevine*, by Jess Stearn, in paperback for $.95
- *Wolfenden Report*, in paperback for $.95

By fall 1968, Craig reported that *The Hymnal* was being mailed to twenty-nine states. Within a year, Craig had added more than a dozen advertisers. While circulation does not appear to be documented, after the Stonewall riots, the Oscar Wilde had a mailing list of around 1,600, and traffic in the shop had put hundreds of hands on *The Hymnal*.

Whatever the success of *The Hymnal* in terms of circulation or advertising, Craig was wedging open society's closet door so that members of the community could gain self-respect, visibility, and the power to stand up against discrimination in whatever way worked for them. *The Hymnal* and the bookshop were advocate, defender, guide, and friend to countless people in need of simple humanity. It was a big mission for a small operation.

Craig had no idea that the Stonewall riots would occur months down the road and that his coverage of the Mafia would be the center of his own flyer during the uprising – or that many others would follow in the steps of the pre-Stonewall lesbian and gay press with new and aggressive publications. But he was paving the way.

The Hymnal continued to be published in 1969, but by 1970, Rodwell was stretched thin with the bookshop, HYMN, and the Christopher Street Liberation Day Umbrella Committee, and it was a challenge to meet a regular production schedule and to achieve the quality he desired. After Stonewall, there was no longer a dearth of news, information, and advocacy; in fact, there was an explosion of gay publications. *The Advocate* would continue to grow, *GAY* (started by Jack Nichols and Lige Clarke and published by Al Goldstein, who founded the heterosexual *SCREW* magazine) would become the leading national newspaper, *Come Out* from the Gay Liberation Front would have a fiery but short history of eight issues. Some of the other short-timers would be *Gay Power* in New York, *Gay Sunshine* in San Francisco, *Gay Times*, and *Gay Flames*.[12]

Craig would find encouragement for his writing and a much larger audience in one of those new publications – George Desantis' *QQ Magazine*. But first, he was about to be consumed by five tumultuous days of that would mark a momentous turning point in gay liberation.

"a publication of the homophile movement"

FEBRUARY 1968 · vol. I, no. 1

the NEW YORK HYMNAL

30 cents

Mafia On The Spot

Mafia Control of Gay Bars Comes to Public's Attention

mafia on the spot

Although it has been common knowledge among New York's homosexual community for many years, the Mafia (or "The Syndicate") control of New York City's gay bars has only recently been brought to the public's attention.

The New York Times, starting in early October of 1967, ran a number of front page articles on the Mafia and, in particular, on the Mafia's control of gay bars. The Times named John (Sonny) Franzese as kingpin of the Syndicate's gay bar operations on Long Island; and in subsequent articles they identified the heads of the Manhattan gay bar Syndicate.

The Stone Wall on Christopher St. in Greenwich Village is one of the larger and more financially lucrative of the Mafia's gay bars in Manhattan. New York HYMNAL received a report from a reliable source over a month ago that the Stone Wall was going to be closed by the Health Department

(continued on page 2)

HYMNAL MAKES BOW

The February, 1968 issue of THE NEW YORK HYMNAL marks the beginning of a new publishing venture directed towards the homosexual community. NEW YORK HYMNAL is published by the Oscar Wilde Memorial Bookshop.

The purpose of HYMNAL is both informational and motivational. Included in future issues will be news articles, theater and book reviews, an advice column, a bar and club column, astrology column, etc. These are the informational aspects of HYMNAL.

The motivational aspect will include voter registration campaigns, special projects to improve the status of the homosexual (such as the 4th Annual Reminder at Independence Hall this coming July 4th), and an overall slant towards getting our people to join and support the work of the movement.

Why was the name HYMNAL chosen?

(continued on page 2)

The cover of the first issue of Craig Rodwell's *New York Hymnal* in February 1968 features reporting on the problem of Mafia control of gay bars in New York, foreshadowing the leaflet Rodwell would write during the Stonewall riots a year and a half later. (Manuscripts and Archives Division, The New York Public Library)

6

Stonewall and Gay Power

What was decisive was not the event itself, but how people responded, the immediate, spontaneous and utterly decentralized flurry of organizing, leafleting and pamphleteering that resulted.... It was this response, and perhaps above all the late Craig Rodwell's determination to commemorate the event the next June with the world's first Gay Pride March, that made Stonewall the shot heard 'round the gay world.

– Michael Denneny,
The Harvard Gay & Lesbian Review, 1994[1]

On Friday night, June 27, 1969, Craig Rodwell and Fred Sargeant closed up shop at the Oscar Wilde and walked down to Washington Square Village, where they would have dinner with friends. It had been a hot, steamy day in New York, and after food and a few hands of cards it was getting late.[2] Craig and Fred stepped out onto the warm sidewalk and headed back to the bookshop to check the door. There had been threats and vandalism, but all was well tonight, and they headed home to their Bleecker Street apartment by way of Waverly Place.[3]

Now sometime after midnight, their route home took them past the hulking Washington Square arch and across Sixth Avenue.[4] As they approached Christopher Street, they could see that a crowd was starting to form outside the Stonewall Inn. The bar had already been raided on Tuesday, and they thought it unusual to have another raid so soon after.

It was in fact another raid, but this time, the raid was being led by Deputy Inspector Seymour Pine of the First Division, who was determined to close down the Stonewall for lack of a liquor license and violation of federal liquor regulations. He was insulted that the Mafia-run clubs would be raided one night and then reopen the next day without consequences. And this time he intended it to be different.[5]

It was different, but not in the way Pine imagined.

When Craig and Fred arrived, they could see that it was already a busy night in the Village – the weekend was starting, and now shortly after 1 a.m., another raid.

They took up a position on the curb across the street, with a direct line of sight to the Stonewall's door.[6] The crowd was growing fast, and Craig and Fred both remembered feeling a tangible agitation on the street.

Inside, Seymour Pine's team of patrol officers and undercover police was in the process of seizing the alcohol and identifying some 200 patrons, separating them into different groups. But they were getting resistance. As some of the patrons were released, they did not scurry away into the night in fear as they would have in previous raids. They stayed, adding intensity to the increasing crowd outside. Pine had called for a paddy wagon from the 6th Precinct to take the liquor and the Mafia and non-Mafia employees of the bar, as well as patrons who hadn't been released.[7]

Craig and Fred were familiar with this pattern – cops would arrive, members of the Mafia would be removed, and staff would be arrested, along with certain patrons who had been singled out for being obviously homosexual or wearing the wrong clothing. Others who hadn't been arrested would vanish into the night, thankful that they had escaped public exposure and all that meant in the 1960s – loss of jobs, families, or home. Craig had been trying to get traction against the Mafia control of gay bars; as mentioned, he had singled out the Stonewall in the first issue of *The Hymnal*, a year and a half before this night. And when it came to the cops, he had already refused a payoff for the Oscar Wilde.

Now, as the police were attempting to fill the paddy wagon, the crowd was growing and shouting. Inspector Pine had never seen anything like it. With the resistance outside, the police took shelter inside and called for assistance, as the crowd began to throw cans, bottles, pennies, and rocks.

From his spot across the street from the entrance, Fred could hear the ping of coins against the door and windows of the Stonewall. For a time, Craig and Fred were both in this position. It was here that Craig, who had a voice that could be something like a bellow, first shouted the words

"Gay Power!" The response from the crowd was tepid. Meanwhile, Fred, who stood several inches taller than Craig, saw two officers heading their way from the direction of the precinct house. He cautioned Craig to "watch it," as he knew the cops would target the loudest voices.[8]

At this point, Craig needed a better look. He couldn't see over the crowd, so he ran up the stairs at 55 Christopher St. for a better vantage point. He tried again with "Gay Power!" and this time, he got a response. Such a moment would have fit right in at an anti-war demonstration, but political outrage at a bar raid was new. A slogan was born.[9]

Twenty-nine-year-old Edmund White, then a staff writer for Time-Life Books, had been walking by with a former boyfriend as the uprising occurred. Not yet politicized, he witnessed the unfolding of the riots. In a letter to friends in the days after, he recalled: "Someone shouted 'Gay Power,' others took up the cry – and then it dissolved into giggles."[10]

Meanwhile, the police were struggling with someone in the crowd, a lesbian who was not going to go quietly. As the cops shoved and pushed her into the patrol car, she looked around and caught the eyes of Fred and others close by – "Why don't you guys do something?" she implored.

There was something about this struggle, an imperative to the people in the crowd to help one person being roughhoused, that caused a flash to electrify the crowd. Craig and Fred could feel it.

Later, that "unidentified lesbian" came forward – it was Stormé DeLarverie.[11] "The cop hit me, and I hit him back," DeLarverie told author Charles Kaiser.[12] In her obituary in *The New York Times*, DeLarverie's legal guardian, Lisa

Cannistraci, remembered, "Nobody knows who threw the first punch, but it's rumored that she did, and she said she did."[13]

Just a few feet from DeLarverie, Fred never forgot the look on her face that night.

As the crowd exploded, the paddy wagon was rocked back and forth. Trash cans were hurled. Someone got lighter fluid from the neighborhood cigar store and lit up some trash. The windows had already been broken, and someone tried to set the plywood interior behind the window on fire. The police inside extinguished it. Inspector Pine was trying to calm his officers. A parking meter was pulled up and used as a battering ram. Every time the cops peered out the door, the crowd grew bigger and angrier. Pine and his crew were under siege and waiting for help to come.

A veteran militant of the homophile movement, Craig knew this was what he had been waiting for. He and Fred would, in fact, "do something." They raced to the bank of phones at the Christopher Street subway station and began making calls to the papers. They called *The New York Times*, the *Daily News*, and the *New York Post*. Thumbing through the phone book, they made more calls to other publications, including *Time* and *Newsweek*.[14] If the movement was going to get a footing and be recognized widely, it needed press coverage.[15] Howard Smith, a columnist for *The Village Voice*, had seen the commotion from his office and rushed over to cover the story. Lucian Truscott IV, a freelance writer who had just graduated from the US Military Academy at West Point and who had done a little writing for the *Voice*, was also nearby at the Lion's Head bar when he saw a crowd gathering.

Meanwhile, one of Pine's undercover agents trapped inside the Stonewall had squeezed out through a back window or vent (there was no back door or fire exit) and called for help, including a call to the fire department. When the officers inside heard the sirens, they breathed a sigh of relief. Seventeen reinforcements from several other precincts had arrived. As the riot intensified, the tactical patrol force showed up with helmets and billy clubs to tamp down the mob and clear the streets.[16]

At this point, Craig and Fred became part of a massive cat-and-mouse chase through the streets near the Stonewall. The crowd had grown to hundreds, and the tactical force formed a wedge on Christopher Street to push them back. But each time the force pushed one way, the mob, taunting them, would circle through the streets and come up from behind. Adrenalin kept Craig and Fred in the chase until it wore itself out sometime before dawn.

Craig and Fred learned later that the whole thing was off balance because Deputy Inspector Pine had brought his six officers in from outside the 6th Precinct to conduct the raid without notifying the local precinct, most likely because Pine did not want the plan for the raid to leak. In fact, Craig and Fred took note of a couple of beat cops who passed on Seventh Avenue as the crowd was lurching out of control, and they seemed to take no interest in what was going on down the street.

The night was not over for Craig and Fred. By dawn on Saturday, Craig knew he had to work to try to keep the momentum going. Everything that had come before had prepared him for this. They returned to their apartment on Bleecker Street for fortifications of coffee, English muffins, and cigarettes. They talked over what would come next, and Craig sat on the floor with his manual typewriter between his legs and spent the remaining early morning hours composing the first of two leaflets. The idea was to let people know what had happened in the previous hours and to bring people back to the Village on Saturday night to demonstrate.

Craig would tap out the leaflet and Fred would get a few hours of sleep in order to open the Oscar Wilde later in the morning. It was going to be a busy day, and the shop would be active, with people wanting to know what had happened the night before.

After Craig finished the leaflet, he called the printer who produced the Oscar Wilde's catalog and got him to open up for a press run of the leaflet, and he asked him to be on standby for more to come. Late in the morning he arrived at the Oscar Wilde with the flyers. Fred would organize the distribution with members of HYMN, and by 4 p.m., Fred was pressing the leaflet into the hands of the Saturday crowd in the Village at Seventh Avenue and Christopher Street. If a leaflet was tossed away, he'd pick it up and hand it to someone else.

Edmund White remembered the scene in his letter recounting Saturday's events: "Some man from the Oscar Wilde bookstore hands out a leaflet describing to newcomers what's going on." Years later, completing a circle, White would sign his books at the Oscar Wilde.[17]

At one point, Fred turned to hand leaflets to three young women approaching him when everyone had a moment of recognition. They had all been high school classmates. Everyone was surprised.

It was, after all, 1969 – no internet, no email, no texting, no cell phones.

No one knew what would happen on Saturday night, but Craig's flyer was getting attention, while New York Mattachine would plead for peace and calm in the Village. As darkness fell, the police presence itself agitated the crowd. This was more than an angry response to the raid and the loss of a place to gather, drink, and dance. There was anger directed at the Stonewall, its relationship to the police and the Mafia, and the fact that gays had become a part of the whole messy structure. The Stonewall represented the societal cubby hole that gay people had been pushed into and cornered.

Meanwhile, the mainstream press began to notice, likely due to the calls from Craig and Fred. On Saturday night, the *New York Post* published a story about the raid under the headline: "Village Raid Stirs Melee."[18]

The account documented a "near riot" outside the Stonewall Inn, with "persons seized" by police and hundreds of passersby. The story in the *Post* also established a record for the shouts of "Gay Power" and "We want freedom." It likewise documented the use of an improvised battering ram and various items from the street that were thrown at the bar.

Craig was thrilled: People had thought of homosexuals as being passive and now a major newspaper was saying they had started a "melee."

"I'm sure it was very jarring to a lot of people. But at the same time, it was very exciting to a lot of gay people. And they would call their friends up: 'Oh, did you hear what happened last night in the Village? And this went on. It was like a grapevine all over town. And that's why more people came every night."[19]

Saturday night was even bigger – the crowd had grown to several times that of the previous night.[20] Gay people filled the streets in the vicinity of the Stonewall, traffic was blocked, fires were set, anger was spilling out. The tactical patrol force was back in much larger numbers to clear the streets, and the fight went on until 3:30 a.m.[21] There was a rumor that Craig and Fred had blocked traffic on Christopher Street, only allowing gay people to pass, which was an exaggeration.[22]

Again in the dawn hours, Craig would pound out a second leaflet, this one digging into the roots of the problem and capturing the outrage of the riot in boldface capital letters:

GET THE MAFIA AND THE COPS OUT OF GAY BARS.[23]

The nights of Friday, June 27, 1969 and Saturday, June 28, 1969 will go down in history as the first time that thousands of Homosexual men and women went out into the streets to protest the intolerable situation which has existed in New York City for many years – namely, the Mafia (or syndicate) control of this city's Gay bars in collusion with certain elements in the Police Dept. of the City of New York....[24]

The flyer included his trademark call to action:

> We at the Homophile Youth Movement (HYMN) believe that the only way this monopoly can be broken is through the action of Homosexual men and women themselves. We obviously cannot rely on the various agencies of government who for years have known about this situation but who have refused to do anything about it. Therefore, we urge the following:
>
> That Gay businessmen step forward and open Gay bars that will be run legally with competitive pricing and a healthy social atmosphere.
>
> That Homosexual men and women boycott places like the Stonewall. The only way, it seems, that we can get criminal elements out of the Gay bars is simply to make it unprofitable for them.
>
> That the Homosexual citizens of New York City, and concerned Heterosexuals, write to Mayor Lindsay demanding a thorough investigation and effective action to correct this intolerable situation.

Under the auspices of HYMN, there was now a documented political anchor to the Stonewall uprising that exposed the Mafia collusion with New York police and called on the "homosexual men and women themselves" to break the monopoly of oppression.

On Sunday, Craig and Fred made a full-court press to distribute the "Get the Cops" leaflet on the street, again with help from HYMN volunteers. Thousands of copies were distributed. They were exhausted.[25]

The news coverage was largely unsympathetic. There was the *New York Post* story, as well as coverage by the *Daily News* and *The New York Times*.

The Daily News, on page thirty in its June 29 edition, reported the riot on the first night under the one-column headline "3 Cops Hurt, As Bar Raid Riles Crowd." Reporter Dennis Eskow's account of the raid on a "homosexual hangout" referred to a "two-hour melee," while the crowd "swarmed over the plainclothes cops."[26]

Eskow reported on the thrown objects, the parking meter battering ram, the smashed windows, fires lighted at the Stonewall windows, and the rocking of the paddy wagon. He reported that Inspector Pine had fresh evidence that alcohol was being sold illegally and that twenty-eight cases of beer and nineteen bottles of liquor had been seized. And at the end of the piece, he reported that police had been watching the inn for syndicate connections.

Then, on page thirty-three of the Sunday edition, *The New York Times* headline read: "4 Policemen Hurt in 'Village' Raid," with the subhead, "Melee Near Sheridan Square Follows Action at Bar."[27] The un-bylined story, which was reported from Pine's point of view, focused on the raid being conducted for the lack of a liquor license. While it noted that 200 patrons had been removed during the raid and that 400 "young men" had gathered outside, the story did not suggest why the crowd was rebelling.

On Monday, the *Times* followed up with somewhat bare coverage of the riot on Saturday, again on the inside pages, with a one-column piece: "Police Again Route 'Village' Youths." This time the story acknowledged "graffiti on the boarded-up windows" which said, "Support gay power," and "Legalize gay bars."[28]

Then came two pieces in *The Village Voice* that hit the streets on Wednesday. Unlike the other stories that focused on the police action, the *Voice* – even though it was protested for the language of its reporter – put the spotlight on gay power. The articles reported the riots from two perspectives – in "Gay Power Comes To Sheridan Square," it was that of Lucian Truscott, who was outside the Stonewall, and in "Full Moon Over The Stonewall," it was columnist Howard Smith, who ended up inside the bar during the riot.[29]

Truscott reported on the political side of the riots and the rising cry for gay power. His story was filled with references to limp wrists, queers, and fairies, and his metaphorical lead – "the sudden specter of 'gay power' erected its brazen head and spat out a fairy tale the likes of which this area has never seen." His second paragraph referred to the "forces of faggotry" that had rallied at the Stonewall. But after running through the details of the riots, he concluded: "Watch out. The Liberation is underway."

Smith, being on the inside of the Stonewall, had the opportunity to know the fear that the police were feeling and the powder keg they were sitting on if they fired their weapons. While he was protected by the police to the extent that was possible inside the Stonewall, his view of the rioters came across as neutral, although he did quote Pine as saying the intent in the raids was not to arrest homosexuals.

For Craig, this was the spark he had been waiting for to publicly light the fire for gay men and women. This was the opportunity for them to see themselves as leading worthwhile lives, not having to subscribe to society's view that they were broken people.[30]

The Stonewall riots continued for five days. Craig and Fred, there for all of it, were spent. They had burned the candle at both ends, night after night. They had stepped – somewhat remarkably – into the middle of the very moment they had anticipated. They barely slept, while producing and distributing flyers, working the streets to pass them out, and keeping the Oscar Wilde open as a central point of information and communication.

The week after the riots, Charles Pitts, who was hosting a series called *The New Symposium II* on WBAI radio, came to the Oscar Wilde with his tape recorder. In the only known existing clip of the interview, Pitts asks Sargeant what happened the prior Friday and Saturday. Fred, just twenty years old, identifies himself as vice chairman of the Homophile Youth Movement and replies that word was spreading through the crowd that kids inside the bar had been beaten up by the police. It was one of the reasons the resistance was boiling over that night – people thought "kids," meaning young gay men, were being beaten up inside and they weren't going to take it. He also relates the circumstances of the two paddy wagons and the extraction of patrons. Decades later, it is easy to forget that just the act of identifying yourself as gay in 1969 was unfathomable to most gay men and women, let alone in a radio broadcast.[31]

After the last night of the riots on Wednesday, July 2, Craig knew that the fifth Annual Reminder taking place in a couple of days in Philadelphia would be the last. There had to be something bigger – and in New York.

"You know, because everybody sensed that nothing's going to be the same after this," Craig recalled thinking. "We just knew."[32]

"[F]or those of us that were there – and there were many thousands of us – we sensed that it was a moment in history. And what does it mean? There was a lot of talks, very animated talks, all over the place.... What's going to happen now? What are we going to do? And people started to organize little things. The second or third night there was a flyer that appeared and said – in big letters it said, 'Homosexuals Are Revolting.' And then in little letters at the bottom it said, 'You bet your sweet ass we are. Come to an organizing meeting.'"[33]

Years later, Fred recalled what was different about the riots: "[F]or Craig and for me, it was the time the gay-rights movement shifted from what we thought of as a 'letterhead' movement of press releases to one of action. Older gays saw the path to equality as going through the power structure. We saw it as going around the power structure. We wanted to exploit the attention this riot received, attention that we had not been able to get before."[34]

The pushback at Stonewall did not stop police raids on gay bars and clubs. Months later, Deputy Inspector Pine was still on his mission and conducted raids on three gay clubs, including one that would be known for its gruesome result.[35]

The first two raids, at 17 Barrow and the Zoo, had gone smoothly for Pine. Management and staff were taken in and customers were released into the night. But then on Saturday, March 8, Pine took his raiding team to The Snake Pit on

West 10th Street to close it down for illegal operations after hours. The customers would not leave, Pine could not sort the staff from the patrons, and so he decided to remove all 167 people and take them to the Charles Street station.

The raid would be known for the attempted escape by Diego Viñales, age twenty-three, who lived in East Orange, NJ, and who was in New York with an expired visa from his home country of Argentina. It was his first visit to a gay bar. When the raid began, Viñales raced upstairs and tried to jump to safety from a second-floor window. Instead, he fell and landed on the iron spikes of the fence below. The fire department had to cut out part of the fence and take it and Viñales – still impaled – to St. Vincent's Hospital.

The new gay liberation groups were not going to stand for such police harassment. The Gay Liberation Front, Gay Activists Alliance, Women's Liberation, and Craig and Fred's Homophile Youth Movement were among those who marched on the Charles Street Station that night to demonstrate against the raid. Afterward, the demonstration evolved into a vigil for Viñales at St. Vincent's.

Viñales survived, and his story helped to reinforce the spirit of Stonewall, but the conditions for a public response were not the same as Stonewall. In spite of the demonstration that followed, there hadn't been the large number of passersby outside the Snake Pit as there had been at the Stonewall. And since the Stonewall riots had already stirred the pot, the militants had their rallying cry.

As for Deputy Inspector Pine, weeks after the Snake Pit raid, he was transferred out of the First Division to Brooklyn.[36] The deputy inspector had been fifty years old when he walked into the Stonewall Inn in 1969. He later said that while police were biased against gays and did boost arrest records by hauling homosexuals away in paddy wagons, the purpose of the Stonewall raid had to do with the Mafia. He said that police believed the Mafia had stolen European bonds and that there was a connection with the Stonewall – that was the point of the operation. He was eighty-four when he made this point at a panel at the New York Historical Society in 2004 in celebration of David Carter's landmark book, *Stonewall*. The mood at the Historical Society seemed to be sympathetic to Pine, who appeared more historian than policeman in this setting, but journalist Andy Humm spoke up, saying what was really needed was an apology. Pine spread his arms wide and, smiling, emoted: "I'm sorry!"[37]

GET THE MAFIA AND THE COPS OUT OF GAY BARS

The nights of Friday, June 27, 1969 and Saturday, June 28, 1969 will go down in history as the first time that thousands of Homosexual men and women went out into the streets to protest the intolerable situation which has existed in New York City for many years -- namely, the Mafia (or syndicate) control of this city's Gay bars in collusion with certain elements in the Police Dept. of the City of New York. The demonstrations were triggered by a Police raid on the Stonewall Inn late Friday night, June 27th. The purported reason for the raid was the Stonewall's lack of a liquor license. Who's kidding whom? Can anybody really believe that an operation as big as the Stonewall could continue for almost 3 years just a few blocks from the 6th Precinct house without having a liquor license? No! The Police have known about the Stonewall operation all along. What has happened is the presence of new "brass" in the 6th Precinct which has vowed to "drive the fags out of the Village."

Many of you have noticed one of the signs which the "management" of the Stonewall has placed outside stating "Legalize Gay bars and lick the problem." This is untrue and they know it. Judge Kenneth Keating (a former U.S. Senator) ruled in January, 1968 that even close dancing between Homosexuals is legal. Since that date there has been nothing illegal, per se, about a Gay bar. What is illegal about New York City's Gay bars today is the Mafia (or syndicate) stranglehold on them. Legitimate Gay businessmen are afraid to open decent Gay bars with a healthy social atmosphere (as opposed to the hell-hole atmosphere of places typified by the Stonewall) because of fear of pressure from the unholy alliance of the Mafia and the elements in the Police Dept. who accept payoffs and protect the Mafia monopoly.

We at the Homophile Youth Movement (HYMN) believe that the only way this monopoly can be broken is through the action of Homosexual men and women themselves. We obviously cannot rely on the various agencies of government who for years have known about this situation but who have refused to do anything about it. Therefore, we urge the following:

1 That Gay businessmen step forward and open Gay bars that will be run legally with competitive pricing and a healthy social atmosphere.

2 That Homosexual men and women boycott places like the Stonewall. The only way, it seems, that we can get criminal elements out of the Gay bars is simply to make it unprofitable for them.

3 That the Homosexual citizens of New York City, and concerned Heterosexuals, write to Mayor Lindsay demanding a thorough investigation and effective action to correct this intolerable situation.

HOMOPHILE YOUTH MOVEMENT — HYMN
291 MERCER STREET
NEW YORK, N. Y. 10003
TEL. (212) 673-3530

Rodwell's flyer, distributed during the first days of the Stonewall riots, crystallized the underlying tensions in the gay community and called out collusion between the Mafia and police. (Courtesy Lesbian Herstory Archives)

7
Dear Craig

August 29, 1969

Dear Mr. Rodwell, I'm 15 years old and homosexual.... I would appreciate any advice on how I could meet other homosexuals.... I don't want to seem pushy or that I'm trying to put my problems on your shoulders. It's just that there are very few people I can turn to at this time....[1]

In the early years, letters poured into the Oscar Wilde from young men seeking guidance and a friend who would understand their situation. Part advice columnist and part pen pal, Craig would do what he could.

One twenty-year-old from Illinois wrote to the shop to say he'd known he was gay since he was thirteen, and now he needed Craig's help:

> I feel silly writing a letter of this nature to a person I've never met but I feel you can help me.

> Three weeks ago I lost my job, or rather I was fired, for no apparent reason. Last week I discovered I lost my job because I'm gay.

He went on to describe his community of 6,000 residents and that no one would hire him, that he had lost his apartment because the landlord heard that he was gay. He also said he had contemplated taking his own life.

"Why are people like that?" he asked. "Can't they accept me as I am?"

He had come across Kay Tobin Lahusen's *The Gay Crusaders* and realized that he was not alone; perhaps he would move to New York. And maybe Craig could help him to cope with the discrimination in his own community.

Craig responded in full. He acknowledged that discrimination in a small community was not uncommon and created a circumstance of loneliness and isolation. He provided a summary of what gay organizations were trying to do around the country to make discrimination illegal. And he had a specific suggestion – a new gay liberation group was forming, and Craig provided the contact.

"Meanwhile," he wrote, "find consolation in the fact that you are wright [sic]. Your strength must come from within. Our lifestyle and our means of self-expression are valid and are good."[2]

With his own personal experience, his work with Mattachine Young Adults, and the Oscar Wilde, Craig was equipped to help. His letters to anxious young men who needed someone to talk to were understanding and supportive. His advice to a teenager from Pennsylvania, who had written to Craig about coming out to his parents, was typical:

I realize the difficulties you may have to face in telling your parents that you are gay. It is likely they have been exposed to many negative attitudes towards homosexuality and their views probably won't change suddenly. You must therefore draw strength from the knowledge that you are right in acting on your gay feelings. The ability to be a good and loving person is admirable and your parents must come to understand that our lifestyle and honest expression of our feelings are valid.

A teenager from Allentown, PA, wrote on June 19, 1969:

I am Eighteen years old, gay (of course), and want to help the Homophile Youth Movement and the Oscar Wilde Memorial Bookshop succeed. With one year of college completed, I now realize that the only thing I definitely want to do is help other gays become proud of what they are and to make them realize that GAY IS GOOD![3]

And someone from Hawaii wrote that he had sought advice from Craig the year before and as a result had sought counseling from a professional in Los Angeles. "I just wanted to inform you that without your initial help, I would probably still be ignorant in matters concerning gay life." He would be graduating in 1974 and would pay a visit to his counselor in Los Angeles, thanks to Craig.[4]

◆◆◆◆◆

In March 1972, an eight-page hand-written letter on Waldorf-Astoria stationery arrived. Another visitor to

New York reflected on how he had been moved by Craig's efforts to help the community. He had seen the Gay Activists Alliance up close and found them "a bit heavy." Greenwich Village had left a new impression on him – "to see a place where gay people can work and live as what they are was a fantastic experience." It was too late to change to be an activist like Craig, but he would do something. "This is to help young gay people in any way I can to enable them to grow and mature in a society which one day will accept them. My lot will be to work within the system, unacknowledged yet satisfied that I did my bit." He was both impressed by "and a little envious" of the life Craig had led. "That which you are doing will have a lasting effect upon the rights of those for whom you work. You were able, it seems to me, to be able to start young enough to do some good."[5]

The impact of the Oscar Wilde was so intimate that it moved a twenty-three-year-old soldier in Vietnam to wonder if he might get a job at the Oscar Wilde when he got out of the military:

Dear Mr. Rodwell,
I saw the article about you and your bookshop in *Queen's Quarterly* and was very impressed. It's good to know someone is really working to honestly improve the outlook for gay life.

An Army Specialist 5 wrote that he had been cut off from gay life for six months, and he was not really sure why he was writing, perhaps loneliness. But also, what were the chances that he might get a job when he got out in December

1970? Meanwhile, he would subscribe to *The New York Hymnal*, assuming he wasn't "too old."[6]

The Vietnam War and the draft were on many gay men's minds in 1969. This letter came in from New York:

> Am I correct in assuming that as a homosexual I have a "legitimate out" from the service? Although during my physical I checked the box which inquires about such tendencies, it seems to have had no effect for I was nonetheless accepted.

Craig turned the letter over to Alfred Gross of the George W. Henry Foundation, who provided advice on how to go about either changing the man's designation or getting out of the service if he had already been inducted.[7]

The importance of comradeship was no more evident than in a letter in January 1970 from Louis, a private in the US Army, who was serving in Vietnam

"Hi Craig!" Louis wrote in buoyant cursive. His order to the Oscar Wilde from November had just arrived at Long Binh military base in Vietnam in a little more than a month. He mused that the US could get troops to Vietnam faster than the mail. "But I've got some bigger news for you," he wrote. He had re-upped for another three years in the Army – through December 1972. He had a good job as a radio and switchboard operator, he had received a chunk of money for re-enlisting, and he was going to buy a new AM/FM stereo cassette system. Oh, and there was a cute guy working in the mess hall who had been "making eyes" at him. Meanwhile, he had a month-long leave coming up and he would be coming home in February or March. Craig should look for him at the Gay Liberation Front dances, although he would be stopping in at the shop to place a new order. It was 90 degrees in Long Binh, so he was sure the cold of a New York winter would be a shock. Louis' full-of-life letter was hand-illustrated with two cartoon figures – one, a bald guy with glasses and a downturned toothy smile admonishing the "Fukkin' Faggots!" in his balloon, and another in which the happy cartoon figure says in his balloon "Gay is a Gas." All signed: "Love, Louie."[8]

Whether Louis found Craig at the GLF dances or whether Louis made it to the shop during his leave is unknown, but a year and three months later, Craig received an enigmatic correspondence addressed to "Occupant" at 291 Mercer St. from the Army's Military Mail Terminal in San Francisco.

The typewritten note, dated April 1971, came from a lieutenant colonel who regretted to inform Craig – rather, the "occupant" at 291 Mercer – that the Army was returning this mail to Craig, as Louis had died in October.

What the letter didn't say was that twenty-one-year-old private had been on leave from combat duty in Vietnam. He had been staying with his family in New York that October and was on his way to his new assignment in Hawaii. Newspaper accounts said he was spending part of his leave in San Francisco before taking the last leg of the trip. He had checked in at the YMCA hotel on Wednesday, October 14. But on Thursday, his naked body was found sprawled behind a San Francisco apartment building. He had been shot once in the head and was identified by three rings found near his body. The joy he had found in the military and in gay life had been snuffed out. Police said credit cards and cash were missing from his wallet and they suspected robbery.⁹

Louis found community inside the Oscar Wilde, and Craig had become a valued friend with whom he could share the details of his life. In a time when there was no social media, no cell phones, and no internet, the letter to a trusted person was a comfort and affirmation that you were, in fact, normal.

8
Let's March

At 8 a.m. on Friday, July 4, 1969, a chartered bus pulled up on Mercer Street across from the Oscar Wilde Memorial Bookshop. In a few hours, its passengers would be members of the New York contingent at the fifth Annual Reminder in front of Independence Hall in Philadelphia. Craig and Fred had barely caught their breath from their participation in the Stonewall riots over the previous week. The coals of the uprising were still glowing, and it was going to be another hot summer day.[1]

Organized by the Eastern Regional Conference of Homophile Organizations and under the direction of Frank Kameny, the Annual Reminder pickets – conceived by Craig at the diner in 1965 – had taken place under the same set of rules for four years. A quiet picket would occur as the marchers walked in a circle, their signs demanding equality under the laws of the United States. Men were to wear suits and ties and women were to wear dresses or skirts and blouses. Kameny was the authorized spokesperson.

Craig had been organizing participation at the reminders through HYMN, the Homophile Youth Movement in Neighborhoods. For $5 ($4 for students), you could have a seat on the chartered bus outside. This year, the sponsors anticipated that a hundred people would show up in Philadelphia for the picket. Now in something of a routine, the expenses incurred by HYMN for the reminder included display advertising in *The Village Voice* for $190, printing of 2,000 leaflets at about $17, the chartered bus at $170, and other miscellaneous charges.

Among the passengers who had signed up for the bus from New York were Kay Tobin Lahusen, Terry Rohnke, Martha Shelley, Charles Pitts, Ernest Hole, and Don Teal (who later decided to drive to Philadelphia). They would meet Barbara Gittings and Frank Kameny, among others, in Philadelphia. They were among the central figures shaping the liberation movement.[2]

The language for the fifth Annual Reminder had been prepared well before the Stonewall riots. The HYMN sign-up form described it as "an annual vigil-type demonstration held every year in front of Independence Hall in Philadelphia, Pennsylvania on July 4th."[3]

Craig had been inspired by the earlier demonstrations in Washington in 1965 and under Kameny's leadership, the reminders took on the latter's approach:

> The purpose is to affirm, on behalf of America's approximately 16,000,000 Homosexual citizens, male and female,

our firm belief in the ideals this country was founded upon as set forth in the Declaration of Independence (which was signed at Independence Hall on July 4, 1776) and the Constitution. We also demonstrate to remind the American people that, nearly 200 years after the signing of that document, our society has yet to grant those freedoms of life, liberty and the pursuit of happiness to all its citizens, in particular, its Homosexual citizens. We also march to affirm our pride, our dignity, and our self-respect as American Homosexual men and women. Concerned heterosexuals are also invited to participate.[4]

As the group assembled outside the bookshop for the trip, a convertible had shown up – four men with bats who shouted that they were going to run them off the road in New Jersey. Craig called the cops, and they got a police escort through the tunnel. In New Jersey, a state trooper boarded the bus and stayed with them the rest of the way to Philadelphia. The whole incident made Craig seethe with the anger left over from Stonewall.[5]

In Philadelphia, under wilting heat at Independence Hall, the picket proceeded as usual, with quiet, respectful behavior, the dress code, the march in a circle, and the carefully prepared signage in block capital letters on a white background.

But this time, Craig was agitated; it was all just too confining.

He was upbeat, though, when two of the women in the New York contingent who were in front of him began holding hands in double file, not single file as prescribed by Kameny. This is exactly what Craig thought should be happening. But Kameny was there in a flash, and with a karate chop–style movement he broke the women apart and admonished them. "None of that," he said.

Years later, Craig remembered what happened next: "Well, I hit the ceiling. Frank hadn't been in New York. He hadn't been through the Stonewall riots. So I got about, oh, ten couples together, to march holding hands. And, of course, the media was going crazy."[6]

Six days later, Kameny wrote to Rodwell to thank him for his participation in the reminder, and to offer an apology for a problem with the picket signs, but he also admonished Rodwell for taking matters into his own hands and airing the dirty laundry of the movement in public. He wrote: "'Love-ins' – homosexual and/or heterosexual, both – have their place, so do picketing demonstrations. Neither is likely to be effective, and both are more likely to be ineffective, if they are mixed."[7]

He told Craig that it was his duty to administer the demonstration in keeping with the spirt of the Eastern Regional Conference, and "that spirit has always been in the direction of a somewhat conservative, image-conscious, conventionally dignified demonstration, designed to get a message across by avoidance of needless abrasion of the sensibilities and sensitivities of the large mass of people."[8]

As incensed as Craig was over the Kameny incident, it was just another example to him that something had to give. Craig knew, before he got on the bus to Philadelphia, that there would not be a sixth Annual Reminder. He also knew before he left New York that the time for peaceful protest and silent picketing was over.[9]

Even during the riots, as Craig and Fred kept the leafletting going and the bookshop open as a convergence point, they had discussed what needed to happen next, and it wasn't an Annual Reminder. Craig imagined a different annual action, building around the riots, not the Liberty Bell, and in New York, not Philadelphia. This was all in his mind before he stepped foot on the bus on July 4, 1969. On the bus ride back and over the next two weeks, Craig put a name to the idea. He would call it the Christopher Street Liberation Day. And as he said, "That became my thing."[10]

Amid the intense focus on what would come next after Stonewall was a new word in the 1960s lexicon – *moratorium*. The Vietnam War had claimed thousands of American lives, and on October 15, 1969, the First Moratorium to End the War in Vietnam was staged across the nation. Craig and Fred, familiar with organizing, arranged for a "gay bus" to take protesters to Washington.

The fall was going to be very busy. The Eastern Regional Conference of Homophile Organizations meeting was coming up the first weekend in November and Craig had been percolating ideas to take a new action. Getting agreement from such a broad membership was going to be unpredictable, but the time had come to put a bold idea forward.

Craig, Fred, Ellen Broidy, and Linda Rhodes, who had become good friends since the early days of the Oscar Wilde, were huddled on the floor at 350 Bleecker. It was October 31 – Craig's twenty-ninth birthday.

As they talked that night in the apartment, Craig had jumped up to get a notepad and pencil. They were going to do something that would change history. Ellen remembers thinking: "This is a powerhouse, and he's going to take us along on this ride."[11]

They began to capture the words – Ellen recalls that they all contributed to the proposal. They wanted to put something forward that they thought that Kameny, chair of the Eastern Regional Conference, would agree to.

Craig described the scene to Kay Tobin in an interview for her book *The Gay Crusaders*:

> We sat here, Ellen, Linda, Fred, and myself; we did up a formal resolution and everything to change the annual reminders to the Christopher Street Liberation Day, the last Sunday in June to commemorate the birth of the gay liberation movement as exemplified in the Stonewall riots. We sat here for hours and worked the whole thing up, coming up with the resolutions, also setting up a committee to put the whole thing together.[12]

While they could all go to the regional meeting under the auspices of HYMN, Ellen would attend as president of the NYU Student Homophile League, which gave her a portfolio and a credential. Under a loophole in the rules, member organizations could bring guests from non-member organizations, which resulted in a large meeting.

The foursome knew by this point that Craig had become a lightning rod on both the left and the right of the movement. Ellen felt that people on the right saw him as too progressive and people on the left saw him as too reformist, reflecting the bridge Craig had navigated between the homophile movement and the gay liberation phase. It was decided that Ellen would stand up to make the official pitch to the conference; she would be the voice of the proposal rather than Craig.[13]

Craig and Fred hopped on the train and the four of them converged in Philadelphia. The meeting took place at "My Sister's Place" on Walnut and 22nd Streets in Philadelphia. Kameny was the presiding officer and Susan Day (who would later have a stint as manager of the Oscar Wilde) was the acting secretary. It was about 11:30 a.m. when things got underway. Kameny announced at the outset that he was done as chair due to other obligations and the fact that he had little help.[14]

Ellen recalls that it was a cold, wet, November day and there seemed to be no heat. As for the members – one looked scruffier than the next. "Looking back at it, it looks completely ridiculous, but not to Craig."

The third item on the agenda after Martha Shelley's motion not to cooperate with *Gay Power* newspaper,[15] and the reports of committees, was the Annual Reminder July 4 demonstrations.

In her trademark jeans, flannel, and light-yellow work boots, Ellen stepped forward into something of a circle. With her Homophile League credentials, she read the first of three resolutions:

> that the Annual Reminder, in order to be more relevant, reach a greater number of people and encompass the ideas

and ideals of the larger struggle in which we are engaged – that of our fundamental rights – be moved both in time and location.

We propose that a demonstration be held annually on the last Saturday in June in New York City to commemorate the 1969 spontaneous demonstrations on Christopher Street and this demonstration be called CHRISTOPHER STREET LIBERATION DAY. No dress or age regulations shall be made for this demonstration.[16]

We also propose that we contact Homophile Organizations throughout the country and request that they hold parallel demonstrations on that day. We propose a nationwide show of support.

Then the second resolution:

> that an umbrella committee be formed to handle the technical end of the demonstration, i.e., permits, publicity, homophile organization coordination, financing. This committee should be composed of one member from each homophile organization supporting the Demonstration (non-ERCHO members included).

And finally:

> Participation in the Christopher Street Liberation Day demonstration will be open to all other organization (s) or individuals desiring to support the Demonstration.

When Ellen was done, she remembered a quick "Right on!" that she thought came from Martha Shelley. She was not used to public speaking, and she was relieved – it was going to happen.

Craig was elated. All three resolutions had passed on roll-call votes. With thirteen groups present, only the Mattachine Society of New York had abstained, and they abstained on all three resolutions.

Shortly after the conference, Fred was designated to head a clearinghouse of ERCHO mailings for distribution among member groups.[17] And back at 350 Bleecker, the organizational meetings began – the apartment would be the headquarters for the first Christopher Street Liberation Day march.[18]

Coincidentally, the very week that ERCHO held its meeting, *Time* magazine published a cover story that reverberated across the country and incensed the militants.

"The Homosexual in America" cover story was disastrous for the community, spreading fear and anxiety to homes across the rural countryside, where many teenagers just becoming aware of their sexuality would get their first taste of what society (in *Time* magazine's view) thought of them.

The inside headline read: "The Homosexual: Newly Visible, Newly Understood." A sidebar asked: "A Discussion: Are Homosexuals Sick?"[19] While homosexuals were becoming more visible, they were hardly "understood" in this reporting.

The article described six "homosexual types" that included "the blatant homosexual," "the secret lifer," "the desperate," "the adjusted," "the bisexual," and "the situational-experimental." None was complimentary. In fact, the section concluded that "[t]he homosexual subculture, a semi-public world, is, without question, shallow and unstable." *Time's* then-brand of reporting included a judgmental tone that came out loud and clear as the cover story concluded: "The Challenge to American society is simultaneously to devise civilized ways of discouraging the condition and to alleviate the anguish of those who cannot be helped, or do not wish to be."

Craig and Fred were outraged. They joined the RadicaLesbians, the Gay Liberation Front, and the Daughters of Bilitis in converging on the Time-Life Building for a new kind of picket in November. They would wear their regular clothes, they would insist on having their photos taken, they would use their real names, they would chant, and they would be unruly.[20]

Ellen Broidy recalled the details. On Wednesday, November 12, 1969, their group of picketers unpacked their leaflets and signs in front of Time-Life on Sixth Avenue near Radio City Music Hall. It was overcast and cold, and Ellen, a member of the Gay Liberation Front, was in her winter wool coat. The Gay Liberation Front had some of its heavy hitters there, too – Lois Hart and Jim Fouratt. Craig was there, and Fred, in his characteristic overshirt and sweater, was unpacking leaflets. They had pulled together without social media, computers, or texting. Instead they used the tools of the day – landlines, bulletin boards, and in-person meetings.

Ellen took up her spot in the demonstration, even though she had yet to come out to her parents. She kept looking over her shoulder, wondering if her father would see her on the picket line. He was inside the very building where they were demonstrating – he worked for Time-Life.[21]

In his "It's What's Happening" column in *The Hymnal*, Carl Lee wrote about the *Time* issue: "If you haven't seen the issue, don't worry about it. While for *TIME*, it was a big step forward, the article generally is a re-hash of all the myths, false impressions and folk-lore about the Homosexual."[22]

Lee was annoyed that *Time* ignored the homophile movement and especially the young people in the movement. Lee also reported that the twenty-five picketers were met by a television crew from ABC, which broadcast locally "about 2 minutes in coverage" that night.

◆◆◆◆◆

The Christopher Street Liberation Day Umbrella Committee pressed forward. Craig sent out mailings to the various gay groups inviting them to send a representative to the first meetings. A core group of about a dozen people formed, and the hard work began. Craig would start each meeting with a speech, saying "all of us come from various different backgrounds, both politically, racially, sexually and what have you. And these meetings are not the time and place to be at each other's throats on those issues. We're here to put together a mass community march and to bring all the elements of our community together."[23]

Disagreements flared up. The issue over whether there should be floats in the march arose from the start. Craig was against it. It went against his lifelong thread that one person shouldn't be valued more than another. The march, in his view, was a way for every single gay person to stand up and be recognized as equal with other gay people.

"[O]nce you start the business of floats or speakers or whatever, you're setting up levels of participation: the stars and the followers. On this one day, let's just be a community. Just a mass march. Just masses of all of us in all of our splendor and ugliness."

Details of the committee meetings were recorded by Foster Gunnison Jr. (He would drop "Umbrella" from the committee's name after several months.) His friendship with Craig had continued after they met at New York Mattachine and when he had participated in the opening of the Oscar Wilde in 1967 by signing copies of his history of the homophile movement.

Gunnison was a portly thirty-eight-year-old, distinguished by his crew cut, bow tie, big smile, and cigar. As treasurer of the Christopher Street committee ahead of the 1970 march, Gunnison kept abreast of the income and expenses and issued regular bulletins from the meetings in Craig and Fred's apartment.[24]

While the members of ERCHO had been invited to send a representative to the planning meetings, attendance was light. John Marshall from Mattachine in Washington had been appointed the official chairman of the ERCHO committee and Gunnison was treasurer, but neither of them were in New York, so much of the work was on Craig's shoulders, with the help of Fred and some regulars at the Oscar Wilde.[25]

At the March 22 meeting, the Christopher Street committee decided that each homophile organization representative would be known as a co-chairman and that a donation of $10 from each group would help get things going, even though future funding would be through the committee itself. Gunnison would be the custodian.

In a press release sent to the homophile movement press in April 1970, just two months before the step-off, he summarized the need for funds:

> Christopher Street Liberation Day, 1970 is Sunday, June 28th. In New York City a massive march will proceed from Christopher Street on through midtown Manhattan to the Sheep Meadow in Central Park for a "Gay-In." This event will be the focus of "Gay Pride Week," which will be celebrated nationwide. Christopher Street Liberation Day marks the anniversary of the Christopher Street Riots – the first time that Homosexual men and women stood up and fought back.
>
> The Christopher Street Riots of 1969 were the beginning of a new spirit among Gay men and women of pride, militancy, affirmation, and solidarity. We march this year to celebrate that spirit.
>
> The Christopher Street Liberation Day Umbrella Committee (CSLDUC) was established to coordinate the numerous activities in New York being planned by various Gay groups.
>
> The CSLDUC needs money – and lots of it – to coordinate and publicize this greatest Gay event ever....

The following month, Gunnison sent a letter to Rodwell, praising the Oscar Wilde's 1,600-name mailing list for publicity and fundraising. Gunnison promised a "full accounting" for all contributors, which he considered standard practice for his role.[26]

Rodwell continued to shepherd the working groups with as strong a hand as possible to keep the planning for the march on track. Less focused on various philosophical approaches, he felt the purpose of the march had been stated and that the goal now was to put all the effort into organizing it.

Equality was at the root of all the planning; when it came time to make the banner for the head of the march, the committee decided that there would be four people holding it, two men and two women. And no one group would be at the head of the march, which avoided confrontations between competing organizations.

By this time, both the Gay Liberation Front and the Gay Activists Alliance had formed in New York with differing agendas and strategies. The Gay Liberation Front, which had organized in July immediately after Stonewall, was radical, revolutionary, and sought alignment with the broad social radical movement of the times. The Gay Activists Alliance split from the GLF and was organized in December to focus more narrowly on gaining rights for homosexuals through concrete actions. While the GLF functioned with a group of cells, the GAA created committees and ran its meetings with *Robert's Rules of Order*.[27]

Craig had attended GLF meetings and was supportive; he put their flyers up at the Oscar Wilde. But he wasn't aligned with their Marxist rhetoric, and he did not warm up to suggestions that they might have a role in operating his bookshop.[28] That may explain why Craig told Kay Tobin Lahusen that the GLF considered him to be "middle class and bourgeois."[29]

Insist That They Love You | 139

Similarly, Craig did not affiliate with the Gay Activists Alliance. He went to their dances and publicized their meetings and militant actions in the Oscar Wilde, but ultimately his only affiliation was with the Christopher Street Liberation Day Committee.

It had been a challenge to get consistent attendance from all the northeast organizations at the planning meetings. But distractions were resolved one by one, with Craig holding everyone to the main purpose.

Another hurdle was that a parade permit was needed. Craig, Michael Brown, and a few others headed for the 6th Precinct on Charles Street to apply for it. The application for a permit to march was submitted to the police department on June 16, 1970. In the cover memorandum, Brown described the member organizations as ranging from social organizations to political activists. He also noted that as a coalition committee, there was no formal chair and there were no formal titles.[30]

When they arrived, the police told them they would not be allowed to march, but Craig made it clear that this plan was going ahead with or without a permit, and they continued to have meetings with the precinct.[31]

The memo said that originally, the marchers were expecting to use the sidewalks for their demonstration up Sixth Avenue but that because the anticipated numbers had grown, they were applying to use the whole avenue. They estimated that between 10,000 and 50,000 people would show up.

The gathering area on the application was "Sheridan Square," and the event was set to begin Sunday, June 28,

1970, 2 p.m. The "dismissal point" was Sheep Meadow in Central Park, and the permit application checked "no" as to whether "rifles or shotguns will be fired for ceremonial purposes."

Typed in the space for "purpose of parade" were the words "Celebration and display of unity."

While Craig and company waited for the parade permit, the permit for the use of Sheep Meadow was approved on June 24, four days before the scheduled march. Permit number 200 allowed the Christopher Street committee to hold a "Gay Be-In (Happening)" of up to 25,000 people at Sheep Meadow from 2 to 7 p.m. Sheep Meadow, at the south end of Central Park, had once been a grazing area for sheep and by the 1960s had been developed into a venue for large events like demonstrations or concerts.[32]

The be-ins, sit-ins, and love-ins of the 1960s were a counterculture expression of resistance to the establishment, whether they were to protest the Vietnam War or social issues or racism. The "gay-in" was an extension of the expressive social conditions of the time, where people could express themselves, and experience themselves together as part of change.

The Oscar Wilde used its mailing list and central location to promote "Gay Pride Week" from June 22 to June 28 and to appeal for funds for the committee. Rodwell took out advertisements in *The Village Voice*, and flyers and posters were distributed.

While the march was the main event, Gay Pride Week would include six days of supplemental activities sponsored by various organizations. Among some thirty events, the Oscar Wilde and HYMN planned a benefit all day on Tuesday, June 23, with proceeds going to the committee. That same day, the GAA would show two movies at the Corduroy Club, and on Wednesday, the GAA scheduled a demonstration for homosexual law reform in front of Governor Rockefeller's office. On Friday, the GLF would put on workshops at Alternate U, and the GAA planned a dance at Weinstein Hall. And after the march and gay-in, Daughters of Bilitis listed a "Gab 'n' Java" on Sunday night for women only.[33]

While it may have come across as a blend of support, Gay Pride Week was the result of differences of opinion as to the purpose of the march. Craig saw the march as a cultural affirmation, where others like the Gay Activists Alliance wanted the day to be about political power. The week of events leading up to the march allowed each organization to emphasize its own goals, while coming together behind the Christopher Street banner on June 28.[34]

Marshals were trained to guide the marchers from start to finish. They were given information on the history of the march, its purpose, and the spirit of the day. They were instructed on the consciousness of their position and their attitudes toward police, hecklers, provocateurs, and the press ("respond as individuals"). They would have instruction on first aid. And they would be given bright orange arm bands with "CSLD" printed on them between the symbols for lesbian women and gay men.[35]

Sargeant was one of the marshals. For $5 and a $15 deposit, he would rent the only bullhorn for the day, which he would carry at the head of the march to coax people off the sidewalks and into the street.[36]

As Craig and Fred (now twenty-nine and twenty-one years old) awoke at 350 Bleecker on Sunday, June 28, there was still no permit for the march. It was one of the many uncertainties that would occur over the next hours as the biggest gay demonstration in history was about to take place. Craig got on the phone to the police – where was the permit? There were crowds of people assembling, and they would be moving out with or without it. Then, about two hours before the march was to assemble, a knock on the door – it was the cop with the permit.[37]

"But we would have marched anyway," Craig insisted.[38]

About a thousand people spread about Sheridan Square – even onto nearby Christopher Street and Waverly Place. While it was not the number Craig had hoped for, there was still time for more people to filter in.

In characteristic Rodwell fashion, participants received a written "WELCOME" leaflet with the key message: "We are united today to affirm our pride, our lifestyle and our commitment to each other," he had written. "For the first time in history we are together as The Homosexual Community. This is the commitment that draws us together; let us not forget it throughout this, our day." It was a quick-read pep talk: "We are Gay and proud. No-one can convince us otherwise."[39]

Fred was positioned at the head of the staging area on Waverly Place, where they had received permission to close the street. There were delays getting started; Craig was working out particulars with the police. The question looming was whether the people who had gathered were ready to march or were they there to witness? No one knew how this was going to turn out.[40]

Time was passing; Fred was concerned that they were about to lose the momentum and that they had to get people onto Sixth Avenue. He and Craig put their heads together and decided it was time.[41]

"Let's march; join us!" they shouted. Whatever was going to happen was in motion.

Up the west side of Sixth Avenue they went, under clear, sunny skies, gathering more brave souls as each block passed. At one point, from the head of the march, Sargeant, with bullhorn and marshal's arm band, climbed the base of a light post and was amazed to see that marchers had filled ten blocks, as far back as he could see.

Gay rights activist and writer Lilli Vincenz was also there. In her twelve-minute documentary *Gay and Proud*, she filmed and narrated images and stories from Greenwich Village to Central Park.[42]

On this day, Frank Kameny's uniform signage of the Annual Reminders was replaced with free-form banners and lettering and typography that reflected the flower power designs of the time. "I am a lesbian and I am beautiful," read one sign. Individualism was exploding into the street.

Instead of one spokesperson for the event, Vincenz talked to dozens of people, each with their own story.

Chants of "gay power," and "out of the closets and into the streets," rang out.

Shirtless men strode arm and arm, almost sauntering their way uptown.[43]

Headbands, T-shirts, vests, bell bottoms, and sandals, along with more traditional Oxford shirts and jeans, had replaced suits and dresses.

At Sheep Meadow, two people were attempting to break the record for the longest homosexual kiss of nine hours.

There was no violence against the marchers to speak of: a man with a "Sodom and Gomorrah" sign and an American flag protested, and a fifty-something woman watching from the sidewalk smiled as the marchers went by, shaking her head but smiling.

Charles Pitts from WBAI was there with his tape recorder, capturing impressions and reactions along the route:[44]

> WOMAN "The same thing they did in Rome; something is wrong with society."
> MAN: "Weird, they have the right to do it, but it's strange."
> MAN: "I think it's wonderful. We're all human beings. Live and let live."
> WOMAN: "It's disgusting, gay relationships."
> MAN: "I'm gay and I'm proud."
> MAN: "I'm a man and I'm holding hands with one."
> GROUP: "Out of the closets and into the streets."
> GROUP: "Gay is just as good as straight."

There was little trouble along the way. Craig recalled how the committee had prepared: "We'd expected all kinds of things. We'd had all kinds of training for the marshals in first aid. We had a first-aid truck."[45]

Mostly, Craig remembered, the people watching the march were stunned – they had never seen anything like it: "[I]n the march if you look[ed] at the sidelines, [you'd] see a lot of people just standing there. You can't get this on tape, but I'm trying to look with a blank face."[46]

George Desantis and the editors of *QQ Magazine* documented the march with the glossy commemorative pictorial booklet *Gay Freedom 1970*. "For the first time in history homosexuals gathered to assert their rights and affirm their lifestyle," they wrote.[47]

In thirty-one photographs, Desantis captured the day. There was Craig conferring with police before the escort. Fred was photographed, bullhorn in hand, at the head of the march in front of the "Christopher Street Liberation Day 1970" banner. The sign "Lesbians Unite" was held high; one woman carried a sign "Everything they say we are – We Are." Eastern cities were represented – the sign "PHILADELPHIA" stretched across the entire side of the street. Despite their earlier "disassociation" with the resolution creating this march, New York Mattachine was there, too.

Three miles later, arriving in Sheep Meadow, a sense of accomplishment, and a release of the march's uncertainties, melted into the grass. People hugged, cheered, danced. There was the strumming of an acoustic guitar. Craig remembered years later: "Half the people were in tears when we got to the park."[48]

In the next-to-the-last image of the booklet, Desantis photographed "two organizers," standing among the masses – sweaty, wrinkled, exhausted – Craig and Fred.

One person was documenting the ballooning crowd at Central Park with a hand-clicker counter – it was Foster Gunnison. His manual count of the total number of marchers was 5,000, which is what he would include later in the accounting of the Christopher Street Liberation Day Committee reports.[49]

Still making ends meet on the lean wages of the Oscar Wilde, Craig and Fred decided to splurge, and they sprang for a cab ride home.

◆◆◆◆◆

The next day, *The New York Times* carried the story on page one. "Thousands of Homosexuals Hold a Protest Rally in Central Park," the headline stated. Reporter Lacey Fosburgh wrote that marchers had come from far and wide "to protest laws that make homosexual acts between consenting adults illegal and social conditions that often make it impossible for them to display affection in public, maintain jobs or rent apartments."[50]

The Village Voice's July 3–9, 1970, edition headlined the page one story, "A Happy Birthday for Gay Liberation," calling it "the first mass coordinated event of the gay liberation movement." While the *Voice* story proclaimed a major accomplishment, the coverage had an old tone. The paper that once referred to the "forces of faggotry" in its report on the Stonewall riots wrote: "And here they were. Out in the streets again, not the precious birthday party queers of 'Boys in the Band,' not the limp-wristed, pinky-ringed, sad-eyed faggots of uptown chic, but shouting men and women with locked arms and raised fists." In 3,000 words, the *Voice* attempted to capture the details of the March, the gains of the movement, the events of Gay Pride Week, its meaning, and the changing psychology around homosexuality in one fell swoop.[51]

Just eight months before, Ellen Broidy had stood before the Eastern Regional Conference of Homophile Organizations in Philadelphia. One of the resolutions had been to contact homophile organizations "through the country and request that they hold parallel demonstrations.... We propose a nationwide show of support."

Foster Gunnison, in his ERCHO report after the "Grand March up Sixth Avenue," stated that it had been "successful beyond all expectations" and that events had in fact occurred in other cities – Chicago, Los Angeles, San Francisco, and Boston. And he provided complete accounting of the Christopher Street Liberation Day Committee.

There had been nineteen contributions from seventeen homophile groups, totaling $290, and twenty-five contributions from twenty-five individuals amounting to $147.40. There were five collections for $62.89 and two benefits for $45.60, with the Oscar Wilde at the top of both of those lists.

The six *Village Voice* advertisements had cost $100. All told, publicity was the main expense, at $278.71. Among the smaller expenses, the armbands and pins for marshals cost $9.99 and the one bullhorn was $5.00.

Total cash receipts had been $575.89, and disbursements were $544.31; minus a bank service charge, they had ended up with a surplus of $26.58.[52]

◆◆◆◆

The march was over – now what?

Craig remembered: "Tremendous excitement that led to another flurry of organizing and a lot more organizations, especially student groups and caucuses within the various religious groups and professional groups. It was like, how can I put it, when something happens once – and I'm referring to the Stonewall riots at this point – it galvanizes people to act on something."[53]

It would still not be smooth sailing, though. To raise money for the second march, the Christopher Street Liberation Day Committee scheduled a set of dances at New York University's Weinstein Hall. After three of five dances were held, the University canceled the fourth, realizing the event was for gays and lesbians. After a protest, NYU allowed the dance to go forward but a fifth dance was not going to be allowed. On Sunday, September 20, Ellen went to the Gay Liberation Front to get their support for a sit-in, which lasted five days, until NYU brought in the police to remove the protesters. While Craig had been in on the organizing of the dances, he was not part of the sit-in, most likely because he needed to keep the shop open.

Gunnison's October 2 bulletin to thirty-seven ERCHO members announced that the first meeting to plan for the 1971 march would be held Sunday, October 11th at 2 p.m. – again in Craig and Fred's apartment.

While there was excitement for another celebration the next year, there was also increasing strain on Craig and Fred's relationship as they considered their commitment to each other after three intense years together.

PERMIT
DEPARTMENT OF PARKS
CITY OF NEW YORK
Borough of Manhattan

PERMIT FOR
GAY BE-IN (HAPPENING)
Type of Event

PERMIT NUMBER 200
DATE June 24, 1970

Permission is hereby granted to Christopher St. Liberation Day Committee
Organization

to hold a Gay Be-In (happening) of not more than 25,000 persons
in Central Park at Sheep Meadow
from 2 P.M. to 7 P.M. on Sunday, June 28, 1970

Francis P. Kelly
Director of Maintenance and Operations

1. Applicant's Copy

Amplification Must Be Reduced At The Request Of Any Police Officer Or Park Department Official

(OVER)

While the permit for the first Pride march did not arrive until a few hours before commencement, the permit for the post-march Gay Be-In and Happening in Central Park was approved four days earlier on June 24. (New York Police Department)

9

QQ Magazine

Several months before the Stonewall riots, a new magazine had appeared for homosexual men. *Queen's Quarterly* (within a year, it was renamed *QQ Magazine*) announced itself as "The Magazine for Gay Guys Who Have No Hangups."[1] The editors' purpose was to support a powerful homophile movement, to get ideas out to thousands of readers, to fight for revisions to laws, and to establish precedents.[2] The magazine would not be a picture magazine, and it was not going to be porn; it was for the "healthy homosexual" and this was its message: "Stop apologizing for yourself ... face the facts and accept yourself as you are ... there is a real place for us in this world ... be proud and excited about being gay – we have earned our place in society and it must now learn its lesson that we are here to stay and that our voice is loud and strong." That's what they meant by no hangups.[3]

For *QQ*, this was the moment of "gay renaissance," and they were going to lead the way.

The gay publication *Tangents* out of California offered a somewhat snarky welcome to the new magazine, calling it a "*Ladies Home Journal* for the gay crowd," but the review recognized valuable information about health and ultimately offered congratulations to publisher George Desantis.[4]

In the summer of 1969, *QQ* listed some of the subjects "of vital interest to real men" that had been published in their pages so far. The list included a story on hepatitis and how to prevent it, an article on "fear and the gay guy," the pros and cons of circumcision, and the dangers of poppers. Lighter fare included pieces on "cooking gay style," "the sexiest bathing suits," and "cruising confidence."

And in this issue, the editors had found one of the gay guys who represented their philosophy – Craig Rodwell. A 1,500-word profile featured a double-page spread under the larger-than-life headline, "Gay is Good." The photo showed Rodwell, leaning against the doorway of the Oscar Wilde, with something of a prep-school style – classic parted-on-the-left haircut above the ears, Oxford shirt, dark slacks, and loafers.[5]

At twenty-eight, Craig was still young and had racked up achievements in the homophile movement – the demonstrations, the bookshop, the Homophile Youth Movement in Neighborhoods, *The Hymnal* newsletter, and the Annual Reminders. His ability to be both friend and counsel to the community was the *QQ* ideal. And to their healthy homosexual definition, he was "completely at ease with himself."

The editors didn't address Craig's personal struggles. He was one of their "young pioneers ... forging a path for us." Advertising was thin in the first issues of *QQ*, but in the back pages – among ads for hair removal, "wet look" bikini swimsuits, and mini-toothbrush "love bristles" for "overnight lovers" – were ads for the Annual Reminder coming up on July 4, 1969, the Mattachine Society of New York, and the Oscar Wilde Memorial Bookshop for "Gay Books, 'A Bookshop of the Homophile Movement.'"

George Desantis was among many who became known as "friends of the shop" at the Oscar Wilde. In 1960, he had been denied an advanced degree at a prominent university because it was learned that he was homosexual. As a result, he also had to resign a position that he had accepted at another university.[6]

Desantis moved on and published *QQ Magazine*, along with spinoffs *Ciao* (travel) and *Body* (erotica) magazines. Ten years after his academic career came to a sudden end, he was also a founder of the Mr. Fire Island Body Beautiful Contest in July 1970. Twenty-seven men competed in that first competition, and Desantis was one of the judges.[7]

It was Desantis who took the photos and published the *Gay Freedom 1970* commemorative booklet after the first Pride march, where Craig and Fred had been featured as "two organizers."

In the spring 1970 issue, the magazine announced that it would increase its publication schedule from quarterly to bimonthly and would change its name to *QQ Magazine*. On the content, the editorial said that "we are not and cannot be a smut magazine.... It is our hope that through *QQ* you will gain a better understanding of yourself, and of our place in a beautiful world."

Desantis' goal was to establish a national lifestyle magazine. And within a year, distribution outlets were listed in nineteen states and Puerto Rico. In the early 1970s, *QQ* regularly claimed to be reaching 95,000 readers.[8] In the December 1971 issue, their advertisement for subscribers claimed the magazine was "Number 1 in the world, outselling all other gay publications combined." Whether that was true or not, *QQ* did make its mark. In an analysis of the gay publications of the 1960s and '70s, published in the *Journal of the History of Sexuality*, author Lucas Hilderbrand called *QQ* a glossy national publication that "might be seen as central to a major cultural transition from a gay *sensibility* to a more formalized and commercialized gay *lifestyle*."[9]

By comparison, *The Advocate*, which had begun as a Los Angeles publication in 1967, is considered the first national gay and lesbian newspaper. In one of its *QQ* advertisements in 1971, *The Advocate* claimed a much larger readership, asking: "What do 120,000 gay people have in common? The Advocate, that's what." *The Advocate* differentiated itself from others, stating that they were "the only gay newspaper that is really a newspaper."[10] Another successful national publication was *GAY*, a lesbian and gay newspaper started in New York by Jack Nichols and Lige Clarke. *GAY* had an impressive circulation of 25,000 in the early 1970s.[11]

These were large numbers, since by the time of the Stonewall riots, all the homophile publications together claimed a circulation of 55,000.[12]

The one-column advertisements for the Oscar Wilde continued to show up in the back pages – one for "Gay Books" and another promoting *The New York Hymnal*, where you could "keep up to date on events in the homophile movement and the rapid changes that are taking place in areas affecting the homosexual community." Desantis knew the Oscar Wilde was a fledgling venture and was struggling financially, and he gave the shop a break on the advertising.

Desantis took the photos that Craig used in his advertising in *QQ*. Craig, Fred, and their schnauzers "Michael" and "Albert" were situated at the counter in the Oscar Wilde, showing their business and their faces. The copy asked: "Gay & Proud? Then you're our kind of men and women." It was still a bold move in 1970, and a step up from the previous copy – "Gay books, A bookshop of the homophile movement."

Having gotten to know Craig and Fred at the bookshop, Desantis found Fred – young and attractive – to be the right person to photograph to illustrate some of the lifestyle articles. With suitcases in each hand, Sargeant looked slightly upward to the New York cityscape in a photo for an article on "New Guy in Town – Tips on Moving to the Big City."[13]

It wasn't the first time Fred had been asked to look up for the camera. As a child living in Bethel, CT, he was a model for the updated "Dick and Jane" books, looking up and pointing toward a plane in the sky.[14]

By fall, in the same issue as the Mr. Fire Island contest and the announcement of the new bimonthly schedule, came a double-page cover story: "50 Years of Gay Life in America." Bracketed on the left by a piece on 1940 and the good old days, and on the right by a forward look to 1990 on how gay times were coming, was the centerpiece: "1970 – How It Is Gay Liberation," the debut article in *QQ* by Craig Rodwell.[15]

It was the first of twenty-one articles and editorials Rodwell would write for *QQ* over the next three years; he now had a national audience.

In his debut, Rodwell pinned the turning point of the gay liberation movement on Stonewall. He clarified for history some of the facts about the raid. First, the street was mobbed with "patrons and onlookers, mostly gay." While the employees and customers were being arrested for the sale and consumption of alcohol, the much-researched purpose of the raid was almost secondary: "the gay crowd interpreted the raid as just another affront on homosexuals." For years later, one of the myths of Stonewall had to do with who hurled the first brick. It took decades to settle this myth about non-existent bricks, but Craig had cleared it up at the start – "We flung pennies, rocks, and bottles at the police," he wrote.

He cited a new spirit that emerged from the riots – when gay people in public "for the first time in history were refusing to run and hide." After Stonewall came "rapid growth of this spirit among gay men and women," and Craig pointed to dozens of gay liberation groups in major cities as well as organizations on fifty college campuses.

A turning point had also occurred for the "expression of pride and self-respect in one's homosexual identity." Gay liberation meant that people should not have to lead a double life and should be able to tell their families, friends, and employers about their sexuality.

Desantis had found someone directly involved – but not part of any one organization – who could bring the heft of the movement to the *QQ* pages. Craig was someone who could interpret the history, the current times, and anticipate the future in approachable and readable terms. After Craig's successful debut on gay liberation, he appeared with a guest editorial in February 1971. In it, he would be the first to coin the term *heterosexism*.

The piece was headlined "The Tarnished Golden Rule." Heterosexuals were not doing unto others as they would have others do unto them, Craig argued, and he had a list of the corrosions. Bombarded by a heterosexual culture, Craig himself was unable to use the word *gay* in his *Village Voice* advertising – he had to use the more acceptable *homophile*. *QQ Magazine* was barred from advertising in the *Voice*, few printers would take *The Hymnal* on as a print job, and when they did, Craig said that he was overcharged. He cited high increases in his Mercer Street lease and lack of action by the FBI and the telephone company to investigate harassment at the Oscar Wilde. He said that the use of a popular beverage sign in the play *The Boys in the Band* was barred for fear that customers would associate the drink with "queers." Craig called for "organized resistance to straight oppression." As he had done in the past, he pointed to the successful example of the Black civil rights movement.

Craig's writing appeared in all the remaining issues in 1971, bringing his well-developed blend of inspiration, education, real-life example, and self-help to his articles and editorials.

In the pages of *QQ*, he would promote one of his most important themes – unity. He had learned a lot about division in the ranks of the homophile movement, and he'd managed to overcome differences within the Christopher

Street Liberation Day Committee ahead of the first Pride march. He had strong opinions but had not wanted to become too closely aligned with the many new political organizations that grew out of the Stonewall riots.

Across the country, readers opened the August 1971 issue to Craig's guest editorial, "Hanging In Together." Here he would explain the differences in the "200 or so" gay liberation organizations. First were the radical groups, who used aggressive actions and sometimes violence to effect change. Then there were the militant activists with orderly demonstrations and even some direct confrontation with elected officials. And third were the social service groups that "almost always function within a straight framework of social acceptability." He identified the main disagreement – a separate society for gay people or integration in society as a whole. Regarding revolutions, he wrote, "Virtually all of the resulting fascist-communist dictatorships which came to power after revolutions ... have resulted in severe and barbarous repression of homosexuals." So there was no other choice but to work within the system of the times. And freedom would only come with unity.[16]

In the June issue that summer, Craig deployed two of his most powerful gifts – his ability to educate with plain language and his compassion to inspire through self-help. The topic was harassment by police. He would reach into his own story to make the first point with his experience at Riis Park in 1962. Pulled by the scruff of his neck off Riis Beach by police due to a bathing suit that did not reach down the thigh, he was ticketed, taken to a private room, called a "faggot" and "queer," and knocked to the floor. After his release, when it came time to pay the fine, it got worse. The judge realized Rodwell was gay, and since he didn't have the right amount for a higher-than-expected fine, he was jailed for three days, where the guard smashed his head into the bars. He had been finger-printed, handcuffed, and his head was shaved. The point he made was that the laws were interpreted by police to discriminate against homosexuals. He called on the community reading this account to recognize that laws were made and enforced for heterosexual men. He asked people to channel their anger and to get involved, because everyone was vulnerable.

For the August issue, Craig had a follow-up: What should you do if you do get arrested? He had a list: Have the telephone number of a lawyer, get the name and badge number of the officer, and give only your name and address if you are arrested. He had heard too many stories of gay men pouring out their stories to a "friendly" officer, only to have the details used against them. He encouraged people to know their rights, to insist on a phone call, and not to give in to the pressure of giving up others to help yourself. And then, he wrote, if you're arrested and you do all of this, sit back and relax and wait for your lawyer – "take a deep breath." He closed with a Christian Science quote from Mary Baker Eddy on the importance of a positive self-image: "Good thoughts are an impervious armor."[17]

Fall brought out a reflective Craig in a collection of "Random Thoughts." First was his review of "sexism," a new term for the times that described "the class structure set up by society concerning certain feelings, desires, actions, and stereotypes which have been applied to 'masculinity' and 'femininity.'" He encouraged gay people to reject the "heterosexist" myths that gay men are feminine, that "all close relationships are 'masculine-feminine,'" and that men can only relate to women sexually or they would be labeled "queer." He called on gay males to reject the notion that sensitivity is feminine and aggression is masculine.

Was there a problem with *QQ* being largely written for gay men? Craig didn't think so. He looked to the women's lib publications and magazines targeting Black audiences to make the point. He said *QQ Magazine* was "leading its own kind of revolution – instilling pride in thousands of homosexuals who never had it," which would free them and give them courage and hope. He then called for unity among homosexual men and women in the movement.[18]

◆◆◆◆◆

As 1971 came to a close and a third of the way through his stint with *QQ*, Craig would have taken stock of the world around him. The gay movement continued to be part of a time of turbulence and change. The Vietnam War had not ended, *The New York Times* had published the Pentagon Papers, the Attica Prison riot had occurred in New York, and Gloria Steinem had made her "Address to the Women of America" speech.

Personally, his relationship with Fred Sargeant had come to an end earlier that year. Craig had had two lovers in his life, Harvey Milk and Fred.[19] His relationship with Fred was the longest and the only time Craig had lived with another man beyond a short stint. While they were eight years apart, their relationship was more like contemporaries than Craig's relationship with Harvey. While Harvey (twelve years older) had wined and dined Craig at ethnic restaurants and introduced him to cultural activities, Craig and Fred found intimacy in a meager existence, with an occasional dinner at Fedora's, a shoulder-to-shoulder life at the bookshop, and an occasional game of Stratego, which was a favorite of Craig's. They had been a young couple who lived an open life together in business and at home.

Unlike what had happened with Harvey, the relationship did not collapse due to unfaithfulness or militancy. Craig reflected on this in an interview with Kay Tobin Lahusen: "When Fred and I were living together, we were faithful. We never used that term; we didn't have a particular need or desire to run around."[20]

But they had been together through thick and thin, during this tense peak in the liberation movement, and they were wearing out as a couple. Fred had also had enough of the city. On Bleecker Street, as they were parting for good, Craig was in tears – "you're still part of the business, the shop is half yours," he told Fred. But Fred knew that the Oscar Wilde would need all its profits to stay open, and so he was gone.

It was crushing. As Ellen recalled the relationship: "Being with Fred was very special to Craig. It made him feel loved and attractive ... to be with someone who looked like Fred was a real badge of honor."[21]

Craig would need to put his full attention on the shop now, and he began to hire staff. These had been peak years for the two of them, with the reminders, the riots, the first march, and giving encouragement to so many unsure gay men and women.

Fred would move on to a career in policing in Connecticut. After what he had been through in New York, he felt he could make a change if he could rise in the ranks, which he did, attaining the rank of lieutenant. Craig was hardly pleased to hear the news given his own experiences, but in subsequent years, as the two of them joined up for occasional dinners again at Fedora's, the idea of gay people in policing began to make more sense.

Many years later, as the Stonewall story and the birth of the gay liberation movement were being written into new histories, Fred moved to Provincetown, MA, where he successfully proposed one of the first domestic partnership registries and action against hate crimes. He invited Craig to come out for a visit – the ocean breeze would be good for him. Craig wouldn't be doing that, as he put it, but he didn't let on that he was seriously ill. He wanted Fred to have something. In the mail sometime later came a copy of the *Gay Freedom 1970* commemorative booklet from the 1970 Christopher Street Liberation Day, the one with their picture together, almost leaning against each other, exhausted after the first march. It had the Oscar Wilde's price tag on it. From their early relationship, they felt a lifelong connection, even if it had gone largely silent. Once in the late 1980s, on a visit to New York, Sargeant had walked by 350 Bleecker, and he'd glanced at the doorbell and intercom panel in the outer lobby. His name was still there.[22]

◆◆◆◆◆

By February 1972, Craig would use the columns of *QQ* to reflect on ten years of gay liberation and to make some predictions about what would happen in the remainder of the decade. In the rearview mirror, Craig saw more on-the-street acceptance of the existence of gay people in society, albeit through his Greenwich Village lens. People were not shocked to see a gay couple holding hands as they once would have been. Craig's personal news clippings of all things concerning homosexuality proved there had been a rapid growth in news coverage. Ten years before, he searched hard to find anything in print about homosexuality. But in 1972, post-Stonewall, there were dozens of periodicals. Coming out was a new possibility. "Ten years ago, it was almost unheard of for a Gay person to inform his or her family of The Fact," he wrote. This was what he saw as the "healthiest" change in the previous decade – that homosexuals had begun to inform their families and friends of their sexual orientation.[23]

Craig predicted that in the next ten years, gay people would start to be elected to public office. Within two years of his *QQ* article, Kathy Kozachenko, an out lesbian in Ann Arbor, MI, won a seat on the city council. In the same year, Elaine Noble won a seat in the Massachusetts House after an ugly campaign against her. And by 1977, Craig's former lover, Harvey Milk, would win his seat on the Board of Supervisors in San Francisco. Craig also predicted the "coming out of well-known Gay people." This would take much longer than he hoped, but it was happening – musicians like David Bowie and Dusty Springfield were out in the 1970s. Tennis great Martina Navratilova would come out in 1981.

The public would begin to recognize that "Gay people make good parents," Craig predicted. He foresaw changes in the adoption laws around the country, which wouldn't really take hold until the turn of the next century. It would just be a "matter of time," he wrote, before parents would realize that their children should be raised from birth as "free human beings," where male children would not be treated differently from female children and vice versa. "The whole idea that boys should be raised with blue blankets, fire engines, toy soldiers and boxing gloves and that girls should be raised with pink blankets, toy stoves, doll houses and sewing kits will be considered archaic and repressive."

In the meantime, there was a lot to be concerned about in the pages of QQ in 1972 – exploitation of the gay liberation movement, the relationship of God to gay liberation, the coming out of gay people in the arts, homosexual law reform, the election, and the problem of gay stereotyping. Craig had become the anchor for social and political discussion in QQ.

The exploitation of gay people had not been erased with Stonewall or by the other protests that occurred during and after the riots. In fact, by spring 1972, he saw it as one of the major problems facing the gay liberation movement. Frustratingly, control by the syndicates had in fact broadened to include the bars and the bathhouses. Now a system of "fronts" had been established, where a gay person would be listed as an owner, but the financial backing was a syndicate. Craig encouraged readers to look for the front and to see if a business had the right licenses. He warned that the exploitation even reached into established gay organizations.

His model of expose, explain, and act would transfer to almost any gay liberation issue.[24]

The politicians' promise and lack of follow-up was especially irksome to him:

> The most outstanding example of this is US Rep. Bella Abzug (D-Manhattan) who, during her campaign for the House in 1970, appeared before Gay organizations in New York City promising to submit bills to Congress to guarantee to Gay people nationally equal opportunity in employment and housing. It is generally agreed in the Congressional District that the margin of her victory was attributed to her heavy support from Gay people. But, of course, since her election a year and a half ago, she has done nothing for Gay people that she promised.[25]

Abzug was asked to march in the 1971 Christopher Street Liberation Day march, Craig wrote, but when the time came, she was "sitting at home," and he said she shouldn't be supported in the next campaign.

Craig found the position of the Socialist Workers Party the most offensive political exploitation. Having discovered the potential of the gay liberation movement, the party gave the impression that they had founded it, Craig wrote, which led him to emphasize that the gay movement was susceptible to being pigeonholed and hijacked. He called for a common trust and for people to become more sophisticated socially and politically to avoid exploitation.

By summer, Rodwell was ready to turn his attention to the rise of gay churches. He winced at the gay marriages that followed the same model as heterosexual marriages, and the gay churches that followed the same social practices of coffee hours, choir practices, and floral arrangement committees. They were okay, but had "very little, if anything, to do with Christianity." What Rodwell imagined was a gay church movement based on "primitive Christianity." Simple goodness would prevail and one of the most important religious experiences would be a coming out ceremony with a spiritual rebirth.[26]

And there was a very long way to go in the arts. You would think, Craig wrote, that of all places the gay community would assert itself, it would be in the arts:

> But we have yet to see ads in the papers for Thomas Schippers conducting the premiere of Leonard Bernstein's "Homage to a Gay Brother – In praise of Walt Whitman." Or Rudolf Nureyev and Erik Bruhn dancing a romantic pas de deux. Or Rock Hudson and Paul Newman starring in the film version of Gore Vidal's updated "The City and the Pillar." Or Van Cliburn playing Aaron Copland's heroic "Gay and Proud – Free at Last" concerto.[27]

This offered a rare glimpse into his sense of humor, but he pressed on, complaining of the cliches and stereotypes in *The Boys in the Band* and porn in movie houses. And this was Craig's chance to take a shot at George Balanchine for not finding a place for homosexuals in the ballet. Craig had been a student at the School of American Ballet when he first moved to New York. He wrote that it was common knowledge that Balanchine was not pro-gay and that only heterosexual men would become lead dancers (Craig found them to be "the worst dancers") in the New York City Ballet. The solo moments when the men display feats of athleticism underscored the stereotypes of heterosexual women as sensitive and graceful and the men as strong and supportive.

Craig posed the question as to why drag shows were considered the only form of entertainment for gay men. Not that he had "anything – per se, against drag shows," but they reinforced a heterosexual stereotype and contempt for gay life "by reinforcing the stereotype in front of us and actually getting us to think that we're being entertained." He called on gay people in the arts to reimagine their creativity and to incorporate the whole "Gay consciousness" in their work – to mold public opinion with a more holistic attitude.

Returning to homosexual law reform, Craig predicted that there would be a change in the Civil Rights Act of 1964 to make it illegal to discriminate based on sexual orientation. He was decades off, even on partial anti-discrimination legislation. The US Supreme Court wouldn't settle discrimination in employment based on sexual orientation until 2020.[28]

Regardless, Craig believed the real reform was in everyday society. Real reform would be when there was development of gay community, group consciousness of oppression, and interrupting the persistent exploitation of gay people. His imagined that "the you-know-what (would) hit the fan when they suddenly realize that what we're calling for is the end to institutionalized sexism which raised boys to be fathers, soldiers, husbands and providers, and women to be mothers, wives, seamstresses and secretaries."[29]

As the November 1972 election approached, there was something new to be considered – the gay vote. Before the Democratic convention was held, Craig prepared a summary of candidates who had issued statements about their positions on "issues of concern to Gay people" for publication in *QQ*'s September issue.[30]

Craig's review: Shirley Chisholm, the first African-American candidate for president in a major party, would ban discrimination against homosexuals by the federal government by executive order; Hubert Humphrey, the unsuccessful presidential candidate from 1968, was supportive but non-specific with an "I see no reason why homosexual Americans should be excluded from equal protection under the law..."; New York Mayor John Lindsay, who had switched from Republican to Democrat, was quoted as saying that only when the tone in Washington changed would homosexuals receive the better treatment that they deserved; Eugene McCarthy, former congressman and US senator, who had lost the 1968 Democratic nomination, would also issue an executive order to ban discrimination at the federal level; and Paul McCloskey, Republican congressman, would support a limited ban on discrimination at the federal level.

This brought Craig to George McGovern. The US senator from South Dakota had offered the broadest set of guarantees to end discrimination against homosexuals.

"Only George McGovern," he wrote, "has pledged 'the full moral and legal authority of his presidency towards restoring and guaranteeing first-class citizen rights for homosexually oriented individuals.'" Craig thought the nation was going in the wrong direction, not only regarding repression of homosexuals, but because of increasing control of the country by big labor, big business, the military, and the media. Gay people, Craig almost pleaded, had the opportunity to influence the election, and it was through McGovern that he hoped – too optimistically – for serious change.

Gay stereotyping would close out Craig's writing for *QQ* in 1972. He bemoaned the continuing stereotype of gay men as mincing and effeminate, "the exaggerated perfumed 'fag' who caricatures society's definition of what a 'real woman' is." He believed the stereotype was losing its strength but that new stereotypes were appearing, including the radical and unclean disruptive fanatic. Going back to his roots, he argued that gay people just wanted the freedom to live their lives peacefully like other sexual, ethnic, racial, and cultural groups. It was just easier to accept a stereotype than to "relate on an equal and loving basis with their Gay sons, daughters, nephews, nieces, uncles, aunts."[31]

Before Stonewall, press coverage of gay issues had been almost imperceptible; now the movement was faced with "ego-trippers," people who were seeking press for the latest gimmick "to call attention to themselves." The ego-trippers were the ones making the news and they were making it difficult for gay liberationists "to reach our millions of Gay brothers and sisters to confront their oppression and to consciously help in the fight against heterosexism."

Still, Craig remained hopeful, and his call to action was to "know yourself," know that the new stereotypes were not the majority, know that there were thousands of gay people working to end heterosexism and to help others, collectively and individually.

◆◆◆◆◆

In 1973, when Craig opened the Oscar Wilde's second location at 15 Christopher Street, closer to the center of gay life in Greenwich Village, he continued to write for *QQ*. The last of his twenty-one articles or editorials was published in the October issue. With the opening of the new shop, his hands were full. Both locations would remain open until Mercer Street closed in May 1974.[32]

Craig would take another shot at the Mafia's influence and control over gay life. It had been exactly five years since he wrote "Mafia on the Spot" in the first issue of *The Hymnal*. It seemed to him that things had only gotten worse.

In the February and April issues of *QQ*, he laid out his thoughts on what had happened. The syndicate had expanded its control of bars, movie houses, porn shops, and bathhouses. With the "fronts" in place, they were less obvious than before. Craig himself was approached to run a male movie house and finagled his way out from under the pressure. He wrote that gay men were being blackmailed through "call-boy" services run by the Mafia, that they were being introduced to and addicted to drugs at Mafia controlled bars, and that the bars were being used as outlets for other mob-controlled businesses.[33]

It seemed like a lonely battle. Where were the other gay liberation organizations, Craig wondered, when the gay bar was one of the most important social institutions of the time and the community had no control over their own social spaces. It was going to be a long struggle, but he was not afraid to put into words what gay men all over knew to be the truth of the Mafia closet:[34]

> The closet of the Gay bar where we are allowed to stand against the walls and stare at other Gay people while paying exorbitant prices for watered down drinks. The closet of the porno shop where we are allowed to spend $10 for a male-nudie magazine wrapped in cellophane and put quarters into vending machines to see a minute of two men making love. The closet of the drug-induced state where we can attain a euphoric state of temporary bliss. The closet of the Gay movie house where we have the "privilege" of spending $5 to see nude males for a couple of hours.

In the second installment, he promoted empowerment in gay lives. He encouraged people to "like themselves" and to nurture their self-respect and dignity. He encouraged people in business to put an end to payoffs. He asked people to respect pickets of syndicate-controlled businesses, and to support non-mob businesses.

"And if I have not yet managed to communicate my personal anger to YOU," he wrote, "I won't stop trying. I have been in this movement too long and am convinced that until we rid ourselves of outside control, we will never even begin to be a free people."

In the same issue of *QQ*, turning to the re-election of Richard Nixon and the defeat of George McGovern, Craig was unsurprised. While appreciating McGovern's support for gay rights, Craig knew it was too soon and that McGovern would go down for being too radical. Political change could not come from a top-down bureaucratic approach – it had to come from a groundswell of local community voters. So, the long view was to use the Nixon years to build a broad, supportive community.[35]

Over the previous decade, Craig had seen the movement grow from a few groups and a couple hundred people to a national movement of a thousand organizations and tens of thousands of activists, but there was still a "powerlessness at the local level" that needed to be addressed. He called for education and dialogue and the growth of allies and parent groups. He even reflected on his mother, Marion, who – after all the trials and tribulations of her son's youth – had told him that she was proud of him when she heard him speak publicly on gay liberation. And finally, Craig took another jab at contrived protests and "media freaks and ego-trippers." The challenge would have to be met by direct connection with people.

In the June 1973 magazine, Craig would take up the issue of violence against gay men in his article "For All the Jack Staffords in the World." Stafford was a thirty-seven-year-old librarian at the Queensborough Public Library who had been active in the Gay Task Force of the American Library Association. At 10:45 p.m. on November 2, 1972, Stafford was cruising in Rufus King Park in Jamaica, Queens, when he was chased down on foot near the exit to the park and stabbed. He died at the scene.

According to an account in the *Daily News*, there had been witnesses at the Mary Immaculate Hospital, whose windows had a view of the park. The witnesses said they "noticed a group of four or five men, when suddenly two men broke off and ran, with the others in the pursuit. Then the two fleeing men were overtaken and stabbed." Stafford's body was found about seventy-five feet inside the park. He had been stabbed twice. The second victim, Wallace Oxenhorn, age thirty-nine, a cantor at the Sheepshead Bay Synagogue in Brooklyn, had been stabbed three times.[36]

Craig hoped that these deaths at the hands of heterosexual men would ignite outrage over the harassment of the "queers." In the 1970s (and to many gay men for decades to come) the word *queer* was a hateful dagger thrust into their psyche to isolate them and to keep them in the closet. Rodwell remembered when he was in high school: "one of the favorite pastimes of the boys who had to prove what 'men' they were, was to go down to the 'queer' section of Chicago and beat one up." He also remembered for his readers the time he was arrested at the age of fourteen in Chicago for "homosexual activity." His stepfather's only response was that when he was a teenager, he and his buddies would make a sport of beating up some queers themselves.

As always, Craig had a prescription for change and empowerment. "Carry a loud whistle," he advised, "and *use* it." He recognized that cruising the parks was not going to go away. It was cultural that gay people who could not make social connections publicly would find private spaces in public places. So, he continued, learn self-defense, get together with other gay people and demand that the police crack down on gangs taunting gay people, or join an auxiliary civilian police unit and patrol unsafe cruising areas.

"The real tragedy of this kind of violence against Gay people," he wrote, "is that it doesn't arouse indignation in the general community or even among Gay people themselves (yet)."

❖❖❖❖❖

Approaching his thirty-third birthday, Craig had already experienced a life filled with male intimacy and sexual encounters, but he was rarely successful in continuing intimate relationships. So, his question for QQ readers was: "Sex: How Important Is It?" Speaking directly to gay men, he told them that the bars, the baths, and the movie houses they were drawn to were isolating them. He urged them to see these places in their social and historical context: "it is in the public interest to keep us isolated ... where we are permitted to commit our 'perverted' acts out of the view and minds of the general public." With their identities suppressed at work, only afterward in faraway corners could they be "Gay males." Craig asked: "How many times have you gone to a Gay bar, stayed for hours, had too much to drink, and been depressed because you went home alone?" This would be a question many gay men would recognize, and Craig knew they wouldn't like the answer. But he was here to raise their consciousness. What was needed was a new purpose – to interact with people not just for sex, but to support the social, intellectual, and cultural fabric of life.[37]

Craig's 1973 model for change included basics that would be taken for granted today: to talk to people at a bar without the goal of going home for sex, to bring gay friends into your home for dinner and socializing, to seek out other gay people where you work, to develop social contacts with gay women, and finally, "to bring your family and Hetero friends into contact with your Gay life."

Craig's growing awareness of middle age in his early thirties was not uncommon for someone born in 1940. Life expectancy for him would have been somewhere in his sixties, which he did not reach, and not because of the coming AIDS epidemic. In the next decade, life expectancy for gay men would plummet. A diagnosis of AIDS would be considered a death sentence within a matter of months or perhaps a year or two.

But that had not happened yet, and a page had been turned for Craig. The new shop was open at 15 Christopher, his involvement in the Christopher Street Liberation Day Umbrella Committee had receded, and more people than ever were involved in the gay liberation movement. Gray was going to be good.

His next-to-the-last feature for *QQ* (the last would be an editorial on the meaning of obscenity) would be a reflection on "youth cultism," which he saw permeating American culture and Gay culture specifically. In "Gray Is Good," taking off on Frank Kameny's slogan "Gay Is Good," Craig cast aside his previous worries that after thirty no one would want him, and he would have less value in society. "I'm more at peace now with myself than I ever was; I have perspective on relationships and ideas which gives me a degree of 'calm'; I don't have the constant need anymore to 'make out' all the time to prove to myself how desirable I am; I no longer have a need to 'impress' others."[38]

In a tribute to the elders who had influenced him, Craig included Bernard Koten from the early bookshop years (whom he referred to only as "Bernard"), who was a longtime friend of the Oscar Wilde, who passed out leaflets in the Stonewall riots, and who was now in his sixties and still going strong as head of a university library.

The life cycle of gay liberation had come into focus. Craig had lived through the revolution, the beginning, and the middle, but what would the end look like? He asked if there was discrimination against elderly gay people in the Social Security Administration, and what about other government programs for senior citizens, and their social and economic needs? The equality he sought in these questions wouldn't come about for decades.

Craig wasn't the only one writing in the 1960s and 1970s – there were voluminous contributions, including those from Kameny, Gittings, and Lahusen. By the end of the year, thanks to the work of Gittings, Kameny, and others, the American Psychiatric Association would remove homosexuality from its list of mental disorders.

But Craig was on the front line – framing, encouraging, and advocating the gay identity as a normal state of being, one to be proud of. He spoke plainly and directly to every homosexual to strengthen their confidence, self-respect, and courage – to mobilize them toward whatever public action they could take.

QQ Magazine continued publication until 1980. But these had been four peak years in gay liberation history and four intense years of Craig's life, in which he found alignment in his personal life, his business, and his advocacy for gay freedom.

In its fall 1970 issue, *QQ Magazine* looked at "50 Years of Gay Life in America." Craig Rodwell wrote the centerpiece, describing the impact of gay liberation. (*QQ Magazine*)

10

Christian Science

Craig's childhood at the Chicago Junior School had been infused with Christian Science teachings and lessons from the Bible. From age six, his day had started with a half-hour Bible study in the morning, and there were prayers in the classroom and before each meal. Prayers inspired the huddle on the football field, and prayers were recited at night. The religious studies had been divided equally between the lessons of the Bible and the writings of Mary Baker Eddy. His young mind had regularly questioned the "whys" of the lessons, though, much to the frustration of the house mothers.[1]

It was the "truth is all" message of Christian Science that had led him to pour his heart out to the judge after his arrest in Jacob Riis Park. In his "God & Gay Lib" feature in *QQ Magazine*, he encouraged readers to consider Primitive Christianity and the values that Jesus put forth, which is the basis for Christian Science. Craig reasoned that if Mary Baker Eddy believed that God was the "father/mother," then gay people should certainly be recognized by the church. The Oscar Wilde itself was modeled on the concept of the Christian Science reading room.[2] But the teachings of the church in the 1970s stated that homosexuality was something to be healed; if a person couldn't be healed, then they couldn't be members of the church.

When Kay Tobin Lahusen interviewed Craig for her book *The Gay Crusaders*, he told her that he had imagined someday that he would travel to the Mother Church in Boston and protest the church's condemnation of homosexuality.[3]

Around the time that Lahusen was publishing her ground-breaking book, a young New Yorker named Bob McCullough was contending with his own homosexuality. He had moved to New York from Houston in 1964 and eventually found employment as a financial analyst. To address the anxiety in his life, he had turned to psychology, but it was a mismatch, and he headed for the Christian Science Church. Like Craig, he thought the concept of the father-mother God seemed a perfect spiritual fit for a gay person. Attending a branch church, he heard the testimony of Bob Mackenroth, who referred to himself as a bachelor, a key word for someone who was gay in the early 1970s. Mackenroth was describing a Christian Science healing – he had had a tumor on his head, and having turned to prayer, he awoke one day to find the tumor had disappeared. The two Bobs linked up right away, and after church they went to McDonald's for coffee.[4]

Soon they would meet Lahusen, who had been raised by her Christian Science grandparents. She had graduated from Ohio State University and moved to Boston, where she worked in the *Christian Science Monitor* research library. She met Barbara Gittings and had a lifelong relationship with her, had contributed to *The Ladder*, published by the Daughters of Bilitis, and was a founding member of the Gay Activist Alliance after the Stonewall riots, before writing her now-famous first collection of gay profiles.

A coalescence was about to occur:

- Lahusen, who worked for a couple of years in the Oscar Wilde, mentions Craig Rodwell to the two Bobs as someone they should meet.
- At a meeting at the Ninth Church in New York, Bob McCullough is introduced to Craig.
- Craig places a copy of Robert Peel's biography of Mary Baker Eddy in a conspicuous spot in the Oscar Wilde.[5]
- Ray Spitale, who had recently come to Christian Science himself, visits the Oscar Wilde, spots the Peel biography, and wonders about the significance of its placement in a gay and lesbian bookshop; he meets Craig.
- A friendship circle of the Bobs, Ray, and Craig emerges.[6]
- Craig posts a notice in the Oscar Wilde's new bulletin, "Signs of the Times": "Christian Science Discussion Group forming – Gay people with some background in Christian Science, write CSDG, c/o Oscar Wilde Mem. Bookshop."[7]

During the early and mid-1970s, Bob McCullough and Bob Mackenroth made attempts to get the Mother Church's attention on inclusion of gay members, with attempts to meet with the Board of Directors and Board of Trustee members, largely to no avail.

The view of homosexuality by the Christian Science Church in the 1960s and '70s was clearly stated in editorials in the *Christian Science Sentinel*, a weekly publication of the church. The *Sentinel* has been published continuously since it was founded by Mary Baker Eddy in 1898 and its purpose is to "hold guard over Truth, Life, and Love."[8]

Carl Welz, later to become editor of the *Sentinel* and other publications, wrote in an editorial in April 1967, "[t]hat homosexuality is a deviation from the moral law is made plain in the Bible." Welz wrote that "the healing of homosexuality ... comes, like the healing of any other abnormal condition."[9]

Naomi Price, a Christian Science practitioner writing in the *Sentinel* in 1972, reiterated the position that Christian Science follows the word of the Bible, and "[t]he Bible is undeviating in its stand for the clear definition of individuals as either male or female, and the absolute restriction of marriage relations to individuals of the opposite sex."[10]

And Steven Lee Fair recounted in a *Sentinel* article in 1979 the story of a young man who was healed of his homosexuality after a life of despair, having begun the piece by stating: "Today many people are asking if homosexuality is right or wrong. The Bible and Christian teaching in general take the latter position."[11]

This was the backdrop to the friendship that McCullough, Mackenroth, Spitale, and Rodwell had formed. One connection was leading to another, and to another, and they were all going to converge in a confrontation with the Mother Church in Boston, perhaps a fairly conservative action to those who had witnessed previous demonstrations, but a major protest within the traditions of the church. They planned to turn the tide, and in 1978, they formed the group Gay People in Christian Science to do it.[12]

Ironically, they would follow the example of Reginald Kerry, a longtime Christian Scientist from Santa Barbara, CA, who had been hired by the First Church of Christ, Scientist to perform a security survey of all church practices and departments, including management and personnel issues. He was to investigate all potential threats to the cause of the church. Over many months, Kerry audited the practices of the church and found great concerns in its finances, predicting bankruptcy if something was not done. The Board of Directors received Kerry's critical report and essentially shelved it, thanking him for his work. Kerry, astonished, tried to get the Board to act on its finances, without success, so he decided to take matters into his own hands. Since the Christian Science Church published the names and addresses of all its practitioners and branch churches in the *Christian Science Journal* directory, Kerry had a ready-made mailing list to get his findings – and now grievances – out to Christian Scientists all over the world. He sent out a blistering letter outlining his research. After Kerry sent his first letter, the Board responded with an attempt to mollify Kerry and work with him, but surreptitiously they sent out a letter of their own, implying that the issues were being addressed. That prompted Kerry to send out a second letter that provided further details of financial problems in the church. And then, about two years before Gay People in Christian Science formed, Kerry sent a third letter he intended would protect the cause of the church by exposing immorality within its ranks. He targeted homosexuality in the church itself – in the church leadership, membership, and staff. He even put his finger on the church organist at the Mother Church in Boston.[13]

The friends had a plan.

They would work to publish and distribute their own pamphlet. On Sundays, Bob, Bob, and Ray would join Craig in his Bleecker Street apartment to frame the concepts and words for the pamphlet. Craig was at his typewriter, and it was a familiar place. He had already written the features in *QQ Magazine*, articles for *The Hymnal*, and he had his background from the Mattachine newsletter. He had addressed the topics of God and gay liberation, and even the Golden Rule had made its way into the headline of one of the *QQ* pieces. He had coined the term "heterosexism" as "straight oppression."[14]

Craig's influence was all over the eight-page pamphlet.

Entitled *Gay People in Christian Science?*, the pamphlet opened with the fact that gay men and women were active in the Christian Science movement. A polite argument for the proper treatment of gay people was directed at Christian Scientists everywhere and to the Board of Directors of the church "to rectify the present wrongs being done to Gay people in the name of Christian Science."

Next, the authors identified what they called "incorrect literature" on the subject, singling out immediately Welz's *Sentinel* article that claimed homosexuality could be healed. They called the publication of the piece "a day of great sadness," especially because it quoted the Leviticus passage in the Bible suggesting homosexuals be put to death. They also singled out Price's 1972 article on the Bible and

Craig Rodwell in an early Roger Sullivan High School photograph in Chicago around 1955. (Craig Rodwell Papers, Manuscripts and Archives Division, The New York Public Library)

Marion Dunlop in 1931 in Rochester, NY, at twenty-two years old, four years before she married Louis Rodwell. (Craig Rodwell Papers, Manuscripts and Archives Division, The New York Public Library)

Craig in his high school Junior ROTC uniform in 1957. (Craig Rodwell Papers, Manuscripts and Archives Division, The New York Public Library)

Craig in a ballet position in 1957, before he would study dance in Boston and New York. (Craig Rodwell Papers, Manuscripts and Archives Division, The New York Public Library)

Craig (top row, fourth from left) with his senior class division in the 1958 Navillus yearbook. (Rogers Park/West Ridge Historical Society)

At Jacob Riis Park beach in Queens in 1960, wearing the bikini-style bathing suit that would get him arrested two years later. (Craig Rodwell Papers, Manuscripts and Archives Division, The New York Public Library)

At the first homosexual picket, protesting the lack of confidentiality of draft records (Craig is second in line, behind Randy Wicker) at the Whitehall Street Army Induction Center in New York on September 19, 1964. (Craig Rodwell Papers, Manuscripts and Archives Division, The New York Public Library)

After three attempts to demonstrate that gay customers were denied service at New York bars, Mattachine Society members (second from left) John Timmons, Dick Leitsch, and Craig Rodwell, and joined by Randy Wicker, were successful with their "Sip-In" at Julius' Bar in Greenwich Village on April 21, 1966. (Fred W. McDarrah/Premium Archive via Getty Images)

Conferring with Frank Kameny at the fifth and last Annual Reminder demonstration in Philadelphia on July 4, 1969. (Photo by Nancy Tucker, Lesbian Herstory Archives)

May 1969, in front of the Oscar Wilde Memorial Bookshop at its first location at 291 Mercer Street, in New York, one month before the Stonewall riots. (Craig Rodwell Papers, Manuscripts and Archives Division, The New York Public Library)

Conferring with the NYPD prior to the start of the Christopher Street Liberation Day march up Sixth Avenue in New York on June 28, 1970. (George Desantis/Gay Freedom 1970)

Under the banner for the first Pride march prior to commencement. No one knew how many brave souls would step onto the street and stride openly from Greenwich Village to Central Park. (Diana Davies/©NYPL)

Ellen Broidy (in Lavender Menace T-shirt), who made the proposal for the march to the Eastern Regional Conference of Homophile Organizations the previous November, with Dolores Bargowski and Rita Mae Brown. (Diana Davies/©NYPL, Courtesy of Ellen Broidy, Courtesy of Rita Mae Brown)

Fred Sargeant (far left, with bullhorn) was a parade marshal and organizer at the head of the march. When he jumped onto the base of a lamppost, he saw that marchers had filled in as far back as he could see. (George Desantis/Gay Freedom 1970)

Exhausted and exhilarated, the 5,000 marchers poured into Sheep Meadow in Central Park, including "two organizers," Sargeant and Rodwell. (George Desantis/Gay Freedom 1970)

GAY & PROUD?

THEN YOU'RE OUR KIND OF MEN AND WOMEN!

★ Gay Guides ★ Homophile Periodicals
★ Fiction & Non-Fiction
★ Gifts, Funthings, Etc.
★ Personalizing Service on Matches, Napkins, Etc.

OSCAR WILDE MEMORIAL BOOKSHOP
291 Mercer St.
(1 blk. west of B'wy off 8th St.)
New York, N.Y. 10003
(212) 673-3539

STOP BY OR SEND 25¢ FOR CATALOG

A "gay and proud" advertisement for the Oscar Wilde in April 1971 features Sargeant, Rodwell, and their schnauzers "Albert" and "Michael," who welcomed potentially anxious customers. (*QQ Magazine*)

In the new shop at 15 Christopher Street in 1973, Craig and his mother sit, together again, having set up the first shop together on Mercer Street six years before. (Kay Tobin/©NYPL)

Author Jonathan Ned Katz signs copies of his landmark book *Gay American History* at the Oscar Wilde in 1976. (Diana Davies/©NYPL)

Tennessee Williams, in fur coat and fedora, visited the Oscar Wilde on Thanksgiving weekend in 1975 for a meet-the-author day. This photo on the steps of the bookshop with Craig and company was later memorialized on the cover of the shop's catalog. (Barbara Gluck Treaster/Craig Rodwell Papers, Manuscripts and Archives Division, The New York Public Library)

Speaking out against the portrayal of gay men in the Al Pacino film *Cruising* at the Judson Memorial Church in New York in July 1979. (©Bettye Lane/Manuscripts and Archives Division, The New York Public Library)

With the staff of the Oscar Wilde Memorial Bookshop in 1984. Seated, left to right: Rodwell, Fred Carl, Ellen Turner; standing: Amina Rahman, Nan Buzard, Chris Madonna, Calvin Lowery. (Sheila Ryan/Craig Rodwell Papers, Manuscripts and Archives Division, The New York Public Library)

Portrait of Rodwell at the Oscar Wilde Memorial Bookshop on Christopher Street in January 1992, when Rodwell was fifty-two years old. (Photo by Robert Giard/Copyright Estate of Robert Giard)

homosexuality, among other pieces. This was the incorrect literature that they said misstated Christian Science:

> Gay women and men are depicted as "promiscuous," "bizarre," "abnormal," "immoral," "unseemly," "unhealthy," "unnatural," "cursed," and "perverted." Nowhere is there even the slightest recognition that the basis of same-sex relationships is love, the exact same human need for love and mutual respect that is the basis for heterosexual relationships.[15]

They continued making their case, citing Bible quotations that women shouldn't address the meetings, that they didn't have a license to speak, and that if they needed to know something, they could ask their husbands at home. How, they asked, could Mary Baker Eddy have founded the Christian Science Church if she were to be punished and silenced through literal interpretation of the Bible? They wanted it recognized that selective use of passages from the Bible could be used to oppress women or justify racism, and now such a tactic was being used to punish gay people.

This "cruel hypocrisy" toward gay people furthermore broke the Golden Rule, they wrote, and they introduced new terminology – freedom to express "affectional orientation." How could it be, they asked, that Christian Science recognized the "place of sexuality in the human experience," but the gay person needs to be healed from intimacy while heterosexuals are free to express themselves?

Among the pamphlet's conclusions there was one that was most certainly Craig's: "Just as racism had a strong hold on the Christian Science movement until very recently, today heterosexism appears to be thriving." And then there was a parenthetical definition: "(Heterosexism is the erroneous concept that only people of the so-called opposite sexes can and should express the full range of love.)"

The plan was to distribute the pamphlet at a demonstration at the annual meeting of the Mother Church in Boston in June 1979. Also, they decided that if Reginald Kerry could use the mailing list from the *Christian Science Journal*, so could they. The idea was to send out about 8,000 copies to churches, practitioners, and college organizations throughout the world, hand-addressed, with the Oscar Wilde as the return address. But there was a glitch; the printer could not complete the job in time for the 1979 meeting, so the distribution at the annual meeting would have to be moved to the following year. Disappointed but determined, they would go ahead with the mailing in the intervening months. The response was largely positive, no thanks to the Board of Directors, which responded with a letter of its own in September. The Board stood its ground on church teaching that homosexuality must be healed, and they were particularly irked by the "affectional orientation" mentioned in the pamphlet. It was a euphemism, they said, and the answer was obvious – the affectional orientation was what needed to be healed.[16]

The polite approach of the Gay People in Christian Science continued as the annual meeting in 1980 neared. While this was a throwback to the Annual Reminder demonstrations, the group was trying to appeal to conservative Christian Scientists. They were Christian Scientists themselves, so they were trying to be as non-threatening as possible. Rodwell wrote to the Board of Directors to alert them of the plan, to let them know that the demonstration would be peaceful, and that they would set up on public property. Dressed in suits and ties, the group had begun to set up their tables with the pamphlets and other literature when the Boston Police and a representative of the Mother Church showed up. The tables would have to be taken down. The year 1980 was also the 350th anniversary of the founding of Boston, and a year-long celebration included a visit by the Tall Ships to Boston Harbor.[17] As a result, the city had prohibited public displays on the sidewalks, and it was a convenient excuse to prohibit the set-up. Rodwell was incensed – he wanted to fight it – but the group resolved to comply with the order and continue the demonstration by passing out leaflets while standing on the sidewalk – that certainly wasn't prohibited. As Rodwell remembered it, the whole thing "created quite a stir."[18]

They had succeeded, at least, in getting a discussion going. The friends had stood up for a positive statement for gay people in Christian Science for the first time. They had given hope to lesbian and gay members around the world with their comprehensive pamphlet. For Craig, who often hoped throughout the trials of his activism that officials would come around if only they were presented with logic and fact – well, that did not happen in 1980 and it would not happen until years after his own life had ended.[19]

Craig continued his involvement with Gay People in Christian Science and participated in actions to support Chris Madsen, a young reporter at the *Christian Science*

Monitor who had been fired in January 1982 for being a lesbian. Madsen had contacted the group after seeing an advertisement in the *Gay Community News*.[20]

Madsen's treatment by the Mother Church sparked a series of actions by Gay People in Christian Science that June – a protest at the First Church in Boston at the annual meeting, participation in the lesbian and gay Pride march in Boston, and attendance at the Sunday service.[21]

Craig remembered the moment at the service after the Pride march – the group sat together, wearing pink triangles, the reclaimed symbol of strength once used to identify and persecute homosexual men in Nazi concentration camps.[22] While others remained seated during the postlude, they stood up to make their presence known. And when they got outside, they unfurled their banner.[23]

Chris Madsen sued the *Christian Science Monitor* for wrongful termination, discrimination, and defamation, but in 1985, the Massachusetts Supreme Court ruled that the *Monitor* was within its constitutional right to dismiss Madsen, calling the case a religious matter. The Court left the door open for Madsen to seek a new hearing on other charges, though.[24]

Madsen did file another suit against the church, this time for invasion of privacy, and a settlement was ultimately reached, but not disclosed.[25]

Gay People in Christian Science had made their mark. They had raised their voices, they had spread the word, they had gained publicity, and they had found their place in the annual Pride march.

Gay People in Christian Science?
Pamphlet – 1979

Gay People in Christian Science?

Today, many Gay women and men are active in the Christian Science movement – serving as Readers, practitioners, branch members, employees at headquarters, and workers in the Field. The purpose of this pamphlet which is being distributed at the Annual Meeting of The First Church of Christ, Scientist, in Boston, Massachusetts in June, 1980, is an appeal to all Christian Scientists and especially to The Christian Science Board of Directors to re-examine their thought on the subject of human sexuality in the light of Christian Science and to take whatever loving and practical steps are necessary to rectify the present wrongs being done to Gay people in the name of Christian Science.

Incorrect Literature

(Please refer to *The Mother Church Manual*, p. 43:21)

To many loyal Christian Scientists, April 22, 1967, was a day of great sadness. It was on that day that the first article on the human expression of love between people of the same sex appeared in one of our periodicals. In that piece ("Homosexuality Can Be Healed," *Christian Science Sentinel*, p. 681), a particularly uninspired quote from Leviticus (Lev. 20:13) was used to suggest that homosexuals be put to death.

Since then similar pieces have appeared in the Christian Science periodicals. (See *Christian Science Sentinel,* November 18, 1972, p. 2051; *Christian Science Sentinel,* March 20, 1976, p. 457; *The Christian Science Monitor,* November 8, 1977, editorial page; *The Christian Science Journal,* October 1978, p. 609;

Christian Science Sentinel, March 5, 1979, p. 377; *The Christian Science Journal*, April, 1979 p. 211; and especially *The Christian Science Journal*, October 1973, p. 607.)

In the above-cited examples of incorrect literature which mis-state Christian Science and violate the Golden Rule, Gay women and men are depicted as "promiscuous," "bizarre," "abnormal," "immoral," "unseemly," "unhealthy," "unnatural," "cursed," and "perverted." Nowhere is there even the slightest recognition that the basis of same-sex relationships is love, the exact same human need for love and mutual respect that is the basis for heterosexual relationships. Indeed, not one of the articles has in any way shown how same-gender relationships are unacceptable in the light of Christian Science. In the negative and hostile atmosphere created by our periodicals, it should come as no surprise that so-called "healings" of homosexuality should appear. This naturally prompts one to ask what exactly has been "healed"? Has the person been "healed" of love, companionship or friendship?

Incorrect statements of Christian Science are the most obnoxious and damaging kind of literature in the world today because they blind the reader to the applicability of Christian Science to every human situation. They would foist upon us the notion that Christian Science is a cult to which only those who subscribe to a certain regimented lifestyle need apply. And when a form of mental malpractice is directed at a group of people – in this case, Gay women and men – in the Christian Science periodicals, it is time to speak out and keep speaking out.

Spirit and Letter

I Corinthians 14:34,35. The New English Bible: "As in all congregations of God's people, women should not address the meeting. They have no license to speak, but should keep their place as the law directs. If there is something they want to know, they can ask their own husbands at home. It is a shocking thing that a woman should address the congregation." What a tragic loss to the world, had our Leader, Mary Baker Eddy, considered the above citation as inspired! She could not have been the Discoverer and Founder of Christian Science. If a literal interpretation of the Bible had been enforced as it had in centuries past, she would have been silenced and even severely punished for having dared to speak out and start her own church.

Many scriptural prohibitions and injunctions were merely social and political conveniences of the time. Mary Baker Eddy states in the Tenets of the Mother Church that "As adherents of Truth, we take the inspired Word of the Bible as our sufficient guide to eternal life" (*Science and Health* p. 497:3). In *The First Church of Christ, Scientist and Miscellany* on page 266 in an article called "Insufficient Freedom," Mary Baker Eddy warns that the most threatening danger that we are faced with in this century is the using of the Scriptures as authority to strip people of their very lives and liberties – substituting creed and ritual for the Golden Rule. Certainly, an example of this is the mass extermination of thousands of homosexuals by the Nazis. In addition, thousands of Gay people in Europe were interned in concentration camps and were forced to wear patches with pink triangles on them to denote their homosexuality. Hitler's justification for this action was that it was necessary to maintain the "morality" and "Christian environment" for the youth of Germany.

Many passages in the Old Testament as well as the one quoted above from the New Testament can be used to justify the oppression of women. Racists quote the story of Ham as proof that Black people were "cursed" by God to eternal inferiority. In short, there is something in the Bible that every zealot can use to justify every prejudice imaginable.

Today in the Christian Science church, new applicants are not accepted into the membership if they are openly Gay. Members of long standing who are openly Gay are being thrown out of branch churches. Others who have concealed their homosexuality and are members of the church would not be permitted to work in any capacity at The Mother Church Center if their orientation were known. Although Christian Science recognizes the place of sexuality in the human experience, on what grounds is the Gay person asked to be "healed" immediately or refrain from any intimate relationships while heterosexuals have freedom to express their affectional orientation?

Mary Baker Eddy's forceful reminder in *Miscellaneous Writings*, p. 223:15 speaks of this kind of cruel hypocrisy that ignorantly or maliciously breaks the Golden Rule.

How does one determine morality in the spirit of Christian Science? Our Leader quotes from Shakespeare at the beginning of *Science and Health*, "There is nothing either good or bad, but thinking makes it so." This quotation does not imply that one can justify immorality. However, in the practice of Christian Science, we learn that the First Commandment and the Golden Rule are the all-in-all of Christian Science (*The First Church of Christ, Scientist and Miscellany*, p. 512). It is the application of the First Commandment and the Golden Rule which determines whether "something is either good or bad" or moral or immoral. In the case of Gay people as well as heterosexuals, it is the quality of the love in their relationships which is the prime consideration.

Can we be responsible Christian Scientists and at the same time demand of Gay people the relinquishment of their affectional orientation in order for them to be worthy of church membership? Is this not a violation of the "all-in-all" of Christian Science?

Morality, Love and Sexuality

Christ Jesus taught his followers to work faithfully within their own human circumstances to understand Truth and from that basis to achieve salvation. This point is shown clearly in his teachings and in his own life. In the parable of the talents in the twenty-fifth chapter of Matthew, those servants who worked to increase their human understanding of the divine idea received increased harmony in their lives and then found heaven, i.e., at-one-ment, with divine Mind. The servant who failed to use or understand his human gift in a meaningful way lost it and delayed his eventual salvation. In Jesus' own experience he rebuked Peter soundly for suggesting that as Savior of the world, he, Jesus did not need to go through the crucifixion (Mark 8:31–33). Jesus knew that it was precisely through living out his own God-established mission that he would find his resurrection and ascension.

This teaching and actual demonstration by the Master has an important message for Gay women and men. Simply stated, it is: Make use of the gift you have, love as only *you* can, for in so doing you have embarked on the road to heaven, harmony.

Our Leader, Mary Baker Eddy, also counsels her students to start working with what they understand. On page 288:13 of *Miscellaneous Writings*, she says, "Wisdom in human action begins with what is nearest right under the circumstances, and thence achieves the absolute." On page 234 of the same book, she says in substance that the *only* way to find the Love which is God is through love for man.

Furthermore, Christian Science teaches that the individuality of man is eternal and unique, unabsorbed in matter or stereotyped by mortal mind. Science promotes the flowering of our individual gifts and condemns attempts to reduce them to bland theological posturings.

The human expression of love is indeed subject to healing, not through the obliteration of one's affectional orientation but through the operation of divine Truth and Love, bringing enrichment and refinement to one's affections. Homosexuality and heterosexuality may be positive or negative depending upon the degree of spirituality and the demand upon each of us to relinquish whatever blocks the realization of our highest selfhood. For both Gay and non-Gay, the standards with which to judge and elevate motives and actions are the First Commandment and the Golden Rule, as both Christ Jesus and Mary Baker Eddy have taught.

Conclusions

Our dear Leader, Mary Baker Eddy, was far in advance of human thought. Her revolutionary discovery that the real nature of God's man is not divided into males and females – but rather each of us is the full reflection of our Mother-Father God – is beginning to dawn on the world thought.

She challenges us to grasp the full import of our real spiritual nature – to combine the best of femaleness and maleness in each of our characters.

It is clear that in our daily application of Christian Science to all human needs we must understand and acknowledge that the full human expression of divine Love is not limited in any way to people of mortal mind's two sexes, male and female. Rather we have the responsibility to be examples to the world in demonstrating the completeness of creation by practicing the wonderful truth of our reflection of God as Mother-Father.

Just as racism had a strong hold on the Christian Science movement until very recently, today heterosexism appears to be thriving. (Heterosexism is the erroneous concept that only people of the so-called opposite sexes can and should express the full range of love.) Heterosexism is a devise of mortal mind to enslave us into thinking that creation originates from an egg and sperm.

Christian Science challenges us to throw off the yoke of mortal mind and to demand of ourselves and the world a higher and more real concept of our being as the image and likeness of our Creator.

Mary Baker Eddy counsels us in *The First Church of Christ, Scientist and Miscellany*, p. 268:24–5: "Truth, canonized by life and love, lays the axe at the root of all evil, lifts the curtain on the Science of being, the Science of wedlock, of living and of loving, and harmoniously ascends the scale of life. Look high enough, and you see the heart of humanity warming and winning. Look long enough and you see male and female one – sex or gender eliminated; you see the designation *man* meaning woman as well, and you see the whole universe included in one infinite Mind and reflected in the intelligent compound idea, image or likeness, called man, showing forth the infinite divine Principle, Love, called God, – man wedded to the Lamb, pledged to innocence, purity, perfection.

(Text of the pamphlet courtesy Bruce Stores)

11

Inside the Oscar Wilde – Christopher Street

The opening of the Christopher Street shop in May 1973 marked the start of a new phase in Craig Rodwell's life, a shift from the Mercer Street days, the Stonewall riots, and the first marches.

As Craig looked back, the planning and preparations for the first march had been homegrown, with meetings in his and Fred's apartment and at Mercer Street. There had been no roadmap for the first march, and no one even knew if there would be a second. The Christopher Street Liberation Day Umbrella Committee was a fledgling organization. Many opinions, many debates, and many personalities had come together for a single purpose.

But there would be a second time. Foster Gunnison, as treasurer of the Christopher Street Liberation Day Committee, announced the plans in his Eastern Bulletin for October 1970.

"The first, and very important meeting in the preparation for 1971 will be held this coming Sunday afternoon, Oct. 11th, 1970 at 2:00 PM at the following address in New York's Greenwich Village: Apartment #3-V, 350 Bleeker St. [sic]...." – Craig and Fred's small, L-shaped apartment.[1]

Other meetings that year were held in different locations. Craig continued his involvement on the coordination committee, and he also oversaw the calendar of events. The second celebration was a success – Foster was present with his clicker once again and counted 8,000 people in the march, up from 5,000 the first year. Expenses had risen from just over $500 the first year to more than $2,000 in 1971.[2]

Everything was getting bigger – more people, more leaders, more money. In his bulletin from January 1972, Gunnison was joyful:

> The enthusiasm for this year's march is unprecedented. There have been many new gay lib organizations that have sprung up throughout the eastern US since last year's march, all eager to get in on the next one. Response has been so great – even before this first announcement bulletin has gone out – that already the original place for the first planning meeting has had to be changed to a larger location.[3]

It was the third year of the march, and the signs of a turning point were coming. Craig's vision of a march of individuals was being challenged. Foster captured some of the debate at the April 1972 meeting, when representatives of lesbian organizations from New York showed up. Like Craig, they were not happy about a decision to allow floats in the march, especially floats sponsored by gay bars or other commercial groups. Among the dissenters was Martha Shelley, already a longtime activist, whom Gunnison referred to as one of the "old homophile hands."

"This all set off a lively discussion which was finally resolved by a general decision to withdraw the float idea and limit displays to banners, signs, and other less controversial paraphernalia. But not before exasperated Ed Trust, who chaired the meeting, had thrown up his hands in despair at all the turmoil."[4]

Then there was discussion about the conclusion of the march at Sheep Meadow. The first year, it had been a climatic emotional convergence of just being in the same place with other gay people. Just two years later, Sheep Meadow was now a "let down," without some kind of entertainment. As he concluded his report, Foster acknowledged some missing faces, including – just two years after the first march – the old hands of Craig Rodwell, Breck Ardery, and a few others "from earlier years."

Stormy weather had lifted just before the step off for the third march in 1972, most likely depressing the turnout. Foster was again positioned with his clicker at 42nd Street – he counted just 2,000 marchers. *The New York Times* counted 3,500 and reported that the marchers arrived at a sodden Sheep Meadow. Still, in his notes to the committee, Foster deemed the march a success. When he provided the official accounting of income and expenses, there was no sign of the Oscar Wilde or HYMN or Craig Rodwell, names that were all over the accounting of the first and second marches.

Then came 1973.

The poster announced that the Christopher Street Liberation Day '73 march "proudly assembles at 11 a.m., Sunday, June 24 on West 64th, 63rd, 62nd and 61st Streets between B/way and Central Central [sic] Pk. West...." Instead of assembling in the Village and going up Sixth Avenue, the marchers would proceed down Seventh Avenue. Instead of ending at Sheep Meadow in Central Park, they would end in Washington Square Park. Everything was going to be different.[5]

As Arthur Bell reported in a front-page story in *The Village Voice* on June 28, disagreements among the liberationists and new members of the organizing committee "came out of the closet." He reported that the committee was now led by "bar people and disillusioned ex-members of Gay Activists Alliance." The focus was entertainment, not political speeches. Activists who wanted to speak were denied. Jim Owles, formerly of GAA, wasn't allowed to speak; neither were the Lesbian Feminist Liberation representatives. And Bella Abzug, whom Craig had criticized in *The Hymnal* for not keeping up with her promises to the gay community, was absent from the march.[6]

Bell summed up the complaint, saying the liberationists thought it was a mockery, with more emphasis on promotion and performances rather than gay causes.[7]

Halfway through the story, he gave the founder of the committee the floor, and Craig did not hold back:

> The basic idea of the parade was to bring the spirit of the Stonewall riot to the people so they could stand up for themselves, independently and individually. After the first

march, a lot of parasites and leeches who literally kicked me out of their bars for passing out leaflets and who were constantly putting us down saw that we represented the yearnings of their customers and that we were affecting their earnings. They had to get in there to save their own necks. So they did. They switched the direction of the march this year, geographically and physically, so we're back to supporting our local syndicate bars and we're back to the ghetto again. We've gone the full circle.[8]

Just three months before the 1973 commemoration, Rodwell had written the two-part series in *QQ Magazine* on the struggle to wrest control of social institutions from Mafia-run businesses. He'd been trying to get the message across since the first days of *The Hymnal* in 1968. The changes in the 1973 march demonstrated how hard it was going to be.

Craig was now into his thirties, when he once thought he would be past his prime. The peak of the liberation movement and his involvement in it had passed. His business partner and lover, Fred Sargeant, whose presence had made it possible for Rodwell to devote many hours to liberation causes, had moved on. He was alone.

Still, there would be new gay rights work ahead, new people to inspire, and a bigger bookshop to run. The Oscar Wilde had grown out of its tiny space on Mercer Street. Kay Tobin Lahusen loved the new spot at 15 Christopher Street, with its gay neighbors and walk-in traffic at a perfect Village junction: "Christopher and, believe it or not, Gay Street, so he had a wonderful intersection," she remembered. Kay, the fellow Christian Scientist and friend who had featured Craig in *The Gay Crusaders* in 1972,[9] worked in the shop for a couple of years. She was upbeat. The shop was popular, pleasant and "people loved to drop in there." The new shop was just doors from the storied Stonewall Inn at 51–53 Christopher, in the heart of the gay movement.[10]

After the opening in May 1973, there would be many stories to tell over the next two decades as people found their way up the four steps into the old rowhouse to find a book, join a debate, or belong to the movement. For about a year, Craig kept both shops going – the advertisements in *QQ Magazine* referred to both locations – but the Mercer Street shop closed in the spring of 1974, as it was not financially feasible to keep both locations open. Craig told his landlord that he had kept Mercer Street open for sentimental reasons.[11]

Financially, the Oscar Wilde was in the red. Kay was having discussions with Craig to decide what to do about it, and she drew up a plan. Craig felt they could get out of the hole if they could become fully stocked, and he favored a slow recovery that wouldn't require a loan. But Kay favored quicker, more drastic measures – take out a loan (perhaps even from Craig's mother) and pay off all the debts, incorporate the business, write job descriptions, and get advice from the Small Business Administration.[12] While the shop openly announced some financial help from family, it is unlikely that Craig followed Kay's advice, as he was known by staff for keeping poor records and for working out of a cash box, but the shop would survive under his methods for twenty more years.[13]

Despite the financial problems, Craig and the Oscar Wilde would be a model for bookstores to come. In the summer of 1973, Tom Wilson Weinberg, who had been a customer at the shop, went up to New York from Philadelphia. Weinberg and two friends had decided they wanted to open up a shop of their own. He found Craig "so friendly and interested and wanted to help."[14]

With $500 in cash, Tom and Craig headed to Bookazine, the wholesaler from which Craig and Fred had first sourced their meager orders for Mercer Street. Tom had a list from Craig of books that Craig thought would be good sellers, and a list from Barbara Gittings of books she thought were most important.

Back in Philadelphia with an inventory, Tom, just twenty-eight, and friends Dan Sherbo and Bernie Boyle opened Giovanni's Room – with a big plate-glass window in the front, inspired by the Oscar Wilde – which, over the succeeding decades, became the oldest operating LGBT bookstore in the US.

During that time, the Oscar Wilde continued to be influential in advancing gay rights. Wearable buttons that made a statement of one's social or political beliefs had exploded in the 1960s and '70s. More than a frivolous decoration, they gave the wearer the power of daring openness. One of those button designs would be the reclaimed pink triangle of the Nazi concentration camps, used now as a symbol of gay liberation.

In New York, beginning in 1970, activists had been agitating New York City Council for anti-discrimination legislation. Ethan Geto, a longtime gay activist from New York, had gotten involved in the movement in 1971. He was part of a group of gay men working behind the scenes in politics and government. A study group was formed and often met in his apartment to coordinate and collaborate on various initiatives to advance gay rights.[15]

By 1975, when a bill banning discrimination in employment, housing, and public accommodations was introduced once again, the study group had a new idea. There would be a "Pink Triangle Campaign."

The "Coalition of Conscience," the study group's advocacy vehicle, would produce pink triangle buttons and ask people to wear them in solidarity, in hopes of shaming the city council by raising their awareness of the treatment of homosexuals in German concentration camps in the 1930s and '40s.[16]

Meanwhile, Geto wrote an article for the study group that he hoped would be the basis for an op-ed in *The New York Times* under the byline of "some prominent person."[17]

The prominent person was Ira Glasser, executive director of the New York Civil Liberties Union, who wrote: "Today, and every day until Intro. 554 is passed, the pink triangle is being worn not only by homosexuals, but also by those who believe that the tolerance of good people is what permits bigotry to persist."[18]

Geto had been a regular visitor to the Oscar Wilde Memorial Bookshop and knew Craig. After the first buttons were produced, the group did not have the resources to keep them coming, so the campaign turned to Craig, who was more than happy to spearhead the initiative. They then became available in the Oscar Wilde, produced by the N.G.

Slater Corp., and were listed in the shop's catalog, reaching thousands of people and helping to establish a gay consciousness symbol.[19]

By the time the spring 1978 catalog was in the mail, the pink triangle button and others expressing lesbian and gay solidarity slogans had claimed a regular spot: "Item 6102. Pink Triangle buttons. Gay prisoners in the Nazi extermination camps, before extermination, were required to wear a pink triangle patch. Ten for 2.50." While the lambda symbol continued to be a popular item in the bookshop for many years, by this time it was considered a much tamer statement by the Oscar Wilde.

The takeover of the pink triangle would spread throughout the 1970s and beyond. It would show up in the 1979 gay march on Washington and made a poignant appearance in Martin Sherman's play *Bent*, which premiered in London and New York, also in 1979.

Later, the Oscar Wilde carried ACT UP's pink triangle "Silence=Death" T-shirts to raise awareness of the destruction of AIDS.[20]

Over the years, Rodwell developed relationships with lesbian and gay authors, who would come by to sign their books. Jonathan Ned Katz, who had anxiously walked into the Oscar Wilde in 1970, was now here on Christopher Street just six years later, signing his newly published *Gay American History: Lesbians & Gay Men in the USA*. He remembered how happy he was to see the book in the Christopher Street window. Photographer Diana Davies captured the day: Jonathan with his curly hair and moustache and turtleneck, signed all the books with his longtime motto: "Love and struggle." Craig, looking somewhat rumpled in his flannel shirt and jeans, stood opposite, delighted with the new volume.[21]

The Oscar Wilde's "Gay Is Good" catalog from 1977 featured a cover photo of Tennessee Williams in a big fur coat and fedora with Craig and the shop staff on the steps of 15 Christopher. Williams had an appearance on Thanksgiving weekend, 1975, during a "meet the author" day.

The influence of the Oscar Wilde was far and wide. Letters were coming in from across the US and all over the world.

One of them was from a twenty-two-year-old foreign-language bookseller in Budapest, who had heard from a friend in Iceland that the Oscar Wilde had a good selection of gay books. In the summer of 1977, he wrote to Craig asking for catalogs and information. He provided a detailed look at gay life in Hungary, and it was not as oppressive as one might think, he told Craig. Responding in kind, Craig sent catalogs, and he requested information himself on gay publications written in Hungarian for the small foreign-language section at the Oscar Wilde.

Recognition for the work of the bookshop was also coming in. Rodwell had heard from the West Side Discussion Group that they would like to honor the tenth anniversary of the Oscar Wilde at one of their meetings in November 1977. Craig had planned to send two members of the bookshop staff to the event, but it went sour. He laid it out in a letter. First, he learned that West Side "was annoyed with me for sending a woman who has worked for the bookshop for less than a year to represent the shop; and that therefore, the focus of the meeting had been changed to Gay bookshops in general rather than the OWMB's 10th anniversary." Then, "to add insult to injury, I have found out that we are expected to appear on a panel with a representative from a peep-show and sexploitation outlet on Christopher Street." And finally, Craig's temperature was rising: "Under no circumstances will the Oscar Wilde Memorial Bookshop appear on a panel with such people...." And in a by-the-way, he reminded those reading that the first meeting he had attended in New York was a West Side Discussion Group meeting in 1959 when he was just eighteen years old, and so he had an affection for the organization. And with that, he withdrew from the event.[22]

In June the following year, Rodwell received a short note from the Christopher Street West Association in Hollywood. He was being nominated for the Ralph Schaffer Memorial Award for the business that has "done the most for the gay community during the last year."[23] They asked Rodwell to please confirm his or a representative's attendance as soon as possible. Eight days later, Rodwell responded: "It is financially impossible for us to send a representative to your Awards ceremony on July 2nd. However, thank you for the kind thoughts."[24] He signed with his full signature.

To at least one person, Rodwell's full signature was a telescope into his complex and compartmentalized personality. A few years after the Oscar Wilde had opened, a handwriting analyst wrote to Craig with an idea for a business venture. To share his credentials, he offered a detailed analysis of Rodwell's full signature from a recent correspondence, which turned out to be remarkably true to life.

To the analyst, Craig's signature showed he was expressive and warm and that he would probably wear his feelings on his sleeve. Perhaps he knew something of Craig's history. He suggested that Craig could easily feel blue and like "the bottom has dropped out." And surprisingly, he captured a luminescence that Craig could impart individually, even if briefly, that drew people to him. Lastly, he had a sense that Craig was becoming easily annoyed, maybe secretive, and insistent.[25]

One thing that was true was that the cranky Craig was getting a reputation.

Meanwhile, Larry Kramer was writing his manuscript for *Faggots*, his explosive satiric novel about the gay underworld of New York and Fire Island. The book exposed a vapid, hedonistic sex and drug-induced culture in vivid detail. After 300 pages and one of the more over-the-top pornographic scenes, protagonist Fred Lemish reflects to himself: "I'm tired of being a New York City–Fire Island faggot, I'm tired of using my body as a faceless thing to lure another faceless thing…."[26]

Author John Lahr, reviewing the book in *The New York Times*, said: "Mr. Kramer wants the book to be a rambunctious farce; but his frivolity isn't valued and so it becomes an embarrassing fiasco." He called it some of the worst writing he had ever seen.[27]

It has come down as legend that Craig didn't place the book on his shelves, and that he was unamused by the book's title and its intentions.[28]

Two men from Brooklyn who had noticed the books' absence in a recent visit were piqued. In a letter to the shop, they said that they were "shocked and offended" when they asked for the book and were directed instead to a review from the *Washington Post* on the wall.

They had not found the book "self-loathing" or "anti-gay," and believed that the novel supported the sexual freedoms of the gay community. They concluded that the bookshop was having a "plight of insecurity" and that they would switch their allegiance to Giovanni's Room in Philadelphia.

A couple of months later, Rodwell typed a polite response:

> Your comments and descriptions of this book are certainly the most flattering I've heard. Although that's not saying much, I admit, considering the overwhelming condemnation of the purposes of this title by concerned Gay people.
>
> If I believed that Kramer's purposes were as you describe them, I certainly would carry the book and highly recommend it.

He concluded with messaging that essentially said "sorry to lose you, but happy that Giovanni's Room will get your business."

Rodwell explained his thoughts on exploitation in gay media to Vito Russo in 1983 for Russo's television series, *Our Time*. Rodwell told Russo that most of the gay periodicals being published in the early 1980s were part of the sex industry – "there's hundreds of them."

"I feel that a clear line has to be drawn between the gay and lesbian independent movement and what's coming out of it, and that which is done strictly to exploit our sexuality."[29]

Other authors were more grateful and stopped into the shop to thank Rodwell for carrying their books. A year after the Larry Kramer tempest, a quickly scrawled note left in the shop from *City of Night* author John Rechy had a decidedly friendly tone:

> Dear Craig, I just dropped in to see the famous store – and to thank you for carrying my books. Sincerely, John Rechy.[30]

Not everyone was so thankful for the Oscar Wilde's books. In the spring of 1978, Craig had sent a shipment of books and other items to a Canadian bookstore in Edmonton. Customs officials, though, considered the shipment controversial, and it was seized. According to a report in Boston's *Gay Community News*, the seized books included *Lesbianism and the Women's Movement*, *Homosexual Oppression and Liberation* and *The Joy of Lesbian Sex*. Craig protested to the Canadian consulate in New York City, not only about the seizure but also opposing the Canadian government's "attempt to close down the best Gay liberation newspaper in the world, *The Body Politic*."[31]

Shop life was regularly punctuated by the impact of national news about gays and lesbians. One of the biggest stories to strike the gay community would hit close to home and heart. On November 27, 1978, Craig's former lover Harvey Milk was shot and killed at City Hall in San Francisco, along with Mayor George Moscone at the hand of former supervisor Dan White. Harvey had been elected supervisor just a year before. He had been the first openly gay person to serve on the board. The *San Francisco Examiner* reflected on his accomplishments during his short tenure – a ban on discrimination against homosexuals, an opponent of new condominiums, a sponsor of a dog litter law, and a proponent of legalizing marijuana. He was the most talkative member of the board.[32]

The *Examiner* also reported on the memorial service. Harvey's assistant, Anne Kronenberg, read a poem by Harvey that she had discovered in his desk:

I can be killed with ease,
I can be cut right down,
But I cannot fall back into my closet.

I have grown.
I am not by myself.
I am too many.
I am all of us.[33]

Harvey Milk's ashes were transported out the Golden Gate and scattered at sea on December 2. The following day, a rainy candlelight vigil was held in Sheridan Square in New York, and a protest meeting followed at the West Village Metropolitan-Duane United Methodist Church.

"How typical of Harvey!" Rodwell wrote about the scattering of ashes at sea. "He was an incurable romantic."[34]

Craig recounted the evening he met Harvey Milk. He recalled the Christmas gift of the ceramic vase for Craig to help civilize his lunches, Harvey's love of music and cooking and plants, the phone calls, and Valentine's Day. He wrote: "To be in love with Harvey Milk was an incredible experience because Harvey was a real man, a term often and usually misused in Gay male culture today. A real man to me is one who does not despise or fear the feminine aspect of his being."

"The twins of death – misogyny and heterosexism," he wrote, "have taken Harvey Milk's life as they have the lives of millions of Lesbians and Gay men before him throughout the ages."

The "true" tribute, he continued, is action. He called on everyone to do more, and in Harvey's memory to go forward with a sense of renewal, not danger, and a commitment to battle heterosexism and misogyny.[35]

Accounts of the vigil and protest appeared in *The Village Voice* and in *Gaysweek* newspaper, which estimated the crowd at 200.

Accumulating the milestones of his life, Craig moved on, increasingly world-weary but still involved. The shop continued to expand its inventory, new people were hired as managers, and the Oscar Wilde occupied a sentimental place in the lesbian and gay heart.

The shop's catalogs tell part of the story of Craig's twenty-five years in the business. The mail-order catalog from 1968 on Mercer Street had included a typewritten list of ninety-five items – fifteen of those items were different buttons, nine were pamphlets, thirteen were hardcovers, and forty-one were paperbacks.[36] A decade later on Christopher Street, the pamphlet-style catalog included 129 nonfiction titles, eighty-two books of fiction, seventeen records, two sample packets of gay and lesbian periodicals, pink triangle buttons, and gay bookmarks.[37]

For the tenth anniversary, the bookshop announced the slogan "Think Straight/Be Gay" as its motto for the year. "It is a call for all people not just those who are already Gay, to think clearly and recognize their basic Homosexual nature." The small version of "Think Straight/Be Gay" on a button was twenty-five cents. Writing pens were being offered with the inscription "Say It Loud – Gay and Proud, Oscar Wilde Memorial Bookshop, 1967–1977" – three for a dollar.

The number of gay and lesbian titles had increased dramatically since the early days. The list included Jonathan Katz' 1976 comprehensive *Gay American History* in both hardcover and paperback. To make books like these readily available to the public, Rodwell discounted every book costing more than $6.95, which became a standard practice in the shop.

Now there were books on gay life, guides to talking with your parents, and a section on gays and religion, including Father John McNeill's *The Church and the Homosexual*.

Gertrude Stein's *Dear Sammy* was on the shelf, as was *The Biography of Alice B. Toklas*. And Kay Tobin's *The Gay Crusaders* from 1972 was still available in hardcover. In fact, where Craig had once struggled to balance the stock with gay and lesbian titles, the dearth of titles for women had changed dramatically. On the tenth anniversary, the catalog's content offered 45 percent of its titles for lesbians, 34 percent for gay men, and 22 percent for all readers.

In 1978–9, the catalog would include *The Black Unicorn*, poetry by Black lesbian writer, poet, and activist Audre Lorde. Fourteen available records included an LP by Sweet Honey in the Rock. The Gay Yellow Pages were available, as was *Damron's Address Book*, and lambda pendants were being offered in sterling silver.[38]

In addition to the spring and fall catalogs, the Oscar Wilde periodically published supplemental catalogs. One of those, in 1983, focused on love stories. For gay men, the titles included Harvey Fierstein's *Torch Song Trilogy* paperback and playscript, Armistead Maupin's first two volumes of *Tales of the City*, and the script for *Bent*, Martin Sherman's heartbreaking story of two gay men in a Nazi concentration camp. Notations on the list indicated that the most popular were *The Wing and the Flame* by Emily Hanlon and *A Different Love* by Clay Larkin.

Alice Walker's *The Color Purple* had just won the Pulitzer Prize. *A Piece of the Night* by Michele Roberts had won the Gay News Book Award in 1979. There was *The Cruise*, by Paula Christian, and "Portrait," a new LP from Cris Williamson.

Meanwhile, Tom Wilson Weinberg, who had long since sold Giovanni's Room, had gone on to become a musician and singer, and in 1979 produced the "Gay Name Game," album, which he brought to Craig to sell in the Oscar Wilde.

"Craig was there, and I had 25 LPs in a box, and he said, 'I'll take the 25, and you should have brought more.' He paid me cash and said I'll sell them." And he did.[39]

Tucked into each catalog was a section for "Catalog Notes," a few bullet points from the shop's perspective. In 1985, Calvin Lowery was the manager of the shop, having first visited the Oscar Wilde when he was sixteen years old and later doing some part-time work. Craig noted in the catalog notes that Lowery, who was featured on the cover, was one of his finest managers.

The shop continued to offer a wide range of titles, from the biography of Alan Turing to a new anthology of writings by former and current lesbian nuns. Nancy Garden's teenage love story *Annie on My Mind* was billed as one of the best lesbian love stories ever written. In addition to buttons, there were now stickers – "A Lesbian Was Here," "A Faggot Was Here," and "This Is Offensive to Gay People."

Craig would not carry materials from the North American Man/Boy Love Association, which had been founded in 1978 and advocated for the removal of age of consent laws.

Incensed, three of the NAMBLA spokesmen wrote to Craig in August 1980: "NAMBLA has requested that you carry our Journal in your bookstore. You have refused to do so and have slandered NAMBLA by referring to its members and supporters as 'agents with the movement.'" They requested a meeting with Craig within the month, and if no meeting was forthcoming, they promised a press release.

There was no meeting, and the press release followed in a few weeks. It read in part: "NAMBLA views Mr. Rodwell's policy as nothing more than censorship and a form of bigotry. NAMBLA has decided to inform the lesbian and gay community about this." They said Craig was suppressing ideas and "dangerous and antithetical to the goals and spirit of gay liberation."[40]

The next month, Craig appeared on a WBAI radio program panel to address the issue. He told moderator Rudy Grillo and panel members that from his perspective, NAMBLA was an organization that was there for adults seeking to connect with young people for sexual purposes, and that was wrong. He spoke against the power that adults have that is unfair to young people. David Thorstad, a founder of NAMBLA who had been active in the Gay Activists Alliance, was also on the panel. All of the examples and rationales he put forward were dismissed by Craig when he summed up his thoughts: "Leave young boys alone."[41]

The association's opposition continued. In the catalog notes from 1985, the shop included the message: "WARNING: We are pleased to tell you that the Oscar Wilde Memorial Bookshop is under a boycott by the North American Man/Boy 'Love' Association (NAMBLA)...."[42] The antipathy toward NAMBLA was well known among shop staff and even mentioned years later at Rodwell's memorial service.

Two supplemental catalogs in 1985 reflected the growing crisis of AIDS. By 1985, the disease had been given its name – acquired immunodeficiency syndrome – and its cause had been discovered, but the cases were hitting an all-time high and there was no effective treatment. Actor Rock Hudson and B-52s guitarist Ricky Wilson would die in 1985. Actress Elizabeth Taylor would step forward with her celebrity to bring attention to the crisis with the American Foundation for AIDS Research.

The number of AIDS titles at the Oscar Wilde increased over the next years. Among the publications offered in 1985 were a comprehensive guide to understanding AIDS, an examination of the presumed connection of inhaled poppers (amyl nitrate) to infection by HIV, a series of meditations for AIDS patients, the playscript for Larry Kramer's

The Normal Heart, and Robert Bourcheron's *Epitaphs for the Plague Dead*, traditional verse for fictional gay men who died of AIDS.

For 1986–7, the catalog featured on its cover an illustration of a labrys, a double-headed axe of ancient Amazons and symbolic of lesbian strength. It was superimposed on a pink triangle.

Now there was a heading for health issues, including the following titles:

- *Understanding and Preventing AIDS*, by Chris Jennings
- *Mobilizing Against AIDS*, from the National Academy of Sciences
- *Death Rush*, by John Lauritsen and Hank Wilson, on the use of poppers and presumed connection with AIDS
- *Sex and Germs: The Politics of AIDS*, by Cindy Patton
- *The Screaming Room*, by Barbara Peabody, a true-life AIDS mother-son story
- *Out of the Shadows*, by Patrick Carnes, on compulsive sexual behavior
- *You Can Heal Your Life*, by Louise Hay, on New Age healing for AIDS patients
- *AIDS: A Positive Approach*, a cassette tape with Louise Hay[43]

It was an agonizing and desperate time, as gay men saw the sunken faces in their circles of friends disappear one by one. Randy Shilts documented it in *And the Band Played On*. AZT, the controversial drug treatment, was just coming on the scene. Larry Kramer started ACT UP as an action group to force the government to respond to the crisis. Michael Bennett (*A Chorus Line*) and Liberace died of AIDS.

Meanwhile, the namesake of the bookshop had become the subject of a monumental biographical work. Richard Ellmann's 688-page *Oscar Wilde*, published in 1988, had taken its place on the bookshelves at 15 Christopher Street and at the top of the supplemental catalog listings. Alison Bechdel's *More Dykes to Watch Out For*, Edmund White's *The Beautiful Room Is Empty*, *The Orton Diaries*, edited by John Lahr, and *A Burst of Light*, essays from Audre Lorde, were among sixty-three other mail-order items.

In that catalog there was also a short but sweet tribute:

> The Oscar Wilde Memorial Bookshop would like to publicly pay tribute to a woman who has done more for the preservation and encouragement of Lesbian writing than anyone in history. Her name is BARBARA GRIER. She has been active in the Lesbian movement for more than 30 years and is a founder of The Naiad Press.[44]

The shop, like its catalog, brought people together in a way that otherwise wouldn't have existed. Over its four decades in operation, it was listed as a resource in countless directories nationwide, and it was a reliable source of tickets for community events, from the Broadway production of Vito Russo's *Celluloid Closet* to an ACT UP demonstration at President George H.W. Bush's summer home in Maine. Tickets were almost always listed in the fine print as being available at the shop.

Central to these connections were the people who managed and worked the shop. Among them was Fred Carl.

Late in 1979, twenty-something Fred was discouraged that he wasn't getting the position he wanted in the kitchen at the restaurant where he was working because he was Black. Originally a flute player from New Haven, CT, who had attended Brown University, he had come to New York in 1978. He knew of the Oscar Wilde, and after educating the managers at the restaurant about their discriminatory hiring practices, he dropped by the bookshop. Was Craig hiring?

Yes, he was. Fred filled out the application and a week later he was on the staff. Two years after that, he was managing the place. The day-to-day activities at the shop included setting the staff schedule, ordering books, being on top of what was coming out, managing the inventory, and paying the bills.

Fred remembered the very first time AIDS was "in my face," and it was at the Oscar Wilde. He was working the shop alone one Sunday when a call came in from Minneapolis. It was someone who knew Craig, and Fred could hear the emotion spilling out over the line. A friend of the caller had developed a cough; it was AIDS, and now he was gone – please tell Craig. There was no internet, no texting. Decades later, the memory of the call lingered.[45]

The shop had become so well known that Craig would often give Fred a nudge and put a slip of paper on his leg with an arrow to point out a notable personality in the shop. And there were signings; Harvey Fierstein with *Torch Song* and Audre Lorde with *Zami, A New Spelling of My Name*, were among them. Alison Bechdel was in the shop, gaining inspiration from a selection of gay and lesbian comics.

In the early 1980s, Fred was inspired by Isaac Jackson, who led the founding of the Blackheart Collective. He enlisted

Fred and others to join him. They formed out of their concern about the lack of available work by Black gay writers and artists. Between 1982 and 1984, the collective published three volumes in a literary journal. The first issue was titled *Yemonja*, named for the Yoruban deity of the sea and giver of life. Blackheart 2, "a journal of writing and graphics by black gay men," brought light to the work of Black men in prison. And the third volume, Blackheart 3, was titled *The Telling of Us*. The journal played an important role for Black writers, poets, and artists to explore their place in the world.

Craig was all in favor, and for the second journal he gave Blackheart space in the bookshop to hold some of their meetings. The journals were carried in the Oscar Wilde, and a new button would join the display – "Black, Gay and Proud" – with the stencil designed by Fred.

Craig and Fred found they were able to work closely together and work out conflict with intense or even raucous conversation. Craig was open to being challenged on questions about race, and Fred remembered occasional arguments that would lead Craig to ponder the debate and return, having raised his consciousness another notch. Fred had never seen that happen like this before.

Fred joined a samba band and marched in the annual parade when it was a looser and more spontaneous event. The band would move about the parade, giving energy to one group after another, especially groups like People With AIDS.

Craig's temper was not a secret, but it seemed to be tolerated by those who knew him, and that seemed to be everybody. The staff, usually one full-time and one part-time employee, comprised men and women; the women self-identified as lesbian and men self-identified as gay. There was racial and age diversity. The shop was ahead of its time. It was unusual to be connected to one's community, which happened at the Oscar Wilde. For Fred Carl, the shop was hiring people who were friendly to activism, so there was a store full of people who had a notion of how the world should be. Craig had hired them partly for that.[46]

But in 1984 Fred decided it was just time for him to go, to do something different. Craig was great for him and to him, but differences led to an endpoint. New bookshops were opening, and it was also becoming harder to run a gay and lesbian bookshop.

The Oscar Wilde was a natural fit for Nan Buzard. She loved the welcoming nature of the place and the fact that it was a center of political activity. As an extrovert, it was easy for her to keep Craig's everyone-will-be-greeted-with-a-warm-hello policy going. She liked seeing the surprised and happy looks on customers' faces when they were welcomed.[47]

Nan had moved to New York in 1975, when she was seventeen, and rented a loft from actor and writer Spalding Gray for $250 a month in what would later be known as SoHo. She remembered coming out that summer, specifically on a day when she was on a bicycle, whooshing down Fifth Avenue from 14th Street to Washington Square, where she was meeting a woman she had developed a crush on. As the wind blew in her face and the evening sun was in her eyes from the side streets, she remembered thinking, "I'm gay! That's what it is, I'm gay!"

That was one of the reasons, she thinks, that Craig hired her to work in the shop – Nan was positive about being gay. She "came out to people every minute. She bonded quickly with Fred Carl, and they worked together as co-managers for two years before Fred left the shop.

Nan found Craig to have a certain deferential-ness about him, in that he didn't want it all to be about him. What always comes back to her is that Craig wanted the Pride march to be the last Sunday of June and that it should be "embedded in the fabric of our liberation movement, not in a committee or person or administration."

She found him to be a true liberationist, which didn't mean that he was easy to work for. She and Fred (and she considered themselves to be the most trustworthy employees you could find) were often on edge when Craig came through the door: "He would come bustling in and always something was wrong, he would come in and fix a shelf or pick up something off the ground; like, clearly, we had failed in our management of the bookstore."

Still, there was a fondness. Craig's thoughtfulness about what people needed, right down to brown-paper wrapping, left a positive memory. She remembered a network of people who would send in handwritten checks, and Craig would fulfill orders and take them to the post office. "It was a personal crusade; it wasn't a business by any means."

For Nan, the bookshop was one of very few gay spaces, and it was sacrosanct. There were times they threw straight people out if they had come in just to gawk at the titles or the inventory.

Edmund White would come in, and he became friends with Fred and Nan. His book *A Boy's Own Story*, which was published in 1982, was one of the popular titles. White would come in to socialize, check on how his book was doing, and sometimes sign books.

Nan gave Alison Bechdel a kitten. When Nan's mother retired to Costa Rica to run a hotel, there were kittens that needed a home, so Nan brought a boxful of kittens to the shop. Craig was reluctantly indulgent, and the kittens were dispersed to happy owners.

The shop was the center of the world. It was a rich and warm place. Craig's knowledge of the movement contributed to that. The world was not yet electronically fragmented, and in-person connections were still necessary and valuable.

How Craig came to focus on diversity in the staff and in the inventory was breathtaking to Nan. She found his attitudes to be clear and forward-thinking. But with that, she felt he was lonely. Perhaps giving his life to a cause and a movement, and fighting to keep the bookshop open, left little room for personal relationships. Plus, he was what you might call a conservative radical.

Over time, the thrill of the gay space began to wane, and Nan went on to be a gardener, a cook, and an international humanitarian aid worker – a gay person using her influence in the world.

Ellen Turner had attended the School of Visual Arts in Manhattan in the 1970s. She developed her artistry as a graphic designer and became active in the lesbian and gay community. She worked at the Lesbian, Gay, Bisexual &

Transgender Community Center, which had opened in 1983. She was active in the day-care movement, and in suicide prevention. She noticed on the cork board at the Center that the Oscar Wilde was looking for help; she answered the ad and was hired to work Sundays.

Ellen's graphic design skills were put to good use on the catalogs and supplements. Typography, spacing, art, rules – everything took a step up. The pages were assembled, photographed, and sent to the printer. The new format was a labor intensive hand-made tri-fold.

In the shop, Rodwell's original concept held firm – everyone was to be greeted with a "hello." The gay and lesbian community should feel welcome, and music should be played that appealed to the community. One of the rules for staff was that they had to read a book during any downtime and then review it for the catalog.

Ellen also remembered the visits by Harvey Fierstein and many other notables who joined the community of books and people. Barbara Gittings and Kay Tobin Lahusen would stop by during the annual Pride march when they came in from Philadelphia. One famous visitor stood out to Ellen, though – a man in a trench coat, hat, and glasses – Barry Manilow.

Craig almost never held back a thought; he had stories to regale the staff, and sayings – one was that there was "no life above 14th Street," which would have been outside of his cultural and historical neighborhoods.

Then, in the summer of 1987, a young Irish immigrant approached the gentle stoop with optimism. The bookshop was among the discoveries that Brendan Fay was about to make, having arrived in New York in 1984 from Drogheda, Ireland, to study at St. John's University and to live a life as a gay man. He had said goodbye to a life of repression in Ireland so he could "go where I can breathe."[48]

Brendan remembered what was going through his mind as he crossed the Atlantic:

> The turbulence outside the plane, nothing like the turbulence inside. I can't wait to see New York with the Statue of Liberty, Liberty Island. Ah, yes, land of the free: Fifth Avenue, St. John's University, Washington Square, Peter, Paul and Mary, Simon & Garfunkel, Bette Midler, the Flintstones, the Waltons, and Batman and Robin.[49]

Now, three years later, he would cross another threshold in a passionate life journey.

Inside was a somewhat preoccupied Craig Rodwell, his bookshop now twenty years in business and brimming with gay and lesbian titles. Whatever weariness may have accumulated from Craig's own struggles, he remained unwavering in his determination to help others find their own pride. He heard Brendan's Irish voice and asked, "What do you know about your Irish gay heritage?" Craig was already planning a response, and he produced a volume of *The Black Diaries of Roger Casement*.[50]

Brendan was taken by surprise: the famous Irish revolutionary and patriot of 1916 was gay? This was not a conversation he would have had in Ireland. And what Brendan knew about his Irish heritage was shame and silence, not freedom and pride. Yet here he was in a bookshop named for an Irish poet and homosexual martyr. The experience would stick for a lifetime.

And no charge for the Roger Casement book.

Like many others, Brendan found the Oscar Wilde's community bulletin board. Craig invited him to post a notice to reach out to other Irish lesbian and gay immigrants, which Brendan did – a small notice with his telephone number. People began calling him, and soon a group formed, part social and part political. They would meet at Irish pubs and wear buttons from the Oscar Wilde, fastened with the Irish tricolor ribbons. Later, they would join the new Irish Lesbian & Gay Organization when it formed in 1990.

But someone else was working in the bookshop that summer day in 1987. It was Jesús Lebrón. Jesús had discovered the shop as many others had – roaming the streets of Greenwich Village and spotting the lesbian and gay titles in the window. In March, having been a regular for about a year, Jesús asked to speak to the manager – was there work available? It was Craig behind the counter, who seemed amused by the inquiry, but that same afternoon, Jesús received a call at home – could he start the next day?[51]

The confluence brought Brendan and Jesús eye to eye and something clicked. The shop quickly became their place. Jesús would lock up for the day, they would turn up the music of Holly Near or Cris Williamson, and Jesús and Brendan would dance among the bookshelves. At twenty-nine years old, Brendan had never danced with another man before.

On Christmas Eve, Jesús told Brendan to dress well and meet him at the Oscar Wilde. They would join Jesús'

Catholic, Puerto Rican family and celebrate together in the South Bronx. Welcomed into the Lebrón home, Brendan thought, "I would do anything to have this."

Holidays were a trying time for gays and lesbians – where did they belong, who could they bring, could they be themselves at family gatherings? At the Oscar Wilde, Craig and Jesús would decorate the shop to be a festive place where the community could feel at home. Brendan remembers the "Peace on Earth, Good Will Toward Women" button, and the knitted pink triangles for Christmas trees. Small gestures during holidays made a difference for gays and lesbians when they were at their most vulnerable. For Jesús, the most special was Valentine's Day, when he would invite customers and couples to paint their names on heart-shaped cutouts, which would be hung from the ceiling as a statement of validation.

Jesús worked at the Oscar Wilde for eight years, right through the years of Craig's illness and death. He was a manager for six of those years.[52]

Jesús would coach and coax Brendan out of the closet to rallies and ACT UP events and the march on Washington. It was a time for consciousness-raising and action. Brendan had arrived in New York in the time of AIDS.

First lovers, Brendan and Jesús later became lifetime friends and activists.

In 1991, Brendan marched with New York Mayor David Dinkins, who had invited the Irish Lesbian and Gay Organization to join him in the St. Patrick's Day Parade, despite being barred by the parade organizers, the Ancient Order of Hibernians.[53] While they marched without their banner,

Brendan was identified and soon terminated from his position as a religion teacher at a Catholic girls' school in Queens. Two years later, when the Irish Lesbian and Gay Organization planned a protest march at the St. Patrick's Day Parade in New York, Brendan was arrested and charged with disturbing the peace. By 1994, he had founded the Lavender and Green Alliance, and after more arrests at the Manhattan parade, formed the St. Pat's for All Parade in Queens. A co-developer of the Civil Marriage Trail with Jesús, he crossed the border to Canada to marry Tom Moulton in 2003 and later helped Edie Windsor to marry her longtime partner, Thea Spyer, in Toronto. In 2016, the Lavender and Green Alliance became the first LGBT group to march behind a banner in New York's St. Patrick's Day parade.[54]

Every July 4, Brendan remembers Craig's influence on his life, what he calls a "gift of legacy," and he imagines the courage it took to protest at the Annual Reminders in Philadelphia. He remembers the community bulletin board at the bookshop where he put the first notice to reach out to Irish lesbian and gay people in New York. He can still feel the warmth from a small button in the shop at Christmas that said "Ho-Ho-Homosexual," and the love from the gay valentines hanging from the ceiling in February. For him, the thread of gay rights was pulled tight more by the Oscar Wilde than the Stonewall Inn.[55]

Brendan was impressed that another book had captured the attention of hundreds of visitors to the Oscar Wilde: *The Church and the Homosexual*, by the Reverend John McNeill, a lifelong LGBT activist and the founder of Dignity, New York, an organization for LGBT Catholics.

The book was a best seller and challenged from a theological point of view the traditional interpretations about homosexuality often cited from the Bible, saying they were misunderstood historical references. In July 1980, Craig wrote to McNeill in praise of the book: "Please let me add on a personal note that I know your book has brought healing to many thousands of Lesbians and Gay Catholics – healing of a false sense of guilt in being Gay." Craig's longtime interest in books was the impact they would have on others. And his concern was the lack of a reprint of the paperback edition. Craig told McNeill that he had sold 600 copies of the hardcover and more than 1,000 copies of the paperback, and he was sure a reprint would continue to sell.[56]

The Church and the Homosexual was also an inspiration to Brendan Fay, who produced a fifty-five-minute documentary on Father McNeill called *Taking A Chance on God* in 2012. Brendan's documentary brought McNeill's story to a wider audience. It recounts his life, from his Buffalo, NY, upbringing, to his experience as a prisoner of war in Nazi Germany, to his years as a Jesuit professor, a gay and civil rights activist, a protester against the Vietnam War, and a leader during the AIDS crisis.

One of the circles in Brendan's life was completed in 2024. For the first time, after decades of activism, every borough in New York City hosted a St. Patrick's Day Parade that included LGBT groups.

Julia Noël Goldman, a young lesbian from New York who had graduated from Sarah Lawrence, remembers the first time she walked into the Oscar Wilde in 1989 to fill out a job application. She was among the last employees of the bookshop to come on during Craig's life. Many years later, she still corrects herself if she refers to the Oscar Wilde as a bookstore; it was a bookshop, and Craig would not have it any other way.

In the last years especially, Craig's eccentricities intensified. His temper could flare, his tolerance or impatience for people he didn't like or trust was short.

Julia remembered, with both admiration and alarm, that on more than one occasion Craig would eject a customer from the shop for some infraction. "Get out of my shop" was something she and her brother, who also worked at the shop, would jokingly admonish each other.

Craig surrounded himself with his staff – they were a captive audience for his stories. Sometimes fun, sometimes too much drama. He worked mostly out of the backroom office on weekdays, leaving the staff to run the shop on weekends. All these years later, his business practices could only generously be considered quaint – he was still running the business out of a cash box. The records were spotty, and the bills didn't always get paid.

Still, the Oscar Wilde was good for Julia. It was a decent job for someone in their mid-to-late-twenties in New York, the co-workers were fun to be with, and it was an honor to be there. Craig was part of what made it an honor. She also worked at the Gay and Lesbian Center, later to become the LGBT Center, for thirty years. She thinks Craig would have appreciated that she stayed in the game for a long time.

In the 1960s, '70s, and '80s, the people who worked in the Oscar Wilde did more than sell books, manage inventory, and greet customers. By their presence there, which was an extension of Craig's activism, they too were activists; many were also activists outside the bookshop.

The shop was still a community center, a voice for liberation, and part of the Village neighborhood. From his vantage point, Craig could continue his part in the movement. He participated in protests, the two national marches in Washington, and the protest of police actions like the raid on Blue's Bar in New York in 1982.

He continued to take on the press for the way lesbians and gay men were portrayed. At one point, he wrote a letter "TO THE REPORTER FROM THE NEW YORK TIMES." In it he complained that the newspaper would not use the words *gay* or *lesbian* unless they were in direct quotes, opting instead to use the word *homosexuals*. In late 1979, it was time to change:

> One of the major causes of the violence daily directed against Lesbians and Gay men in American society is the public perception of us as sexually-obsessed, "diseased" individuals. The *New York Times*, as one of the major public opinion molders in this city, must share part of the blame for this public misconception of us.
>
> We are Lesbians and Gay men, the terms we have chosen for ourselves and which have historical roots and meanings for us; we rarely refer to ourselves as "homosexuals," a clinical term coined by a Hungarian psychiatrist in the late 19th Century to describe deviants to the so-called heterosexual norm.[57]

A few months earlier, the William Friedkin film *Cruising*, with Al Pacino, was being shot in Greenwich Village, and its violence-against-gay-men plot drew outrage. On July 25, several hundred protesters gathered in Sheridan Square and took their demonstration to the on-location scene at Ninth Avenue and 14th Street. Their numbers rose to more than a thousand on the second night of demonstrations.[58]

The protests over the film grew over the perceived anti-gay plot in which a detective (Pacino) infiltrates the gay subculture leather bar scene of motorcycles, power, and sex to apprehend a serial killer who has been targeting gay men. The film outraged the gay community through its focus on the dark corners of the leather bars and haunts, as well as the vague ending that left to the imagination whether Pacino's character was gay himself and may have killed one of his new gay friends to cleanse his soul of this latent sexual discovery.

On July 23, Craig had spoken at a rally at the Washington Square Methodist Church "to alert the Gay community to the fact that a motion picture, *Cruising*, was being filmed in the Village and that the film is a vicious distortion of Gay people which, if released, can only intensify the current wave of violence directed against Gay people."[59]

There were 300 people in the audience and Craig asked them to raise their hands if they or someone they knew had been assaulted in the street in the past year because they were gay. One hundred hands shot up.

Those were the points he made in a letter to Mayor Ed Koch on July 24, asking him to "cancel the various permits obtained by this film ... and make it clear to the world that the City of New York will not now or in the future collaborate with filmmakers or anyone else who seeks to encourage violence against Gay people."[60]

That message was also carried to the mayor by the National Gay Task Force, concerned about the potential for an explosive response in the gay community.[61] Koch refused. On Christopher Street, Craig was unphased by Hollywood and not beyond criticizing celebrities. When a famous opera star was interviewed on a national lifestyle program on television, Craig found her responses homophobic and heterosexist. He wrote:

> I know next to nothing about opera and wouldn't consider for a split second the idea of getting on national television to discuss opera.
>
> By the same token, may I suggest that you are as ignorant of Gay Liberation and its ramifications for the future of all humankind, as I am of opera....

Craig would get responses to his critiques – in this case a terse, tongue-in-cheek note from the star herself.[62]

12

Monuments, Myths, and Memorials

Another "gay liberation" was in the making as the tenth anniversary of the Stonewall riots approached, and it came with its own set of controversies.

Bruce Voeller, a co-founder of the National Gay Rights Task Force, felt there should be a permanent monument to the gay and lesbian rights movement. He approached the Mildred Andrews Fund of Cleveland and proposed the idea of a sculpture.[1] In 1978, Mildred Andrews had commissioned sculptor George Segal to complete a memorial at Kent State University to commemorate the four students killed by the Ohio National Guard during the anti-Vietnam War demonstration on May 4, 1970.[2]

Segal was offered the new commission under the broad guidelines that the sculpture "be loving and caring, and show the affection that is the hallmark of gay people.... And it had to have equal representation of men and women." It also was required to be placed on public land.[3]

Segal's statue would include four bronze figures, two men standing together, and two women seated next to each other on a park bench. They would be life-sized and understated. One of the men would have his arm on the other's shoulder; one of the women would have her hand on her companion's thigh. The sculpture was to be finished with a white lacquer, giving it a plaster appearance.

But the installation would be years and many roadblocks away.

Among the issues was Segal's own sexual orientation. He told *The New York Times* in 1979 before he began working on the project that he was "an unregenerate heterosexual, and my first reaction was a gay artist should do it." However, he reasoned that gay people were "human beings first" and that he couldn't refuse to do it.[4]

It certainly wasn't what Craig Rodwell had in mind to commemorate the people of the movement. In a statement in September 1980, he listed his objections to the "Gay Liberation" statue.[5]

First, he said the sculpture would perpetuate a myth that the gay rights movement was a movement of white people: "As Gay people, one of our major problems is our invisibility and that we are so often ignored. For us to turn around and impose the same kind of invisibility and ignorance on our sisters and brothers who are not white, is unconscionable."

Second was the exclusion of lesbian and gay artists from the opportunity to design the monument. Craig complained that the sponsor of the sculpture had stated that to choose a lesbian or gay sculptor would itself be discriminatory, to which Craig responded: "The only discrimination in the selection of an artist for this statue was directed against Lesbian and Gay male artists and sculptors."

Third, he found the proposed art to be "frivolous" and trivializing to the struggle.

Fourth was an effort to diminish the criticisms within the gay community by focusing on homophobic reactions of the Greenwich Village residents who didn't want a monument to the movement in their neighborhood to begin with.

He concluded his statement by saying how distasteful it was to have to publicly oppose other Gay people over a statue, but he felt the ramifications were too large to hold back.

The next month, Craig appealed to the community to oppose the statue at the Planning Board 2 meeting on October 16, 1980, in the St. Joseph's Church hall.

The New York City Parks Department can sum up the story in two dates: "Cast: 1980" and "Dedicated: June 23, 1992" – twelve years later. News accounts of meetings about the sculpture noted complaints about the gay theme of the sculpture, that it wouldn't fit the neighborhood, that it would be too big for Christopher Park, that it would invite vandals, and then there was a planned reconstruction of the park itself.

When the statues were installed in 1992, Rodwell did not relent. He recounted his complaint one more time to the *Times*: First, the four people in the statuary group were all depicted as white. "To have a sculpture that is meant to commemorate our movement and the community consist of all white people is vulgar." Second, "[t]here was no competition, no attempt to give the commission to any of the thousands of talented gay artists." And third, "the project was just presented to us" – the gay and lesbian community had not been consulted.[6]

At some point in the controversy, Voeller wrote to Craig to state his obvious disagreement with him over the statues. Voeller pointedly told him that if he had been more involved in "any of the major gay organizations," he would have been more aware of what was being proposed. But then he went on to say that despite the heated discussions over the statues, he wanted to acknowledge Craig's "electrifying and courageous" work, saying "the creation of Oscar Wilde has served innumerable people profoundly."[7]

Craig was now an elder of the movement. He had been fighting and advocating and promoting the positive image of gay life for thirty years. It was a crushing disappointment that the Gay Liberation sculpture was going to be the monument.

Craig had become increasingly impatient as the years went by, especially regarding claims on gay and lesbian history. Folklore about who was responsible for the Stonewall riots was one of them: "Certainly, one of the major myths is that the Stonewall was started by any one particular group," Craig said in 1986. He continued:

> I've heard this many times over the years. I always resist it. There were drag queens at the Stonewall riots, there were women, however the vast majority of people there were men. Nobody can deny that. My basic way of answering that question is simply to say that no one group or person was responsible for the Stonewall riots. It was an event that happened in history that came at a time when every component

came together at a certain time. Almost a mystical experience or a spiritual experience. No one group or person is responsible for it.⁸

Years before, Dick Leitsch had been among those concerned about credit for gay liberation, and he remained bitter over his short relationship with Craig. The year after the Stonewall riots, he had a dig at Craig in the *New York Mattachine Newsletter*: "Watch out for some of our more hysterical, more paranoid brothers and sisters who want to make every raid a 'Gay Power' issue," he'd written.⁹

After the meeting of the North American Conference of Homophile Organizations (NACHO) in 1970, Foster Gunnison, always the reasonable one, was so exasperated with Leitsch's approach to the conference, Frank Kameny, and Craig, that he wrote Leitsch a blistering six-page, single-spaced letter that concluded with some harsh advice:

> And if you can marshall [sic] all the energies that you expend in plotting and planning against Frank, and abhorring poor Craig, and erecting your little defensive walls, and channel this into constructive endeavor toward something bigger than yourself and your little home territory of MSNY – whether it be the NACHO, or the CSLDC, or the (we-hope-to-be-resurrected-this-February-but-don't-lose-sleep-on-it) ERCHO, or what else may come, you will have a feeling of accomplishment, and importance, and influence.¹⁰

While Craig had been responsible for or participated in some of the most consequential actions of the gay liberation movement – the pickets, the protests, Mattachine, the sip-in, the Annual Reminders, the Stonewall riots, the Oscar Wilde, and Christopher Street Liberation Day – Leitsch, who had been brought into the movement by Craig, dismissed it all: "The day before Stonewall, everybody in New York except for me was a closet queen; the day after Stonewall, everybody was a gay leader and wide open and a radical," he said in an interview more than forty years later.[11]

It was not as though Dick Leitsch had not had accomplishments of his own. He had been president of New York Mattachine from 1965 to 1971. And he had worked to end police entrapment of homosexuals. He had written his own first-person account of the Stonewall riots, which was published in *The Advocate*. But his relatively short Mattachine years were the peak of his involvement and visibility in the movement.

Reflecting on years of Pride marches, undeniably conceived and started by Rodwell and his Christopher Street committee, Leitsch said, astonishingly, that one year he looked down from the Empire State Building at the march, and thought, "I kind of did this."[12]

◆◆◆◆◆

Rodwell's large and direct influence in the movement, accomplished as a leader without a title, was waning. But as the decade of the 1990s opened, there came an unusual thank you, one that Craig might never have imagined in the Stonewall days.

Eight years before, Sam Ciccone, who had been a sergeant in the Fairview Police Department (NJ) and who had not come out in his fifteen years there, moved to New York and cofounded the Gay Officers Action League. It was there to help gay and lesbian employees in law enforcement. He helped to bridge the hostilities between the organizers of the annual Pride march and the police.[13] Rodwell's attitudes toward police had not been positive from the time he was a teenager. He'd had run-in after run-in, he had written articles about entrapment, and his Stonewall flyer had become legend.

When Fred Sargeant left Rodwell and New York in 1971, he had witnessed the problems in policing, but two years later, he decided he would try to change things from the inside. He joined the force in Stamford, CT, and rose to the rank of lieutenant. When he visited the Oscar Wilde soon after, Rodwell was so incensed at the news that he couldn't even speak to him. But there were gay people who wanted careers in the military, in policing, in firefighting, and emergency services, and Sargeant was one of them, as was Ciccone. Fast forward to July 1990, and Ciccone also stopped in at the Oscar Wilde, as a customer. He purchased some copies of the *Gay Freedom 1970* commemorative pamphlet from the 1970 Christopher Street Liberation Day march, and he wrote to Craig the following day on Gay Officer Action League letterhead:

> Much is owed to you and others of that time twenty years ago. I would probably not be putting my name to this stationery, nor would the above letterhead exist if it were not for your courage and the inspiration you gave to so many who followed you. Thank you for what you have done for Gay and Lesbian freedom.

And he capitalized Gay and Lesbian in his letter.[14]

By 1993, Lambda Literary had been recognizing the contributions of lesbian and gay writers for five years, and in May the fifth annual awards ceremony was held in Miami. Comedian Kate Clinton was the emcee. Among the award recipients that year were Paul Monette, who won in the non-fiction category for *Becoming A Man*, and Blanche Cook, who won in the lesbian non-fiction category for *Eleanor Roosevelt*. A posthumous award for lesbian poetry went to Audre Lorde for *Undersong*.

There were two special awards announced. One was the editor's choice award, which went to Richard Mohr for *Gay Ideas*. The other – the Publisher's Service Award – was announced by Deacon Maccubbin, founder of the Lambda Rising bookstore in Washington and publisher of the Lambda Book Report.[15]

"Sometimes," he said, "this award is granted on the basis of a special project, a unique one-time contribution to lesbian and gay literature, and sometimes it is granted in recognition of a lifelong commitment to our community and to our industry."

This night the honoree would qualify in both categories – it was Craig Rodwell, "for his life's work in promoting lesbian and gay literature, and for his courageous and visionary role as a pioneer in the field."

Maccubbin himself was among the many inspired by Craig, having walked into the Oscar Wilde in 1972, amazed to find a bookshop for his community's literature. Maccubbin decided that Washington, DC, should have a similar bookshop, which he went on to open in 1974.

So, on this 80-degree night at the Intercontinental Hotel, Maccubbin summarized Rodwell's many contributions:

> Craig's vision and courage in 1967 gave birth to a whole network of lesbian and gay bookstores across the country. He showed many of us that such stores were viable and could serve a useful purpose in our communities. He gave publishers an outlet, and authors a home.

Those were emotional words about vision and commitment, but Craig was not there to hear them. He had learned in May 1992 that he was ill, not with AIDS, but with stomach cancer. In less than a year, the cancer would advance, and it was clear that Rodwell was not going to make it.

Maccubbin's tribute concluded with a heartfelt call to action:

> [H]aving dedicated his life to the gay and lesbian community, Craig is now approaching the end of his life. He lies in a bed in New York tonight, unable to move, unable to speak, unable to be here with us to accept this much-deserved accolade. This man who has given us so much now asks only our prayers in return. This Lammy award can be only a token of our appreciation for his work; the real reward will come when each of us rededicates ourselves to continuing Craig's dream and continuing the work he started a quarter century ago.[16]

The award was later delivered to Craig in New York. When Maccubbin spoke to him between the ceremony and his passing, he felt that Craig was appreciative.

In his last years, Craig had given up on the Christian Science Church. Bob McCullough, who had been a long-time friend from the Gay People in Christian Science days, visited Craig in his apartment toward the end. Bob had brought a book on Christian Science but learned that Craig had "followed the medical thing completely." Craig was smoking and watching his beloved Chicago Cubs on television. Bob saw a resignation in him, as well as a light. He thought, "Down deep, perhaps Craig thought Christian Science won't back me up."[17]

In fact, Craig had told Martin Duberman, in the tape-recorded sessions for Duberman's book *Stonewall*, that while he respected the wisdom of Mary Baker Eddy, he no longer considered himself a Christian Scientist and felt that the church had not really changed its position on homosexuality.[18]

As spring arrived in 1993, the letters came in a stream.

In March, true blue to Craig and the Oscar Wilde, Julia Noël Goldman wanted Craig to know a few things in his last days:

> I am writing this to tell you, in case you didn't know, that I am proud to have known you. Even if I did not agree with some of your decisions, even if you were sometimes an asshole. If nothing else, it made me feel better about being an asshole myself sometimes. Knowing you has given me so much more pride in being gay, made me so much less willing to make compromises about it, for myself or the movement as a whole. I so appreciate the work that you have done for lesbian and gay people, and through that, for all

people, and for the future. In your unique way, you have changed the world; no one else could ever again do what you have done.

So know that I will never stop fighting for the things that you believe in. I will miss you very much. Most of all I will miss your stories and that wicked sense of humor.[19]

It was signed, "Love," from Julia Noël Goldman, which must have brought a smile to Craig's face in a dark time.

Then in April, a letter from New York Mayor David Dinkins:

Dear Craig:

Words are small comfort during times of illness, but I would be remiss if I did not let you know that my thoughts are with you.

Your record of service to the lesbian and gay community and to all citizens of our City has not gone unnoticed. You are an outstanding citizen whose efforts have paved the way for many. The founding of the Oscar Wilde Memorial Bookstore [sic] has inspired the minds of generations of activists, and your work in organizing the homophile Youth Movement and the Christopher Street Liberation Day March lives on in the lives of New Yorkers. We all have been blessed with your rich contributions.

May the grace of God be with you, your family and friends. Keep the faith.

Sincerely,

David N. Dinkins
Mayor[20]

And in June, from Nancy Garden:

> ... it's a blow that I'm sure all your friends and acquaintances wish, as I do, that they could somehow absorb, and remove from you. You have given us all so much, from those early days in Mattachine to those first tiny demonstrations (remember the recruiting office in the rain?), to Stonewall and Christopher Liberation Day – and, of course, the bookstore, which has touched countless lives and become a vital center of gay and lesbian life, literary and otherwise.[21]

Nancy closed by remembering Craig's smile, his raised eyebrows, his sense of humor, and the privilege of knowing him.

In the next two weeks at St. Vincent's Hospital, where thousands of AIDS patients had been treated and died, Craig was ready. He told the nurse he wanted to stop his intravenous feeding. According to Craig's brother, Jack, the nurse asked him two questions: First, was there any unfinished business in his life? "No," he answered, "I've accomplished my dream." The second was whether Craig would like spiritual counseling. "No, I am the most spiritual person I know, and I talk to myself all the time." These were the last steps in his march for self-determination.[22]

Craig Louis Rodwell died on Friday, June 18, 1993, at St. Vincent's. The cause was stomach cancer. He was fifty-two years old.

In the days after his death, his obituary appeared in newspapers across the country: from the *Democrat and Chronicle* (NY) to the *LA Times* (CA); from the *Tampa Bay*

Times (FL) to the *Modesto Bee* (CA); and from the *Pottsville Republican* (PA) to the *Wichita Eagle* (KS). In New York, the *Times* headline called him a "pioneer for gay rights." The *Daily News* headline called him a "gay-rights activist" and the lead recognized him as "a principal organizer" of the first Pride march. Wire services UPI and AP carried the story, bringing the news to readers across the country. Such recognition was a remarkable turnaround in the attitudes of the press – one that Craig himself had fought for. From the 1960s – when he couldn't get his bookshop ads accepted – to the week of the Stonewall riots – when any publicity was considered a major victory – to the protests over *Time* magazine's negative portrayal of homosexuals, to the delayed recognition of AIDS in the gay community, times had clearly changed.

The public memorial the following month at The (LGBT) Center on 13th Street – preserved on video and archived – reflected the discrete compartments of Craig Rodwell's life.[23]

It was another sticky New York night with the temperature hovering around 80 degrees. The fans in the Alexander Room were whirring and cotton shirts were wrinkling as the evening service began. But for the seventy-five or so people in attendance, there were stories to tell and stories to hear. Marion Rodwell Kastman, now eighty-three, small in stature, her silver hair in soft curls, sat quietly in the front row.

One by one, people rose to tell their story.

Randy Wicker was first. Aside from family, he had probably known Craig longer than anyone else in the room. Randy recounted the early days of his and Craig's militant involvement with Mattachine and their successful efforts to upend the conservatives in the organization. They took on the establishment to prove they weren't sick. Then the demonstration at the Whitehall Street Induction Center, then the sip-in at Julius'. Then Randy's button shop, which had opened just before the Oscar Wilde, and then the bookshop itself – "our community center." As for Marion, sitting a few feet away, Randy had never met another gay person's mother before and it had changed his life to see her in the shop (applause). He concluded: Craig didn't open the Oscar Wilde because he loved books, but "because he loved us."

A woman who had worked in the shop on Sundays had remained friends with Craig, "which could be difficult [laughter]." She had picked up *The Village Voice*, saw Craig's picture, and she knew that he was gone. She remembered that Craig had brought diversity to the Oscar Wilde; everyone was on equal footing. And he had standards – no books that Craig found to be racist, or anti-woman, or anti-Semitic, or newspapers that had racist advertising. And yes, he was crotchety.

Then there was Martin Duberman, who had most likely spent more time interviewing Craig than anyone else. He was glad to see so many people at the gathering since the publicity of the memorial had seemed sparse. Craig was one of the six profiles in Martin's book *Stonewall*. Martin got to know Craig well through his many interviews and found him modest and self-effacing, but he thought people should know the "enormity of his contribution" to the gay and lesbian movement. Craig's overarching motto – to tell the truth – sometimes got him in a lot of trouble. And it was true that Craig had become contentious and eventually dropped out of the movement to focus on the Oscar Wilde. He left behind a life of "confrontational politics."

Ellen Turner was there. She recalled her time working in the shop and considered Craig an employer, friend, and comrade. She was impressed by his continued determination to fight sexism. And she remembered his opposition to NAMBLA.

Julia Noël Goldman had seen Craig in the last few weeks before he died. He had arrived at the Oscar Wilde, emaciated, in a wheelchair, and wouldn't move for the Al Pacino crew filming on Christopher Street.[24] It was classic Craig. Julia knew that Craig felt the movement had let him down in the end.

Then Jack Rodwell: "We were half-brothers brought up by different mothers in different cities; we barely knew each other." But he remembered a time when they were eight or nine years old in the back of their father's car on a long drive from Chicago to Detroit – an endless game of Twenty Questions.

The last speaker was Joe Roberts, a longtime friend and board game buddy. As he recounted, he knew Craig when *The New York Times* wouldn't use the word *gay* in its columns. Craig wasn't satisfied even when they did, he said dryly, because it wasn't capitalized. The first of a few deep sighs stilled the room – the fans were still whirring. Joe, in short sleeves and in the heat, was ramping up. He wanted people to know that Craig had disdain for hypocrites, religions, funerals, and services. He probably didn't need to remind everyone that Craig wouldn't want to miss the opportunity, though, to make you uncomfortable when you least wanted it. Then, Joe posed a big question:

> What happened to the parade?
> What happened to the event he helped start for everyone to celebrate being gay?

So much had changed from the beginning that Ed Murphy, the former bouncer-manager of the Stonewall, was recognized for his contributions to the movement, the Socialist Workers Party marched in the parade, and even NAMBLA, the man-boy love group, had a presence.

"What happened to his parade?" he asked again.

Joe continued – Craig couldn't bear to go to the end of Christopher Street at the end of the parade anymore. He was disgusted by the "mafiestival." And he wanted to know, where does all the money go from this event? Does it go to gay and lesbian organizations? Who's selling the burgers and beers – are they gay?

Joe's finale: Craig didn't want a service or burial. But Joe took his ashes to a place in the country, in the woods, on a Sunday – on gay pride day, in fact – and on the hour that the parade was to start, he scattered the ashes "to start a parade near the earth again at the roots."[25]

It was quiet, and people were swallowing hard – but there was one more thing.

Bill Offenbaker, the new owner of the Oscar Wilde who bookended the service with announcements, said that a poem had been sent to Marion Kastman from a woman in San Francisco. Marion wanted it to be read that day.

Offenbaker, with a lump in his throat, picked up with the third stanza of Maya Angelou's "When Great Trees Fall":

When great souls die,
the air around us becomes
light, rare, sterile.*

And it seemed that way as he read through the thirty-five lines to the end, as the group breathed in the meaning of this poem and the connection it gave them to Craig's memory. And they departed, with smiles and acknowledgements amid the moving of folding chairs.

---

* Maya Angelou, "When Great Trees Fall" from *Celebrations: Rituals of Peace and Prayer*, copyright © 2006 by Caged Bird Legacy, LLC. Used by permission of Random House, an imprint and division of Penguin Random House LLC.

13

Transitions

Suffering from terminal cancer, and three months before the cancer took his life, Craig put his lifelong dream in the hands of Bill Offenbaker, a twenty-six-year-old from Brooklyn and a bookshop manager. Offenbaker signed his business certificate for the Oscar Wilde on March 17, 1993. Craig signed his certificate of discontinuance two days later.[1] The sale began a string of changes and new owners that would occur during a time of massive disruption for independent booksellers.

Julia Noël Goldman, who was there for the transition after Craig's death, had a sense that the shop needed to find a new path to survive. With Rodwell gone, so was the history that came with the shop. People knew him and would come into the shop to see him. Despite his crotchety behavior, he brought color to the atmosphere.

But Offenbaker wasn't Craig, and he lacked the same support from the staff. Three years after he had taken the reins, the shop was in serious financial trouble.

Larry Lingle, the owner of the Lobo Bookshop in Houston, learned that the Oscar Wilde was on the brink. Lingle had previously operated bookstores in Dallas and New Orleans, and he would own others later in Austin and Oklahoma City.[2] He purchased the Oscar Wilde and kept it going under the trusted management of Kim Brinster. But Lingle told *Publisher's Weekly* in 2003 that the shop lost money every year he owned it, and he intended to close the doors at the end of January 2003.[3]

Enter Deacon Maccubbin, who had delivered the heartfelt words at the Lambda Literary ceremony. He had visited the Oscar Wilde when it was on Mercer Street, and it had inspired him to open Lambda Rising, the gay and lesbian bookshop in Washington, DC, in 1974. Maccubbin had run other stores from a distance in Baltimore, MD, Rehoboth Beach, DE, and Norfolk, VA. He had been in the Oscar Wilde recently and still loved the shop. He made an offer and became the fourth owner of the Oscar Wilde in February 2003.[4]

Maccubbin brought in fresh stock from the Washington shop and added more gift items to the inventory. Being a small location, it was a challenge to stock, but the doors to the Oscar Wilde remained open until the time came for ownership to return to a New Yorker.[5]

Kim Brinster had worked for about a decade for the US Post Office in the West Village in the mid-1980s. The Oscar Wilde was on her truck route, and she remembered regular cash-on-delivery orders to the shop during Rodwell's years. When fate brought her together with Larry Lingle and then to the Oscar Wilde as a manager for Lingle and later Maccubbin, the bookshop became "a great joy" in her life. She met passionate readers from around the world and reveled in the company of loyal customers and authors.[6]

In 2006, Kim Brinster became the fifth and final owner of the Oscar Wilde. She kept the business afloat for another three years, until the pressures on lesbian and gay bookshops and independent bookshops everywhere forced her to close the doors on March 29, 2009, more than four decades after the grand opening in November 1967. She remembered that Marion Kastman had visited the shop after Craig had died. Brinster had made renovations and Marion stood there, remarking that the Oscar Wilde had become a classier place. But on February 4, reporter Sewell Chan reported in a story on page A27 of *The New York Times*: "Venerable Bookstore to Close in Village." In the article, Brinster attributed the closure to declining sales.

The world had changed in many ways since Craig had opened the shop. Large national bookstore chains with broad and voluminous inventories began drawing customers to multi-floor storefronts. The internet made book purchases available from vast warehouses without having to go anywhere except the mailbox or the doorstep. The success of the gay movement itself made it possible for lesbian and gay titles to find a place in the new order, blending in with the travel and cooking and biography sections of the superstores. Then there was a decline in tourism and the effects of 9/11.

When it looked like the Oscar Wilde was going to close in 2003, writer Bruce Bawer wrote in the Opinion section of the *Times* that "the hole in the soul that places like the Oscar Wilde Bookshop once helped to fill is no longer there."

But the legacy of the Oscar Wilde was far from linear, and its measure was deep. As time would show, the gap was indeed still there.

Epilogue

What *did* happen to Craig Rodwell's parade?

As he had advocated from the beginning in 1970, marches were held in other cities outside of New York – in Chicago, Los Angeles, and San Francisco. But as he had feared from the beginning, competing interests from different groups eventually changed the nature of the march. The idea of individuals walking for their freedom, without hierarchies, without entertainment, all equal, would not hold.

Commercialism would win out in the early years, with a change in the direction of the route in New York, so that instead of starting in the Village, it would end in the Village. In the 1970s and '80s, the march would proceed uptown a half-dozen times, but the trend would become a march downtown, from Columbus Circle and down Fifth Avenue, sometimes down Seventh Avenue. Rodwell complained that by switching the direction, they were benefiting Mafia-owned businesses.

The early debate over floats and bars and businesses would dissolve as the Christopher Street Liberation Day Committee changed, disbanded, and was eventually replaced by Heritage of Pride as the organizer of the annual march.

The answer to Joe Roberts' question at the memorial service – "What happened to the parade?" – is the story of the committee that oversaw the annual event. Craig left the Christopher Street Liberation Day Committee late in 1971. After the early marches, the committee was joined by a variety of new members, some causing scandal, others putting the committee back on track. One new member was Ed Murphy, the former mob-connected manager at the Stonewall Inn.[1] Murphy succeeded in reversing the direction of the march so that it would end in the Village, where he led the separate post-march festival committee. The earlier activists were pushed aside so the event could become a party and a money-making opportunity. Jim Owles, who had been an originator of the Gay Activists Alliance and its first president, called out the committee as a mob front.[2] But Murphy himself was gay, and while he had worked in Mafia bars, he was also an informant for the FBI. In the 1970s, he was positioning himself to turn over a new leaf, which he described in a raw tell-all appearance before the West Side Discussion Group in the spring of 1978.[3]

When a letter came to the Oscar Wilde from the 1982 committee, seeking funds and advertising for the Pride Guide, Ed Murphy's name was among the signees. He was listed as "chairman and founder" of the Christopher Street Festival Committee, and Craig circled it in red. The primary signature on the letter was Anthony Gambino, co-coordinator of the Christopher Street Liberation Day Committee.

Tony Gambino, known as the "mayor" of Christopher Street, was also the head of the Stonewall Awards Foundation. The year after the Christopher Street committee wrote to the Oscar Wilde seeking funds and advertising for the Pride Guide, Gambino sent another letter to the Oscar Wilde from the Stonewall Awards Foundation, announcing that the Oscar Wilde had been nominated in the category of "outstanding contribution by a business." Craig wanted nothing to do with Gambino or the awards foundation, and he wrote to them two weeks later, asking them to remove the bookshop from the nominees. "I have made it a policy over the years of neither seeking nor accepting awards," he wrote, and thanked them for the thought.[4]

By 1983, the Christopher Street Liberation Day Committee took formal action to reverse the direction of the march. In the committee's monthly publication, Gambino said the reversal would be a message to the politicians for more visibility. The projected budget for the march was $26,500. Gambino was one of the grand marshals that year.

Then a scandal. In April 1984, the committee wrote to Gambino by certified mail that he was going to be removed for misappropriation of funds, although the letter came back unclaimed. In addition to his positions on the committee and the Stonewall Awards Foundation, Gambino was also the head of the Manhattan Community Athletic Association bowling league for lesbians and gay men. From late 1983 to spring of 1984, he was accused of writing checks to "cash" from the athletic association's account and then loaning the money to other organizations. In news accounts in the lesbian and gay press, Gambino admitted that he had diverted funds to the Christopher Street committee and even to himself during a time when he was ill. The scandal came out in full, and the whole mess resulted in a set of resignations, charges, and countercharges. Gambino himself was removed or resigned as head of the bowling league, the awards foundation, and the Christopher Street committee.[5]

Candida Scott Piel was one of the members of the committee who realized there was no money left in the bank account. She had joined the Christopher Street Liberation Day Committee in 1982 as a parade marshal. She had been working in theater production for The Glines, a non-profit theater company for gay artists. She did not have work that year, so she stepped up to work on the annual march. When she suggested the community had been "miserable enough" and that there should be floats and bands and a more celebratory experience, she was given the job of organizing the units. By 1984, to help put the pieces back together after the financial scandal, she became co-coordinator with Brian O'Dell, and they thought of themselves as the "second wave."[6]

In June, the Christopher Street committee made a change to its constitution. The original purpose, which had been to organize a lesbian and gay liberation march and rally, was changed. The new purpose would focus on a "parade/march."[7]

But it became clear to the committee that there needed to be a clean break from past leadership and money problems, as well as the organizational structure itself. Piel had grown weary of the Committee's paralysis, including long political speeches by people who weren't really involved. That break would result in a new name and a new structure. In January 1985, the Christopher Street Liberation Day Committee voted in a constitutional amendment to change its name to Heritage of Pride, Inc. The wording of the group's purpose continued to evolve. Now, their purpose was to commemorate the Stonewall riots and organize a "parade and rally." And the organization would be a not-for-profit corporation, no longer an association.[8] The directors of the new corporation were Candida Scott Piel, Brian O'Dell, and Matt Foreman. Piel made the application for non-profit status in April. The Christopher Street loans were paid off and a new bank account was opened. That year, the march walked a route designated by a lavender line, conceived by Foreman. Piel dipped her hands in the paint and pressed them into Foreman's T-shirt to commemorate the event.[9]

By November, a new constitution stated the following purpose: "to organize and promote the annual Gay/Lesbian Pride Day Parade/March and Rally in New York City." It also prohibited lobbying and participation in politics. There were to be two co-coordinators, one female and one male. Later, Piel and others moved to become a charitable organization under the 501(c)(3) rules of the Internal Revenue Service.

Meanwhile, the march became an emblem of the fight for life as the gay population was decimated during the AIDS crisis. "Homosexuals Parade in the Face of Death," was the headline in *The New York Times* on June 29, 1987. The eighteenth annual parade marked the deaths of 6,000 New Yorkers from AIDS. Marchers carried funeral bouquets and signs with the names of people who had died from the disease.[10] The next year, there was a release of 10,000 balloons when the march came to a halt on Fifth Avenue, each balloon to honor someone who died of AIDS. Down the lavender line, thousands marched, many wearing pink triangles.[11]

New York mayors began to join the march. Ed Koch in 1985, and later David Dinkins and others. The Empire State Building was lighted in lavender in 1990. On the twentieth anniversary of the Stonewall riots, the march became the largest gay parade in New York's history, with 150,000 people attending.

Gay and lesbian marches on Washington started to occur, with the first event in 1979 with 100,000 marchers, fired up by the assassination of Harvey Milk and the light sentence Dan White received for killing him. Other marches occurred in 1987, 1993, 2000, and 2009.[12]

The 1980s weren't the easiest of times for Heritage of Pride. The attempt to obtain 501(c)(3) status would not be resolved for years in a morass of legal back and forths with attorneys. By 1989, Heritage of Pride amended its certificate of incorporation to become more of an educational organization. The old march/rally concept was not mentioned, and the new purpose was to organize programs or events to commemorate historic lesbian and gay civil rights struggles.[13]

In 1994, the annual event was substituted by a march on the United Nations to celebrate the twenty-fifth anniversary of the Stonewall riots. The community splintered that year into two parades: the march on the UN, to protest treatment of homosexuals everywhere, and an unofficial one, which focused on addressing the problem of AIDS. The two parades joined at 57th Street and proceeded to Central Park, where marchers paused for a "moment of silence" and also "a moment of rage."

The total in cash receipts that the Christopher Street Liberation Day Committee had raised in 1970 was $575.84. As of 2022, Heritage of Pride reported revenues of more than $5 million, a paid executive director, a staff of eighteen, and 850 volunteers.[14]

At the 1993 Pride march, ten days after Craig Rodwell died and more than two decades since he conceived of the idea of a march, Lesbian Herstory Archives co-founder Deborah Edel remarked on the acceptance the community had acquired and the vulnerability it continued to experience. She had a plain but powerful assessment – "we've reached a level of visibility."[15]

Kay Tobin Lahusen, in her own goodbye letter to Craig that spring, had a prescient assessment of how he would be remembered:

> I feel the founding of the bookshop cannot be fully appreciated by today's activists, nor can they realize what a big step out of the closet the first pickets were. The squabbling over the dress code paled beside the larger issue keeping gay people from picketing – fear of the consequences. Thank goodness we were all in the handful of people with the guts to go public.[16]

Three more decades would pass, and Pride events are now held in more than a hundred countries and attended by millions of people. In 2023, Candida Scott Piel recalled the legacy of Craig Rodwell's "hand-made" march as a sentimental experience of the post-Stonewall days when you could join the march with the simple act of stepping off the curb. She wondered, though, about today: "If you're just somebody, can you just show up?" She hoped so.[17]

Craig would have hoped so, too.

It would be hard to overstate Craig Rodwell's impact on the roots of today's freedoms. While his is not a household name, and he is not as well known as pioneers like Frank Kameny or Barbara Gittings, his influence was so broad as to earn him recognition as the un-leader leader and the bridge between the homophile and gay liberation movements.

Recognizing Rodwell's contribution does not negate the pioneering achievements of others to change institutions and laws – the remarkable action to reverse the American Psychiatric Association's definition of homosexuality as a mental illness, or the fight for rights to employment by the federal government, or the Daughters of Bilitis, or the actions of the Gay Liberation Front or the Gay Activists Alliance, or Mattachine, or other revolutionary books, periodicals, broadcasts, or newspaper columns.

But as Tom Wilson Weinberg said, "He was ahead of so many people before activism grew. He was one of the first people to be angry and come forward. He didn't care what people thought."

How did Craig know what to do?

He had been in the movement for ten years by the time he arrived in front of the Stonewall Inn as the police action was unfolding. He knew as the violence erupted that the timing was right for a political disruption to be newsworthy and that press coverage of a disruption was exactly what the movement needed.[18]

He already knew that the Annual Reminders were not reaching the goals for gay liberation. And he had a well-established target – the Mafia, and the cops, and their relationship to gay bars. He had the words and the mechanism to distribute a landmark flyer with the volunteers from HYMN. And he had a plan for a much more radical event than the Philadelphia reminders.

But Rodwell's vision for gay freedom, and perhaps the fact that he did not crave leadership or power, helped him open doors for everyday gays and lesbians to take individual and collective action.

Craig himself believed he was living on a "cusp of history," a transition period where he hoped lesbians and gay men "would have a growing sense of how important this movement is."[19]

In assessing Rodwell's impact, one could almost come to a full stop at the Pride march. The 5,000 souls who tumbled exuberantly into Sheep Meadow in Central Park in 1970, thanks to the planning and encouragement of the Christopher Street Liberation Day Committee, grew into millions across the globe in the subsequent decades.

In the announcement for Gay Pride Week in 1971, the Christopher Street Liberation Day Committee cited an explosion in celebrations: in Albany, Boston, Washington,

Philadelphia, Houston, Dallas, Chicago, Seattle, Portland, San Francisco, Los Angeles, Phoenix, Denver, San Jose, Sacramento, Minneapolis, London, Paris, Stockholm, and Malmo.

"And throughout the world," the committee wrote, "Gay people are gathering in groups from two to tens of thousands to affirm their pride and dignity."[20]

The decades have seen surges in the growth of Pride marches and events. By 1999, the marches and the week of gay activities had officially grown into Gay and Lesbian Pride Month, which was established that June in a proclamation by President Bill Clinton.

By the numbers alone, the Oscar Wilde Memorial Bookshop was impressive, not just for its mailing list of 1,600 addresses prior to the first march, but for its thousands and thousands of customers over four decades. And it is not just that the Bookshop takes its place in history as the first of its kind dedicated to gay and lesbian literature. From the start, the shop was meant to be a nerve center of the movement. After the Stonewall riots, people flocked there for information and camaraderie. Countless individuals, many who would become famous for their own contributions, crossed the threshold of the Oscar Wilde to be welcomed and encouraged. Person after person remembers the bookshop for its cultural heartbeat, a place they could hang out, call their own, and feel at home, unjudged.

As new bookstores sprang up inspired by the Oscar Wilde, the doors of legitimacy opened across the country and beyond. When Tom Wilson Weinberg opened Giovanni's Room in Philadelphia, it was paramount to him that the shop have a large plate-glass window on the first floor, transparency into the lives of gay people, like the Oscar Wilde.

It was similar for Ernest Hole, the Londoner who had boarded the bus for the fifth Annual Reminder in 1969. He had lived in New York from 1968 to 1969 and became friends with Craig. Ten years later, he opened the United Kingdom's first gay and lesbian bookshop, Gay's The Word. In 2012, in the online *Polari Magazine*, Ernest wrote: "Craig is credited with radically influencing [Harvey] Milk's politics, and he certainly influenced mine. His example inspired me to try and create a similar bookshop in London." Gay's The Word also had a storefront similar to the Oscar Wilde on Mercer Street – a door to the left of a large plate-glass window, filled with gay and lesbian titles. Like the Oscar Wilde, the bookshop became a community center as well.

Harvey Milk didn't open a bookshop, but when he opened Castro Camera in 1972, it would be more than a camera shop and, like the Oscar Wilde, would be a gathering place for the community and for Harvey's political causes.

The many volunteers and paid staff who worked at the Oscar Wilde found a place for their activism. The thousands of customers in the US and around the world found refuge through the shop's storefront space and mail-order connection. How many people like the Army private, Louis, found their footing through the Oscar Wilde and through individual letters of support from Rodwell himself? The buses that rolled from the doorstep of the Oscar Wilde to Philadelphia for the Annual Reminders made it safe and respectable for the community to gather and speak out.

Thousands of readers would have become grounded on the issues of gay liberation and the how-you-can-live guidance Rodwell provided in *QQ Magazine* and *The New York Hymnal*. As he banged away at his typewriter, he had no fear. He did not fear the Mafia and sought to expose their control of gay bars and the negative impact that had on the community starting with the first issue of *The Hymnal* in 1968. He did not fear them when he wrote the signature leaflet of the Stonewall riots – "Get the Mafia and the Cops Out of Gay Bars." Nor did he fear what might happen if he bellowed into the crowd on Christopher Street – "Gay Power!" He had no fear of the press and regularly tried to change their discriminatory policies. It is likely that his and Fred Sargeant's calls to the newspapers during the Stonewall riots were crucial in raising awareness of the bubbling gay rights movement. Rodwell had no fear of being first – at the first picket at the Induction Center, creating the Annual Reminders in Philadelphia, participating in the 1965 pickets, or sitting with Dick Leitsch and John Timmons at the sip-in at Julius'.

Rodwell did not put himself in these positions for self-aggrandizement. He did not seek leadership positions in the movement; in fact, he shunned them. He did not seek awards or recognition for past successes; he often turned them down. As an organizer, he could have positioned himself at the front of every Pride march in New York. He did not.

In 1986, as he was wrapping up his life story with historian Michael Scherker, he said his life and his job were one and the same:

> I'm sure a lot of other people would like to live their lives as openly and totally as a gay person as I have the privilege of doing. It's only because and through the support of other gay people and my family that it's been able to happen. I struggle. Many times it's been a struggle. But it's like you said, it is a constant progression.[21]

The thread through Craig's life and his impact on the community many years later is his lesson on how to think. His influence was cultural – at the big turning points in the movement, in the one-on-one support for individuals, and in the day-to-day skirmishes to root out the seeds of prejudice ... always pushing, guiding, and demanding dignity as the conscience of gay liberation.

Acknowledgments

I want to express my sincere thanks to the University of Toronto Press for bringing Craig's story to life, to Carli Hansen for believing in the project and taking the manuscript in, and to Janice Evans and Jenn Harris at UTP.

I am especially grateful to Martin Duberman for his early support and for granting me access to his hours of recorded interviews with Craig for use in this work, which made it possible for me to hear Craig's story in his own voice. Similarly, I was supported by the late Michael Scherker's oral history with Craig, which is central to this biography – thanks to Elliot and Steve Scherker. Kay Tobin Lahusen's interviews with Craig for *The Gay Crusaders*, archived at the New York Public Library, were also an important resource. Foster Gunnison's voluminous records at the University of Connecticut provided important insight into the details and accounting of the liberation movement, and my thanks to

Florence Search for making them available. Tim Wilson at the San Francisco Public Library, along with Bonnie Nadell and Joe Denneny, made it possible to access Randy Shilts' interview notes with Craig. I also had help from the Pacifica Radio Archives. Roger Williams at the Chicago Public Library helped me with some of the early orientation materials.

My sincere thanks go to all of those who set aside time for an interview with a writer they had never met before – Julia Noël Goldman, Fred Carl, Nan Buzard, Ellen Turner, David Stienecker, Deacon Maccubbin, Edmund White, Dean Oswalt, Jonathan Ned Katz, Candida Scott Piel, Ethan Geto, Ora McCreary, Kim Brinster, Bob McCullough, Jack Fritscher, and Tom Wilson Weinberg. I hope that their trust in me has been earned.

I was fortunate to speak with Ellen Broidy, who knew Craig well in the early days of the Oscar Wilde and whose insight was central to understanding the activism of the time. I am grateful for her patience with back-and-forth questions and details and to know of her own pivotal role in the movement. Thanks also to Ellen for graciously agreeing to read the manuscript.

My first editor was the great Michael Denneny, who knew Craig and believed a biography was overdue. I had hoped to rely on his expertise and friendship over the long term, but he passed away weeks after he concluded work on the manuscript. I was honored that he took it on and by his supportive comments. I continue to be inspired by his ground-breaking career.

The arrival of the COVID-19 pandemic made public research a challenge, but I was helped over this hurdle

Acknowledgments | 273

especially by Tal Nadan and the welcoming staff in the Manuscript and Archives Division at the New York Public Library, who patiently retrieved batch after batch of documents from Craig's papers, the Barbara Gittings and Kay Tobin Lahusen gay history papers and photographs, and who directed me to the Gale Archive of Sexuality and Gender. Thanks also to Lou McCarthy at the LGBT Community Center in New York for optimistically and kindly guiding me through the impressive documents, video, and audio records of The Center's archives. I am grateful to Eric Cervini for assembling and making available the massive Frank Kameny archive at the Library of Congress through the researchable Deviant's Archive.

I want to acknowledge the importance of the digital archives of dozens of printed newspapers to understanding the decades of news around Craig's life. They are truly the first draft of history.

I had valuable research help from Micah Farman in New York, who went on various missions at The Center and at the New York Public Library. And thanks to Scott Burgh for his expert research into court records in Chicago. I am also grateful for the assistance from Columbia University, Tim Wilson at the San Francisco Public Library, Jesús Lebrón, Steven Payne, and the Bronx Archives at the Bronx County Historical Society Research Library, the Lesbian Herstory Archives, and Dona Vitale and Stephanie Barto at the Rogers Park/West Ridge Historical Society.

I was fortunate to have access to Fred Sargeant's collection of George Desantis' *QQ Magazines*, which included Craig's essays and editorials and which brought context to gay life in the 1970s.

Many people took time to help me track down friends, colleagues, or acquaintances who had insights into Craig's life and activism. I'm grateful to Fred Carl, Tracy Baim, Randy Wicker, and Michael Glasser for taking the time to open the right doors. I'm especially grateful to one of those acquaintances, Brendan Fay, who not only shared his own inspiration from Craig and the Oscar Wilde Memorial Bookshop, but regularly unearthed items or articles that shed light on the importance of both. Special thanks also to Bruce Stores, who provided access to the Gay People in Christian Science pamphlet and other details of this lesser-known chapter in Craig's life.

I drew inspiration for this project from many people who had documented the gay liberation movement, but especially from Martin Duberman, David Carter, Kay Tobin Lahusen, Diana Davies, Fred McDarrah, Randy Shilts, Arthur Bell, Tracy Baim, Kate Davis and David Heilbronner, Rodger Streitmatter, Lillian Faderman, John D'Emilio, Eric Cervini, Toby Marotta, Michael G. Long, and Charles Kaiser. I also had help and direction from Duncan Osborne, Marc Stein, Mason Funk, and Mike Wasco.

The picture of Craig's life could not have been assembled without the help and permission of the caretakers of our historic photographers, the New York Public Library for the Kay Tobin Lahusen and Diana Davies collections, Saskia Scheffer at the Lesbian Herstory Archives, Gary O'Neil for Bettye Lane, Jonathan Silin for Robert Giard, and Amanda Kerner for Barbara Gluck Treaster. Likewise, Marion Rodwell Kastman's photo albums at the New York Public Library provided a candid look at her son's life.

Acknowledgments

I have done my best to track down permissions for documents and items related to this historic time, through archives, interviews, databases, internet searches, public records, newspaper accounts, and many cold calls. Despite my efforts and the accessibility of the digital age, there were times when people or organizations could not be found, and the trail went cold, but my appreciation has not.

I express deep gratitude for my first reader, my good friend and former public broadcasting colleague Heather Dieringer, who patiently listened to chapter after chapter, provided an ongoing reality check, and encouraged me to push through the rough patches.

I am, as always, sincerely grateful for the support of my longtime friend Debbie Bookchin, who added the role of beta reader to her own work as journalist, author, and editor.

The unwavering support of my family kept my spirits up as hurdles came and were cleared, as they suspected they would be.

But most of all, I am indebted to the support of my longtime partner and spouse Fred Sargeant, who introduced me to Craig's life and who endured a series of interviews starting in 2001 for some future project that finally took shape twenty years later. And for answering my almost daily questions about some detail or memory that would illuminate Craig Rodwell's life as the conscience of gay liberation.

Appendix A: *The New York Hymnal*, 1968

Editorial
February 1968

Across the United States, the homophile movement is expanding and maturing at an ever increasing rate.

However, New York lags behind in that none of the homophile organizations in this area have found much in the way of active and enthusiastic support among the homosexual community of New York (at least 500,000 in number).

Why?

Possibly because the present organizations are for the most part exclusionary in nature. They each limit their area of concern to either discussions, politics, counseling, etc.; this does not demean the fine work of these groups or say they aren't serving a highly useful and commendable function; however, the time has come in New York for the establishment of a homophile organization which will have a place in it for everyone, no matter what their particular area(s) of interest may be. In other words, the building of a sense of community and common concern.

A perfect example of what New York needs is the Society for Individual Rights (SIR) in San Francisco. In three years, it has opened a community center with varied social activities, a theater, a storefront and has become a force to be reckoned with in San Francisco. Candidates for public office seek their support and, in turn, SIR supports candidates who show a genuine and involved concern with the particular issues facing the homosexual community in that city. SIR now has the active support of 3,500 of San Francisco's homosexual community, which is proof positive of the effectiveness of their work.

The same thing can and must be done in New York City.

Mafia on the Spot
February 1968

Although it has been common knowledge among New York's homosexual community for many years, the Mafia (or "The Syndicate") control of New York City's gay bars has only recently been brought to the public's attention.

The New York Times, starting in early October of 1967, ran a number of front page articles on the Mafia and, in particular, on the Mafia's control of gay bars. The *Times* named John (Sonny) Franzese as kingpin of the Syndicate's gay bar operations on Long Island; and in subsequent articles they identified the heads of the Manhattan gay bar syndicate.

The Stone Wall [sic] on Christopher St. in Greenwich Village is one of the larger and more financially lucrative of the Mafia's gay bars in Manhattan. *New York HYMNAL* received a report from a reliable source over a month ago that the Stone Wall was going to be closed by the Health Department because it was alleged that a number of cases of Hepatitis (which has reached epidemic proportions among the homosexual community) had been traced to the Stone Wall's bar. It was reported that the Stone Wall does not wash the glasses.

In an attempt to check out these reports, *New York HYMNAL* made a number of calls to the Health Department's Sanitary inspection Office. To put it mildly, we received a "runaround" – and doubletalk, lines being disconnected and a direct refusal to connect us with the Legal Department. Similar calls to the State Liquor Authority received the same treatment.

The case of the Stone Wall only points up the fact that the Community cannot rely on governmental agencies to break the Mafia control of gay bars until the day comes that pay-off and collusion between the Syndicate and governmental agencies are ended.

How can you identify a gay bar as being Mafia?

1. When you walk in, there will be at least one or two "gray goons" sitting near the door checking out everyone as they enter. If it's a Mafia "private club" like the Stone Wall or the Bon Soir, and you are wearing a jacket and tie and don't fit the Mafia's stereotype of a "fairy," the goons at the door will refuse to let you in.

2. The bar will be dark – to hide the filth and to give the place an atmosphere of "anything goes."

3. On Friday and Saturday nights, it will cost you $3 or $4 to get in and they will give you 2 tickets for drinks.

4. There will very likely be dancing in a back room hidden from view when you enter the bar.

5. Policemen will make periodic and mysterious appearances to talk with the goons at the door.

6. The general atmosphere will be one of licentiousness and gloom.

Gay bars in Manhattan's Greenwich Village that fit generally the above description include the Stone Wall, Bon Soir, Danny's, The Den, The Skull, Telstar, Keller's, Checkmate, 17 Barrow and the Sea Colony.

The situation as it now exists makes it virtually impossible for a legitimate businessman to open a gay bar with a healthy social atmosphere. And the only way the situation is going to change for the better is for homosexuals to stop patronizing bars run by concealed Mafia interests. We cannot rely on governmental agencies in this fight. The Mafia monopoly on gay bars has existed in New York for decades and the City government has shown no interest. When the Department of Investigations of the City of New York was asked if they were planning any steps to break the Mafia monopoly, we received the standard, "No Comment."

Mafia Control of Gay Bars
March 1968

Since the founding of the Tavern Guild of San Francisco, the gay bars in that city have become models for the rest of the country of what a gay bar can and should be.

Founded in 1964, the Tavern Guild of San Francisco (TGSF) quickly became the focal point of the homosexual community in San Francisco in its fight to improve the operating conditions and atmospheres of the bars. The TGSF is composed of owners and operators of gay bars and taverns. It protects its members' businesses from harassment or abuse by authorities, which has virtually eliminated the problem of payoffs. The TGSF's main contribution to the improvement in the social atmosphere in San Francisco has been its firmness in resisting infiltration efforts by organized crime (the Mafia, Cosa Nostra, Syndicate, or whatever-you-want-to-call-it).

The result of the TGSF's work is evident to anyone who visits San Francisco's gay bars. Many of the bars have benefit nights for the various homophile organizations and donate one night's profits to them. They also show old movies, have ten-cent beer nights, support the homophile publications of S.F. by advertising in them, and in general, make their customers feel welcome and "at home."

A Tavern Guild of New York is impossible at the moment for the simple fact that there is only one gay bar in the city which is not Mafia-run. However, the day is coming when there will be a number of legitimate gay bars in New York who will form a Tavern Guild, or something similar. Until that day, one of the major problems of the homosexual community will continue to be the lack of a healthy social atmosphere.

Martin Luther King Jr.
April 1968

Many of us who are homosexual and who have grown up in the past ten years, a period in American history that has seen the rise of the civil rights and civil liberties movement as embodied in the spirit and ideals of Martin Luther King, feel a special loss at his assassination.

Tens of thousands of homosexual Americans, particularly those of us under 30, have come to realize that we, too, like the Negro, have a right to claim our share of the American dream. Also, like the Negro, we are beginning to assert our dignity and self-respect as witnessed by the rapid growth of the homophile movement in the past few years.

While Martin Luther King directed his efforts in behalf of the Negro cause, those same ideals and principles he represented are just as applicable to homosexual Americans: For it is the same kind of thinking in society that denies dignity and self-respect to Negroes and homosexuals – a society which feels it must have a scapegoat to justify its own short-comings.

To paraphrase Martin Luther King, a man dies when he refuses out of fear to assert his dignity and self-respect. America, and the homosexuals in particular, would do well to heed the lesson and example of this man's life. America is the most noble experiment in the history of man, and we must make it work.

McCarthy Wins Poll
May 1968

In the first sampling taken in New York City of the preferences of homosexual voters, Sen. Eugene McCarthy (Dem.–Minn.) has emerged the winner with 23% of the total vote and 50% of the Democratic vote. Runner-up to McCarthy was Sen. Robert Kennedy (Dem.–N.Y.) with 18% of the total and 39% of the Democratic vote. Among GOP voters, Gov. Nelson Rockefeller won with 37% of the vote. Mayor Lindsay was the second choice of GOP voters with 31% and Nixon a poor third with only 10%.

The results:

	#	%		#	%
McCarthy	61	23.0	Reagan	6	2.0
Kennedy	48	18.0	Benjamin Spock	5	2.0
Rockefeller	34	13.0	Chuck Percy	5	2.0
Lindsay	28	11.0	Dick Gregory	4	1.5
Nixon	9	3.0	Fulbright	3	1.0
Johnson	7	2.5	Undecided	31	12.0

(The remaining votes were one or two for General Gavin, Ted Kennedy, Martin Luther King, George Wallace, George Kennan, Fred Halstead, Winthrop Rockefeller, Henry Cabot Lodge, Romney, Goldwater, Mark Hatfield, Margaret Chase Smith, Adlai Stevenson, Jr., Humphrey, Pat Paulsen and Snoopy.)

The poll of 263 homosexual voters was conducted by the Homophile Opinion Poll, a project of the Homophile Youth Movement (HYMN).

Both McCarthy's and Kennedy's popularity among homosexuals is another evidence of their respective appeals to minority groups. The two candidates who lead the national opinion polls, Nixon and Humphrey, received between them only 10% in the Homophile Opinion Poll.

The poor showing of so-called "conservatives" such as Reagan and Wallace puncture another hole in the myth that the homosexual voter is more conservative than other minority groups. The total "conservative" vote in the poll was 3%.

Mayor Lindsay's good showing, with 31% of the GOP votes, is seen as a reflection of his civil libertarian policies which have had a great effect on the lives of homosexuals in New York City in the past couple of years.

Although Kennedy came in second, many people expressed their hostility to him because of his role in the Army-McCarthy hearings in the 50s, which had anti-homosexual overtones.

One of the purposes of the Homophile Opinion Poll and of HYMN is to encourage homosexuals to participate in our country's political life. Other surveys of homosexual voters have shown that a minority of homosexuals are registered to vote and that less than 35% actually vote.

The Homophile Opinion Poll will conduct two more polls – one which will be released before the conventions in August and the other before the election in November.

Robert F. Kennedy
June–July 1968

Once again our nation has been degraded by an act of political assassination, Robert F. Kennedy only being the latest in a series of such acts of violence during the past decade. However, in a society where it is socially acceptable for gangs of so-called men to go out on the town and "beat up a queer," or for a jury to let a defendant off on a murder charge because the man he murdered was a homosexual, the increasing tone and acceptance of violence is not surprising.

And this is the society that paradoxically calls the homosexual "sick." To the contrary, *we* live in a *sick* society, and only a concerted effort on the part of millions of people can begin to reshape it into a decent and healthy society where respect for our fellow man is practiced.

We live in an era where nothing is more needed as a commitment by millions of people to stand up for what they believe in, yet up to now have been either afraid or too timid to act on that belief. We contend that society's psychosis regarding sexuality, and particularly homosexuality, is one of the factors contributing to the general "sickness" of society. For too long, the homosexual has hidden in dark corners and let himself or herself be blackmailed by society into a silent and demeaning submission to prejudice and hate.

By the homosexual's silence he inadvertently lends his support and encouragement to society to go right on keeping the homosexual minority in an inferior position. Many homosexuals, particularly younger ones, are beginning to ask themselves which is more important, to stand up to society and demand justice and equal treatment or to cower in the shadows in fear. The best job in the world or all the money in the world cannot buy self-respect and dignity – only a commitment on our part to become active in the forces of what is good in our society can give us self-respect and dignity.

For those of you who have decided to become committed to a decent society, one of the first steps you can take in that direction is to join the hundreds of people, homosexual and heterosexual, who are going to Philadelphia on July 4th to remind the American people that there are approximately 15,000,000 homosexual American citizens who demand the application of our Constitutional guarantees on their behalf.

Gay Power Gains
August–September 1968

On July 17th, the *Wall Street Journal* printed a lead, front-page article on the growing militancy of American homosexuals in their fight for "a piece of the action" in this country. Considering who reads the *Journal* – members of Congress, the

President, leading businessmen and opinion makers – this is one of the most significant developments concerning the homosexual to date. It is said that the *Wall Street Journal* is six months ahead of society in indicating trends. They obviously received a wide reaction to the article because in August, they devoted an issue's "Letters to the Editor" column to the article.

Another development in the growth of Gay Power was the adoption by the North American Conference of Homophile Organizations of the slogan "Gay is Good." The NACHO held its 4th Conference in Chicago the week of August 13–17 and received national publicity, particularly on its program to seek out the various candidates for office this Fall and elicit their views on issues of concern to the homosexual communities. The Homophile Youth Movement (HYMN) is a member of NACHO. In adopting the slogan "Gay is Good," the NACHO took a cue from our black brothers' slogan, "Black is Beautiful."

The homophile organizations in New York City, through the New York Committee of Cooperation, are considering publishing a directory of businesses and professional individuals who support the homophile movement and urging the homosexual community to support those establishments listed as another way of developing Gay Power. Considering the billions of dollars that homosexuals put into the economy every year, this idea has a tremendous practical use.

Other recent developments in the growth of the Gay Power concept have been the success of the WBAI (99.5 FM) radio program, "The New Symposium," on Mondays at 11 PM; a civil suit instituted by two individuals in New York City to stop the Bureau of Social Services to end their discrimination in hiring homosexuals as case workers; the establishment in New York City of a Council on Religion and the Homosexual; the increasing sensitivity of politicians of not offending the homosexual voter (Nelson Rockefeller, in a press conference, said that he saw no reason for discriminating against homosexuals in government employment, except for the blackmail angle); and, most important of all, a trend among our homosexual youth not to settle for a "double life."

Appendix B: *QQ Magazine*, 1970–1971

How It Is Gay Liberation
Fall 1970

Gay power is at best a nebulous concept. To some it signifies the coming of a new day, when homosexuals will no longer bear distinctive labels or be (singled) out as being significantly different from society at large – when homosexuality will be just one more sexual expression. To others gay power means liberation within an establishment framework, freedom to live freely as a society within a society, with its own rules and on its own terms. Still others are not as concerned with social acceptance as they are with sexual freedom; this group is primarily concerned with the elimination of laws forbidding sex between "consenting adults of the same sex."

The means of achieving these goals vary widely, ranging from passive dialogue in intellectual circles to Marxism to militant violence on the streets. Collectively, individuals and groups actively engaged in accomplishing the above-mentioned goals are known as the Gay Liberation

Movement – and it all started in New York late one Friday evening in June of 1969.

When I arrived on the scene the police were raiding the Stonewall, at that time the largest and most popular gay discotheque in New York City. Christopher Street, just off Sheridan Square in Greenwich Village, was mobbed with the patrons and onlookers, mostly gay. The help and some customers were being arrested for the sale and consumption of alcohol on unlicensed premises. But the gay crowd interpreted the raid as just another affront on homosexuals, and for the first time in our history united and made their feelings known publicly: "Gay Power" and "Get the Mafia out of Gay Bars" we chanted. (Because of an "unholy alliance" between some law enforcement agencies and the syndicate that controls many gay businesses, gay people are often caught in the middle when "internal conflicts" lead to raids, etc.) We flung pennies, rocks, and bottles at the police (who were greatly outnumbered), forcing them to withdraw inside the Stonewall for protection.

What happened then and on succeeding nights for the next week is now history. Thousands of gay men and women went into the streets (primarily Christopher Street) in a display of anger and determination to turn a new leaf in homosexual history. It was a beautiful sight to see hundreds of gay couples holding hands and chanting "Gay Power," closing down Christopher Street from Greenwich Avenue to Sheridan Square (about three city blocks) and only letting cars with gay people in them get by. To put it mildly, it was an embarrassment for the police to have to call out the Tactical Patrol Force (riot police) for seven nights in a row to control homosexuals. There wasn't much violence – a few fires, a couple of broken store windows, some minor police injuries – but the new and entirely unexpected spirit of gay people, who for the first time in history were refusing to run and hide, was being publicly displayed.

This new pride and determination among our people was the lesson and example of the "Christopher Street Uprisings of 1969." Since then, the rapid growth of this spirit among gay men and women throughout the country has been astounding. There are now dozens of Gay Lib groups (which function under various names) in major cities across the country, as well as on 50 campuses. To name just a few colleges which have formed homophile organizations: Northwestern University; University of Chicago; University of Illinois; University of Wisconsin; University of Minnesota; University of Michigan; MIT; Harvard University; Boston University; New York University; Columbia University; City College of New York; University of California; Stanford University.

The primary effect has been on young people, but a questioning of old fears and assumptions is also evident among the over-25 generation. Some of these are:

The idea that gay men and women must bear distinctive labels which have unattractive connotations. Helen Niehaus is the president of the Society of Anubis in California, which is one of the largest gay social groups for men and women, and she said recently: "I am not a citizen of the Isle of Lesbos. I am a female homosexual and wish to be called such." As a direct result of Miss Niehaus' comments, the Western Regional Conference of Homophile Organizations passed a resolution urging the use of the term "male and female homosexuals" as opposed to "lesbians and homosexuals." The term "lesbian" is rapidly going the way of such labels as Negroes and Jewess as more and more gay people realize the need for unity among homosexual men and women in our common cause.

The idea that gay people, of necessity, should lead a double life to function in society. Before the Christopher Street incident it was rare to find anyone who told his or her parents, friends, and employer that he was gay. In the past year it has become quite common to hear of someone who has just declared himself. It is important, however, to point out here the thinking behind this: It is not to shock or alienate, but rather it is an expression of pride and self-respect in one's homosexual identity. There is a realization that the double-life idea is self-defeating and indicative of a deep-seated guilt instilled in one by a society which attempts to force on all its citizens the heterosexual lifestyle ethic.

The idea of role-playing in a homosexual relationship, e.g., butch and femme. What is emerging, in my opinion, is a definition of the homosexual relationship as a partnership of equals, emphasizing their commonality in personality, character, and sexual awareness. The idea of "butch" and "femme," or "husband" and "wife" roles is clearly an intrusion of heterosexual values on the homosexual personality.

There is not, of course, unanimity among the many Gay Lib groups on any of these ideas; only time will determine whether my observations are correct or not. If I may quote Henry Hay, founder of one of the first homophile organizations, who said recently at a California Gay Lib conference:

> The first (homophile) movement called homosexuals to a brotherhood of love and trust. It called on homosexuals to rediscover their collective – as well as personal – self-respect and integrity. It raised into consciousness, for the first time, the concept of the homosexual minority, complete with its own sub-culture, with its own lifestyles. It struggled to perceive – however dimly … that, in some measure, the homosexual minority actually looked out upon the world through a somewhat different window than did their heterosexual brothers and sisters … a world view neither better nor inferior….
>
> It took 16 years for the movement to return to that first gay liberation ideal, after a long interval of seeking respectability rather than self-respect; parliamentary individualism rather

than the collective trust of brotherhood; law reform and quiet assimilation rather than a community of rich diversity with the Family of Man. One might say that they sought to be exactly the same as the DAR – except in bed.

Hay called upon his audience to "recognize that homosexuals are and always have been, through their oppression and in spite of brainwashing, a Free People ... a minority that shares each other's dream, that redirects the aggressive fighting instincts, competitiveness and inherited animal maleness and femaleness of the parent culture into appreciation of – nay, even a lifelong passion to call forth, the grace and tenderness ... the humility and compassion ... (of our) shared commonality of outlook ... challenging us to break loose from the lockstep expectations of heterosexual life patterns so obliterating of our own natures. Our homosexual liberation movement must consist of far-ranging communities of free spirits." Amen.

The Tarnished Golden Rule
February 1971

A common argument against the gay liberation movement offered by some gay people goes something like this: "What do I need gay lib for? I *am* liberated. Sure, I have to play it cool at the office and reassure my family that I just haven't met the right girl yet, but I've got a good job and a groovy lover ... I'm liberated!"

After a few years of this kind of "liberated" existence such people become oblivious and completely unseeing of straight prejudice and – to coin a phrase – the "hetero-sexism" surrounding them virtually 24 hours a day. We are all bombarded incessantly with heterosexual-supremacist subliminal advertising from the happy hetero family pictures on our breakfast cereals in the morning to the commercials on the late news telling us that this or that after-shave lotion will get us a big-bosomed woman.

As gay people living in 1970 America, we are being called upon to reexamine our own lives with all of our compromises to hetero-sexism and to become conscious (at the very least) of the prejudices directly or indirectly confronting us. We should recognize that straights do *not* do unto others as they do unto themselves. A few examples may shatter your illusions about some of our American institutions as they pertain to homosexual citizens.

In 1967 I opened a "bookshop of the homophile movement," my small contribution to the battle against hetero-sexism. While my commercial interests were not as strong as my desire to carry books, pamphlets, periodicals, etc., all with a positive gay theme to help raise the self-image of gay people, I still needed to advertise, mainly because the shop was and still is on a side street and could not exist on sidewalk traffic. Assuming our local "liberal" weekly newspaper, *The Village Voice*, would accept my ad, I delivered it to a clerk. The following day I received a phone call: The clerk dutifully informed me that I could not use the word "gay" in my ad, and that furthermore, she thought we were all "sick and perverted." I then wrote to the publisher, explaining my position in a long and thoughtful (I think) letter, asking for a few minutes of his time, at his convenience, in order to discuss the matter. No response. Only by submitting the euphemism "homophile" for "gay" did I manage to get my ad in – which was stripped clean of "offensive expressions" according to the *VV* dictate. More recently the *VV* was forced to permit the use of the word "gay" in advertising, thanks to the efforts of gay lib groups who picketed and met with the editors. In spite of this *QQ Magazine* has never been permitted to advertise, because those in charge feel its editorial nature is offensive. Moreover, *QQ* has been denied advertising space in other publications even one which is notoriously gay in its choice of subjects and whose editor is as gay as pink ink. These incidents are typical of the prejudice in advertising in general, especially those businesses run by closet queens who are especially fearful of gay associations.

I also publish a small periodical, which has the same purpose as the bookshop but which extends its influence beyond New York City. It contains no physique photos, no lurid stories, no sex ads, etc., and yet I always have difficulty finding a printer to run it. When I do manage to get someone who is willing, I am overcharged – a consequence of existing prejudice which puts the printer in a position to demand more, and myself in a position to pay up or give up. I know other small publishers of gay materials constantly experience the same problem. Difficulty is also encountered at the post office whenever mailing permits are applied for – all part of a carefully orchestrated resistance against homosexuality by straight society.

Recently I had to renegotiate a lease on my store front and was made to pay considerably more than other shops in my area – because my landlord knew I would have trouble locating elsewhere and could demand an increase and get it. My shop does not pretend to be straight. It must therefore be subjected to the prejudices of straight society, and specifically to those exercised by landlords who prefer not to have "perverted" tenants. I have also been denied insurance because my shop has been classified "political," hence, subject to violence.

My shop has been vandalized on these occasions. Windows have been smashed, shelves torn down, books ripped and piled on the floor. Once a swastika was painted on the door, along with a charming slogan, "Kill All Fags!"

We receive threatening phone calls at least 10 times weekly. Just recently we had a rash of hate letters and calls, threatening to kill us and burn the shop down. While my clerks and I have become used to such threats, this particular individual, what with his six letters and 20 phone calls a day prompted me to seek help from the "Annoyance Call Bureau" of the New York Telephone Company (I got the grand run-around after the nature of the calls was learned) and the FBI, because I had been able to determine that the threats were originating from another state, making it a federal incident. Several days after making my report the FBI informed me it would make "no active investigation in the matter." Why should it? After all, consider how many killers of "fags" are automatically given light sentences by most judges – because "indecent homosexual advances" prompted murder.

Homosexuals are crucified by straight society in many ways. It's done in small ways. For example, a major cola company refused to permit the producer of "The Boys in the Band" to display a cola sign at the party which takes place in the play – in spite of the fact that the sign is so established no one would notice it anyway because the directors of the cola company did not want to give the impression that "queers drank their soda."

A new movie called "The Bar" takes place in a gay bar. It examines the lives of various patrons. One is an airlines pilot. Naturally, the director had hoped to use an airport for some scenes. Not one major airline would consent. Everyone approached did not want to convey the impression that their planes were being flown by "fairies." The same director was denied clothing by a major haberdasher in New York, because he felt if homosexuals were shown wearing his clothes it would affect his national sales adversely (he has a mail order business in addition to running shops) – in spite of the fact that he has gotten rich on gay money and is gay himself.

Sometimes straight prejudice cuts deeply. Eleven years ago, when QQ publisher George Desantis was 23 and had two years of teaching college speech under his belt, and two years of class instruction for his master's, it was learned he was a homosexual. In spite of the fact that he had been an excellent teacher and had already completed his courses and was only hours away from receiving his diploma, he was confronted by officials and asked to leave. His diploma was denied because Purdue University did not feel "a person of his kind should represent the university." A teaching job which he had already accepted at another university had to be chucked. A brilliant career was squelched. Being strong-willed, he recovered in a time when gay liberation could hardly be imagined and through the years has turned defeat into success through multiple business enterprises which are all gay.

And so, dear reader, if you ask what gay liberation is all about, it is simply this: Only through organized resistance of straight oppression and insistence on our rights as human beings will we ever win a rightful place in society. Not just one of tolerance or mere acceptance, but of total integration in a world which must eventually provide equality for all – be black, white, yellow, straight, or gay. The movement needs your support. It desperately needs the support of responsible homosexual citizens. Gay lib groups are springing up everywhere. I urge you to pitch in and lend a helping hand – in silence if you must. No one likes revolutions. But we must look to history for our lesson, to Blacks for their advancement in recent years, and we must also strive to find our place in a world which is ours as much as theirs, and in doing so find a new kind of freedom for ourselves and those who follow our way of life.

Hanging In Together
April 1971

The gay liberation movement is not monolithic or of a single mind; there are many sharp differences in approach, style, and goals among the 200 or so gay lib organizations around the US. There are even gay people in some of these groups (notably the Gay Liberation Front) who don't regard other gay groups who don't mouth a "radical rhetoric" as being part of gay liberation. (Personally, I think that view is myopic at best and authoritarian-minded at worst. To my mind, any group of gay people who join together to improve our collective or self-status is a part of the gay liberation movement.)

For the purpose of clarifying the differences between the various organizations, I will divide them into three general categories – radical, militant activist, and social service:

Radical. Gay lib groups that fall into this general category include the Gay Liberation Front (branches in Los Angeles, Berkeley, New York, Philadelphia, and a few smaller cities around the US); radical lesbians; and many of the college campus organizations (Gay Students Liberations, New York University; Madison Alliance for Homosexual Equality, University of Wisconsin; Gay Liberation, San Francisco State College; and GLF, Iowa State – among others). Some members actually advocate physical violence as a means of achieving goals, and while this attitude is not typical of so-called "gay radicals" (who identify with Marxism, etc., and support such groups as the Black Panthers), the general public usually attributes violence to these groups because they have come to regard certain aggressive acts performed by a handful as typical.

Militant Activist. Generally included in this group are the Gay Activist Alliance (New York); Chicago Gay Alliance; Metropolitan Community Church (Los Angeles, Miami, Phoenix, Chicago, Honolulu, San Diego, and San Francisco); Homophile Union of Boston; Kalos Society (Hartford); and some of the student groups. Orderly demonstrations, sit-ins, direct confrontations with politicians, etc., are typical examples of how these groups operation.

Social Service. Included in this group are the organizations which primarily deal with the homosexual on an individual basis through social activities, discussion groups, counseling, referrals, etc., such as the Mattachine Society (San Francisco, Chicago, New York, Washington); West Side Discussion Group (New York) Daughters of Bilitis (Los Angeles, San Francisco, Cleveland, Reno, New York); Institute for Social Ethics (Hartford). These groups almost always function within a straight framework of social acceptability.

One of the main issues dividing people in the movement, both intraorganizational and interorganizational, is the question of gay separation: Should we work toward a separate society for gay people, or should we work to integrate the homosexual into society at large? The leading advocates of separation are Don Jackson of Berkeley and Craig Schoonmaker of Homosexuals Intransigent (New York). You have surely read of Don Jackson's involvement in getting gay people to take over Alpine County in California. His plan works something like this:

First, about 400 gay men and women will move en masse to Alpine County (located on the California-Nevada border near Lake Tahoe) to establish residence and after three months' residency they will register to vote. The next step would be to have a recall election to throw out of office all the straight politicians (at present there are only about 300 registered voters in Alpine County) and then elect gay people to all the vacated offices. After the takeover of Alpine County is effected, they would then work to take over the state of Nevada through much the same process, only, of course, involving tens of thousands of gay men and women.

On the east coast, Craig Schoonmaker is working to get gay people to move into already-heavily-gay-populated areas in New York City (Greenwich Village, Manhattan's West 60s and 70s, Brooklyn Heights) and eventually to elect gay congressmen or congresswomen to represent gay people in the national government.

The principal opposition to the gay separatists has come from the social service groups and various gay newspapers; and most of the support, particularly for the takeover of Alpine County, has come from individuals. At this writing, over 500 people have signed up to move into Alpine County in the first wave, scheduled for early 1971. I heard on a TV newscast the other night that already the County officials have threatened to call out the National Guard to repel the "invasion."

While I personally would not be about to take up roots and move to Alpine County, I can see great good coming out of the effort if it is not dominated and dictated to by the "radical rhetorics." None of us would even be thinking of the idea of gay ghettoes if we did not live in a society which legislates against our lifestyle, denies us our self-respect (or, at least it attempts to), denies us employment and justifies murder if the victim is "queer."

Another issue which is stirring up dust in the gay lib movement (as it is in other movements) is whether we, as homosexual men and women, should work within the present system to further our goals or whether we should, to put it bluntly, support the "revolution."

Again, this issue crosses organizational lines except for the social service groups, which are wholly committed to working within the system. While the radical groups describe themselves as revolutionary, many of the individuals in them are, to varying degrees, in favor of working within the system.

It was over this issue of revolution vs. evolution that a number of the militant activist groups were formed as a breakaway from the "revolutions" in the Gay Liberation Front – e.g., Gay Activists Alliance. Good points on both sides have been won: Through the support of GAA in New York, a congresswoman and a New York state assemblyman were elected; and through the pressure of GLFers, Huey Newton issued a statement in support of gay liberation and Castro has apparently relaxed his harsh treatment of homosexuals in Cuba.

My personal opinion is that we as gay people should look to the examples of what has happened in other revolutions around the world. Virtually all of the resulting fascist-communist dictatorships which came to power after revolutions (Cuba, Russia, Algeria, Indonesia, etc.) have resulted in severe and barbarous repression of homosexuals. While, admittedly, we have a long way to go in the United States before gay people are granted even the most basic rights, I feel we have no other viable choice for the time being, at least, but to work within the present system. Of course, if a fascist dictatorship comes in this country, as recently predicted by Billy Graham, I will be the first one to support a revolution as I think most other gay people will. It is no secret that we are not any better liked by the extremists on the right than we are by those on the left. Homosexuals seem to be the only universally accepted scapegoat for the right and the left; and for that reason, we have much more to gain through peaceful and orderly change.

In spite of the many differences on issues and methods which divide the organizations and people, in general, it is important to remember that our commonality is much greater than the sum total of our differences. All of us, as gay people, suffer from basically the same prejudices, myths, unjust laws and policies. We must strive to join together to demonstrate our solidarity – and in unison win our freedom.

Johnny Cop Wants You!
The Homosexual and the Law
June 1971

The law as it applies to homosexuals has been the subject of numerous articles and books in recent years. Most of them have dealt with law reform; that is, removing from the statute books the laws which attempt to proscribe what consenting adults of the same sex may do with each other sexually. While it is quite true that we have advanced somewhat concerning law reform (an example being Illinois, where homosexuals have experienced greater legal rights for years), the fact remains that interpretation of the law has remained virtually unchanged.

The laws in this country and in most other places function according to heterosexual dictate, and within a straight framework. Wherever the term "consenting adults" is used there is great room for individual interpretation because the concept is subject to prevailing social mores and cannot be enforced. There are so many loopholes that an extremely hostile law enforcement agent can interpret the law to suit himself and legally wreak havoc on homosexuals.

For example, Riis Park – a bathing beach, which is located about an hour from mid-Manhattan, by public transportation – has an entirely gay section which is packed on weekends. On the busiest Sundays of the summer – the Memorial Day and Labor Day weekends – plainclothes lawmen station themselves on the boardwalk outside the bath house and give tickets for violation of park regulations which specify that the "legal" limit for men's bathing suits is mid-way between the knee and thigh, and covering the navel. This is only one of countless laws regulating "decency" which have remained on the books for decades, and which have little general application today. Straights would not stand for enforcement of such a silly law, and would react swiftly and even violently if the matter were pressed, but the average gay guy who is ticketed for violation of this law usually does not object and simply pays the fine. The police have a "quota" of tickets to give out on these particular weekends. Naturally, gay guys – who are always "up" on the latest swimsuits – are easy marks.

Nine years ago, I was ticketed. I objected strenuously and accused the officer of "harassing gay people" and he knew he was doing just that. But it wasn't as safe to speak up in those days as it is today, and I was grabbed by the scruff of my neck and hauled off to a private room in the bath house. There he called me a lot of names, such as "Faggot!" and "Queer!" – knocked me to the floor and pressed me for my name and address. I decided to remain silent. He picked me up and literally dragged me to the local precinct, where I was locked in a cell. Later that night I was taken to Night Court in lower Manhattan.

As I stood before the judge, bare-footed and in my swimsuit, I was asked why I refused to speak. I related my story. The judge took me aside and in a fatherly way apologized for the treatment I had received and informed me that I was free to go but that I would have to appear in court a couple of weeks later and pay a $10 or $15 fine. (It should be noted here that this judge was the only kind lawman I encountered during my ordeal.)

To make a long story short, when I appeared in court two weeks later the judge realized I was gay and immediately became hostile. He ordered me to pay $25 or spend three days in jail. I tried to explain that I had only $21 with me, because I was led to believe (by the first judge) that the fine would be $15 or less. He yelled for the bailiff and ordered him to take me away.

I was fingerprinted and handcuffed and put in a van. When I arrived at the Brooklyn House of Detention I heard one particularly big and menacing officer say to a guard "This faggot refuses to speak." Word had gotten around. The guard smashed my head against the bars and knocked my wallet to the floor. "Pick it up, Faggot!" he yelled. I really couldn't believe it was happening to me – for "violation" of a silly law which in no way is applicable in the usual sense today – but it was. Then I was put in a "Queen's Tank," which every jail has – a separate cell for homosexuals. I didn't mind this (in fact, it probably protected me from being raped by aggressive straights – a common occurrence in all jails), but I did mind denial of certain "privileges" for the three days I remained imprisoned – commissary rights (for toilet paper, sugar, candy, etc.), movies, outdoor recreation. Moreover, my head was shaved – something which is not done to straight "prisoners."

My point in relating this incident is that regardless of what the law books say, we as homosexuals are discriminated against by individual law enforcement interpretation – and we are at the mercy of Johnny Cop. Old laws are being used to harass gay people. Just recently, a specific interpretation of a valid law, but a law which would not have been used if a heterosexual were involved, was applied to deny a homosexual a driver's license in Connecticut. The law, concerning the rights of ex-convicts (the man was imprisoned on a morals charge), would not have been used had the applicant been straight – as "society had been paid." But because the man was gay and had a "gay criminal record" – discrimination was based on his homosexuality.

As a child growing up in the Midwest, I was taught to respect the police and the courts. But as a homosexual adult in New York City, I have learned that a gay person must always be on guard against the police and the courts. I have seen too many payoffs to policemen by Mafia-types in gay bars; I have noted too many incidents of harassment of gay people without justification; I have read about too many murder cases involving gay victims where the heterosexual killer got off light because he "resisted homosexual advances." To top things off, the International Association of Police Chiefs in convention recently voted unanimously to actively oppose political candidates who favor homosexual law reform.

It has become painfully clear to me that "laws" are made and enforced by and for heterosexual men. One of the goals of gay liberation is a just society in which laws are made and enforced by and for all people. Gay people have been historically patient and quiet, and meek – but the anger and frustration that is daily building in our community must be recognized and channeled. The Christopher Street Riots in 1969 put the nation on notice that we are not as patient and quietly and meek as they believed. Since then we have made some advancement if only in increased concern and involvement in law reform among gay people who are protesting loudly. We must be heard … we will be heard.

In future issues of *QQ Magazine* I will discuss other aspects of the homosexual and the law which concern our community. And the law should concern all gay people because we are equally vulnerable. There are certain "basics" we should be aware of. For example, in the area of arrest, while it might serve a heterosexual to cooperate with the police by giving whatever information is asked for, the homosexual being arrested should be reasonably cooperative, but should not give out more information than his name and address until he sees his lawyer – lest that information be misinterpreted and used against him by the prejudiced. Moreover, homosexuals must always be on guard against certain ploys used by the police, an example being the "Beauty and the Beast Approach" used to interrogate homosexuals. Two officers will question you, one pretending to be especially hostile, the other trying to be your "friend." As soon as the hostile guy leaves, the homosexual – believing he has found a kind ear – tells everything ... and finds himself in a lot of trouble.

Then there is the matter of finding a lawyer, which I will also discuss at length later on. Generally speaking, finding a good lawyer is like finding a good doctor – and you just can't do it by running to the Yellow Pages in an emergency. Ask around. At least one of your friends has probably had an experience with a lawyer. It's a good idea, when you're not in need, to visit that lawyer, in order to "size him up." Most lawyers are happy to meet prospective clients, and there is no charge. If you haven't done this, and if you are arrested, contact the nearest branch of the American Civil Liberties Union; they will assist you in finding someone who is experienced in your kind of cases. If you are indigent, seek help from the Legal Aid Society (note: similar organizations operate under various names in different cities). If, after being arrested, you have time to seek help from a local homophile organization, all the better. But don't go in "blind." Never pour out your life story to someone you are not sure of (and this you must base on the past experience of friends, and hearsay). For instance, among certain homophile "leaders" there are individuals who misuse their position and milk those in trouble for information – which they use to their advantage ... by passing the information on to criminals who use it to blackmail you later on, or rob your apartment when you're out. The fact that a man heads a homophile organization is no mark of his personal character. Another common practice among these unscrupulous few men who should be put out of office is to bleed those in trouble by referring them to shyster lawyers who charge outrageous fees, and then "kickback" part of that fee; it's a nice living for some "leaders" who are otherwise unemployed.

We have a long way to go before laws are changed favorably for homosexuals – and an even greater distance before mere interpretation of general laws changes so that individuals cannot twist words to our disadvantage. With each passing day we are gaining strength – and the more YOU become involved in these matters, the faster will we all achieve the rights we are entitled to – and which we so justly deserve.

What to Do When You're Arrested
August 1971

In my 10 years of Gay Liberation involvement I have talked to scores of people who had been arrested for the first time for a Gay-related offense – entrapment in a Gay bar, spied on in a tearoom, "soliciting" on the street, loitering for the purpose of "committing deviate sexual acts," etc., people who wished they had acquainted themselves beforehand of the practices, or malpractices, of their local police regarding the homosexual. Just because you've never been arrested, don't think it can't happen to you; you owe it to yourself to become familiar with your local police attitudes and practices concerning treatment of Gay people.

Law enforcement and judicial attitudes differ greatly from state to state and city to city. The only common denominator is that if you're a Gay man living in the United States your chances of being arrested for a "crime" which for a heterosexual man would be considered excusable, or non-criminal (holding hands and kissing in public; going to "singles" bars to make out, approaching someone on the street you are attracted to), are much greater. So, before you are arrested, become familiar with local conditions. Talk to other Gay people in your area about it, contact your nearest American Civil Liberties Union branch for any information they may have (such as a "What To Do If you're Arrested" brochure), see if any of your local Gay Lib organizations have pamphlets on arrest procedures and local police attitudes, and, if possible, become familiar with a lawyer you can contact if you have any trouble (carry his phone number in your wallet).

But if you are arrested and haven't done your homework, here are a few rules to follow which hold true for any community in the United States today.

1. At the very moment of your arrest, before even giving your name and address, satisfy yourself that the person arresting you is indeed a police officer. Ask for identification, especially if he is in street clothes. Even after seeing identification, memorize badge number(s). The reason that you should first make sure that the persons arresting you are actually policemen is that there are thousands of instances, particularly in the past 10 years, of phony cops "arresting" Gay people in compromising situations, such as the "bushes" in your local cruising park, and then telling their victims that they will let them go for a sum of money. You may even find legitimate policemen offering to let you go for a fee; but remember, if you do pay them off, the odds are they will be back, again and again, for additional payoffs.

2. If you are arrested in a situation where there are other people around, as in a Gay bar, try to get the name and address of at least one witness, or if the cops won't let you shout your name and/or a phone number out loud so potential witnesses can call you. Conversely, if you are in a situation where a brother is being arrested, give him your name and address or get his. Don't let yourself be intimidated; you have every right to get a witness or to be a witness for another person. If even 10 percent of Gay people stood up firmly for the rights we do have, a good part of the harassment we suffer from local police would cease. As an example, in New York City about five years ago, dozens of Gay men were "entrapped" every day,

say, for "soliciting for immoral purposes," after a cop came on strong as a "Gay guy" and got an invitation to go home to bed. Finally, a group of Gay people and some civil liberties-minded straights formed a committee to end entrapment of homosexuals. The result of the committee's work in a relatively short time was the end of entrapment in all of New York State; in fact, entrapment in New York State is now a crime. Unfortunately, for most Gay people in other sections of the country, entrapment is still a reality which must be dealt with. So don't be afraid to stand up for what rights you do have; be courteously firm in your dealings with local police, but let *them* know that you know your rights.

3. When you are arrested, you are required to give your name and address ONLY. Even if it is a relatively minor offense and the cop tells you that if you plead guilty you will get off with a light fine, volunteer no information other than your name and address. You have much more to lose by volunteering additional information (which may seem harmless to you at the time) than your heterosexual counterpart would. Remember, the odds are that your arrest is part of the cop's "quota" for the day and if he thinks he can get by with charging you with a greater offense, he will. While a heterosexual would have a good chance of balancing off conflicting testimony of a policeman, there are very few, if any, judges around who would take the word of a Gay person over that of a policeman.

4. As soon as you arrive at the police station for booking, insist on our constitutional right to a phone call. Do not accept any excuses for any abridgement of this right. This is the time to use that lawyer's phone number you have been carrying in your wallet all these years (haven't you?). BUT – in case you don't have a lawyer's phone number, call a close friend or relative of yours who is most likely to be home and who will contact a lawyer for you.

5. After completing your phone call, you will be locked up – so just sit back, take a deep breath, relax and wait for your lawyer. Do not discuss with anyone, either a policeman

or another prisoner, any aspects of your arrest. You don't have to be unfriendly or discourteous; just inform them politely that you are under instructions from your counsel not to discuss your case with anyone.

6. If you are arrested while in the Armed Forces, you will probably be told that you will receive a General Discharge if you will give the names of other homosexuals in the services. Admittedly, it is a difficult choice you will have to make; but I hope you would refuse to cooperate and not give in to this particular kind of "legal blackmail." Even if you do get a General Discharge, you most likely will not be able to get any kind of government employment as they have other ways of noting on your service record that you are homosexual. Your service record will not keep you from getting most jobs, however, as most employers don't bother checking that far, and many big companies have specific rules regarding fair treatment of homosexuals.

Gay men are the easiest targets for cops who need "quota" arrests. We have historically been a submissive people who have allowed ourselves to be used by "macho" policemen who assert their perverted sense of masculinity. To guard yourself against this type of cop, when you are arrested, at all times maintain your dignity and self-respect, if you are abused – either physically or verbally – in the "back room" of the police station. I can assure you, from my own experiences, it's no fun for a Gay person to be arrested and taken to the local police station, so do your homework NOW!

Get that lawyer's phone number for your wallet; acquaint yourself with local police attitudes and practices; support any effort in your community to make the police more relevant to the community by putting their emphasis on crimes against people and getting them out of the inhuman business of trying to regulate our love lives.

And above all, have a good positive self-image about being a Gay person. To quote Mary Baker Eddy, founder of Christian Science, "Good thoughts are an impervious armor, and clad therewith you are completely shielded from the attacks of error of every sort; and not only yourselves are benefited, but all whom your thoughts rest upon are thereby benefited."

Gay and Free
December 1971

On Sunday, June 27, 1971, tens of thousands of Gay people throughout the world participated in the second annual observance of Christopher Street Liberation Day. Mass marches and parades though downtown areas were held in such cities as New York, Los Angeles, Chicago, Boston, London, Paris, and Stockholm; and there were dozens of smaller observances, mostly "Gay-Ins" at parks and other public places in other cities.

The purpose of Christopher Street Liberation Day (celebrated yearly on the last Sunday in June) is to commemorate and reaffirm the new spirit of pride and determination among Gay people which emerged after the now historic "Christopher Street/Stonewall Riots" of June 1969 in New York City. At that time, about 2,000 Gay people rioted in the streets of Greenwich Village to protest the police raid on a Gay bar, the Stonewall Inn. It marked the first time historically that Gay people didn't run-and-hide, but stayed-and-fought-back. Before June 1969 there had been a few hundred of us struggling along in the "Homophile Movement," but after the riots, thousands of Gay people here and abroad were inspired to stand up, and since that time what was the Homophile Movement as evolved into the beginnings of a mass movement termed "Gay Liberation."

In the 1971 New York City observance, highlighted by a march from Christopher Street in Greenwich Village to Central Park three miles away, approximately 20,000 people participated in the 2 ½ hour walk on a sunny, warm afternoon. The 1971 turnout was about twice that of the 1970 march, and that number is expected to double in 1972.

The general organizing group for the New York march is the Christopher Street Liberation Day Committee of New York. The Committee is composed of individuals from the Gay community and representatives from the dozen or so Gay organizations in the city. I must emphasize here that the CSLDC is not an organization like the Gay Activists Alliance, Daughters of Bilitis, Mattachine Society or the Gay Liberation Front; it is a work-group which comes together every year for the sole purpose of organizing and promoting the Christopher Street Liberation Day march.

At the end of Christopher Street Liberation Day this year, when those of us on the CSLDC sat around Central Park with thousands of other Gay people and relaxed at the conclusion of another successful and joyous march, we almost forgot the problems we had over the preceding months in putting it together. In the hope that some of you reading this will consider forming a Christopher Street Liberation Day Committee in your own area to promote a 1972 observance, let me go over a few of the problems we had this year and how they were resolved.

One of the biggest problems (and this is true of any city that has more than one Gay Lib organization) is getting the various organizations in the city to forget or at least mute their very real differences in the interest of showing a United Front on at least one day in the year, namely on Christopher Street Liberation Day. Until the final weeks of planning during June, the CSLDC's meetings are open to anyone and consequently we were "zapped" by various groups with various "demands" at a number of our meetings. And, of course, these "zaps" have to be dealt with on a very human and personal basis. It takes many hours of talking and reasoning to convince these people that it really is worthwhile to have one day in the year when Gay people and Gay organizations can come together as a community and that the only way to be successful at it is to swallow their personal organizational pride and help build Christopher Street Liberation Day to show the great diversity in our community and to show other Gay people throughout the world that we *can* be together on at least one day in the year.

Another problem which you'll have in any American city (including New York) concerns your dealings with the police department in getting the parade permit for the march. For this year's march, we submitted our "application for Parade Permit" in April and it was not approved and delivered to us until the day before the march, June 26th. In the interim, we had numerous meetings with police people and representatives from Mayor Lindsay's office (Barry Gottehrer and Ronnie Eldridge) asking when our permit would be issued. At each meeting, we received the same assurances that where was no problem but until we got that piece of paper in our hands, we sweated.

The worst scare we had this year was on the Friday before the march. A rumor spread like wildfire through the community that all of the illegal Gay bars in the city were going to be raided on the night before the march as a result of the Knapp's Commission's investigations. (The Knapp Commission is a group investigating police corruption and, in particular, collusion between the police and the "syndicate" in operating illegal after-hours bars.) It goes without saying that if there had been raids on dozens of Gay bars that night, the atmosphere and mood of Gay people at the march the next day would not have been the joyous, relaxed and happy one that it was. At best, the mood of the march would have been indifferent; at worst, there would have been a repeat of the 1969 riots.

Anyway, people from the CSLDC and from the Gay organizations got on the phones and called the Mayor's office, explaining the whole situation to them and appealing to them that if the rumor was true, to please put off the raids until the week after in the interests of peace in our community. We still don't know if the raids were originally planned for that Saturday or not; but they did take place about a month later when hundreds of Federal agents and New York City police swooped down on 9 after-hours, syndicate-controlled Gay bars.

Another problem you'll have in any city are the threats that uptight heteros will make to "break heads" at the march. The first few calls or letters of this type you'll get will probably scare you. But remember, most people who are really going to attempt something of this nature don't call and tell you about it; their real purpose is to frighten you into calling the whole thing off. Keep your cool; go ahead with your work, and take the usual precaution to assist the people by making sure adequate police protection is available and by training "marshals" or "coordinators."

Many, if not most, of the people who come out for Christopher Street Liberation Day marches are doing so publicly for the first time. Therefore, it is doubly important that there be people at the march who have been specially trained to give information to the people and to assure them that everything has been carefully planned and they have nothing to worry about.

I was personally very pleased to see many readers of *QQ* at this year's New York march from a number of states (as a result of the editorial in the August *QQ*). Maybe some of you, especially those I talked to from Ohio and Pennsylvania, will consider forming a Christopher Street Liberation Day Committee in your area to plan a local observance in 1972. It's not too early to start planning now; and if I can be of any help, let me know.

Appendix C: *QQ Magazine*, 1972

Reflections on Ten Years of Gay Lib
February 1972

Ten years, a decade, a tenth of a century – it's still difficult for me to believe I've been active in the movement that long; ten years ago, as far as I know, I was the only person who was under 21, but – now as I was described recently in a book on Gay Lib – I'm considered an "old-timer." And yet, everything seems new and exciting, as it must be in any healthy and historically important movement such as Gay Liberation.

I remember ten years ago walking hand-in-hand with a friend through the Greenwich Village Art Show. Surprisingly (or, on second thought, not surprisingly), the most shocked reactions came from other Gay people. But today it's an everyday occurrence to see Gay couple walking arm-in-arm or hand-in-hand on Village streets. No one is shocked or surprised anymore, except for occasional non-community hets.

Since high school, I've been an inveterate "cutter-outer" of newspaper and magazine articles concerning Homosexuality.

But whereas ten years ago, it was a rare and special moment when I came across such an article, today it is virtually an everyday happening. In fact, I find myself now deciding which articles to cut out and save and which not to. And I fully expect in the *next* ten years to rarely cut-and-save articles because of their tremendous volume, in this same vein, ten years ago it was easy for me to keep complete sets of Gay publications, since there were so few. But today, there are dozens of such periodicals, and it would take a professional librarian to collect and collate complete sets.

Ten years ago, it was almost unheard of for a Gay person to inform his or her family of The Fact. Today, especially among young people, it's a question of when and how to inform family and friends. Personally, I regard this as one of the healthiest changes in the last decade. After all, if we can't educate our families and friends (theoretically, those who already love us as individuals) to support our cause, there really isn't much hope of reforming the politicians, jurists, employers, police, teachers, etc., strangers all.

Even in the Gay organizations ten years ago, most of the controversy was around such questions as: Are we really mentally ill? Are we simply the product of over-protective mothers or fathers? Which psychiatrist should we go to? Today the main questions being debated in Gay Lib are: What Hetero institution should we zap next? Should Gay people work within The System or work for the revolution? How can we get parents to raise their children in a non-sexist way? Should we plan for 40,000 or 50,000 in this year's Christopher Street Liberation Day march? How many thousands of beers should we get for this week's dance?

Yes, for Gay men and women, especially in the larger cities, the past ten years have brought great changes; but what about the next ten years? I don't mean to compete with Criswell, but here's the list of things I think, and hope, will happen in the 70s which will greatly affect the lives of millions of Gay people in this country and elsewhere:

Widespread support by practicing heterosexuals. I think it is only a matter of time before large numbers of parents will recognize the ideal that children should be raised as free human beings, *from birth*. In other words, parents will not feel the need to "brainwash" their offspring with their own particular views and opinions, whether it be religious, political, racial, sexual or what-have-you. Boy-children will not be treated differently from girl-children. The whole idea that boys should be raised with blue blankets, fire engines, toy soldiers and boxing gloves and that girls should be raised with pink blankets, toy stoves, doll houses and sewing kits will be considered archaic and repressive. Some boys will grow up to be good baseball players; some girls will grow up to be good baseball players. Some boys will grow up to be good cooks or nurses; some girls will grow up to be good cooks and nurses; some boys and girls will grow up to be Catholics or Protestants; some boys and girls will grow up to be Jews, Buddhist, Mohammedans. Some boys and girls will grow up to be politically minded. And yes, some boys and girls will grow up to be Homosexuals or Bisexuals; and some boys and girls will be heterosexual.

Colleges and universities for Gay people. At the present time, every major college and university in the world is based on the needs, aspirations, and desires of heterosexual people. Don't be surprised if tomorrow you see an article in your paper that a group of wealthy Gay people have gotten together the funds to start construction of a university for Gay students, a university based on the needs, aspirations and desires of Gay people. (At this writing there are over 100 Gay Lib groups on college campuses already.)

Coming-Out of well-known Gay people. I eagerly look forward to the day (which is not far off) when many Gay people who are prominent in their respective fields – politics, arts, religion, sciences, education – lead their lives openly and proudly. The example this will give our young people and the effect it will have on society, in general, is very great indeed.

Gay people elected to public offices. The first Gay people (publicly known, that is) who will be elected will most likely be from the "Gay ghetto" areas of our large cities. Look for a Gay person to be elected largely by Gay voters, to a public office from the Greenwich Village area in New York. Already there are plans in the works to run an independent Gay candidate for the New York State Senate next year. Also in such areas as Back Bay (Boston), Hollywood (Los Angeles), Near North (Chicago) and Nob Hill (San Francisco).

Gay couples to raise children. Look for changes in the adoption laws around the country to enable Gay couples to adopt children. This will largely come about because of the crisis already existing; there are many more children up for adoption than there are parents willing to adopt. At the same time, the public generally will recognize that Gay people make good parents.

All-in-all, the next ten years will, I am convinced, see great changes in the daily lives of all Gay people and in the public image and attitude toward us. For those of us who are now "old-timers" it will be a challenge to change with the times and not cling to the myths and false self-images we have had to contend with in the past.

There's only one thing I can guarantee you during the 70s. It will be an exciting time to be living – and loving.

Exploitation and Gay Lib
April 1972

Exploitation of the Gay Liberation Movement by criminal syndicates, embezzlers, pseudo-religions groups, and even politicians has in the past year become a major problem which must be faced if the movement is to become a major force in reshaping society, and if the corner is to be turned in the battle against sexism.

Probably the major problem we face at this time is, what seems to many of us, an obvious and concerted effort by the same "syndicates" which have controlled the only social institutions Gay people have been allowed in this country – the bars and baths, to co-opt Gay Liberation and turn it into an advertising and public relations gimmick to perpetuate their control over Gay bars and baths, thus perpetuating and increasing their economic stranglehold on the Gay community and "keeping us in our place."

To fully understand how this particular kind of exploitation is taking place, one would have to be an expert in state liquor laws, licensing procedures and understand how deep the collusion is between the syndicate and the police. This is usually done by using what is known as a "front." To illustrate, a Gay person appears on the records as the "owner" of a particular bar or baths or restaurant. As for outward appearances, the operation looks "clean" – while it is in fact being used as a syndicate dope-drop, or a front for prostitution, or a conduit for hijacked liquor, or blackmail, or you name-it. If there's money in it, they're doing it!

There are a number of ways you can find out if a particular establishment is being controlled by the syndicate; ask yourself some of these questions: Do the people who claim to be the owners have sufficient finances of their own to have opened the place? What is the background of the apparent owners? Have they previously had a history of working in syndicate-controlled places? Is the landlord of the building the same as in other buildings where there are syndicate operations? If it's a bar and they have dancing, do they have a cabaret license?

A number of Gay Lib organizations throughout the country have had their treasuries stolen or funds embezzled in the past couple of years. When any movement starts to attract widespread attention, there are always a few people around who see an easy way to make some money. They get into an organization, talk big about "Gay unity" or "Off the pig!" and before you know it, they're in a position of leadership, and eventually it's discovered that hundreds or thousands of dollars are missing. The most conspicuous example of this is the recent discovery in one of the largest established Gay organizations that the head of it had embezzled thousands over a period of several years.

The only way to keep this type of exploitation in the movement to a minimum is to make sure that your organization has adequate bookkeeping procedures, issues regular financial statements showing income and expense to the members and again, looks into the background and history of people who appear out of the blue and present themselves for leadership positions in the group.

In the name of religion, a new kind of exploitation of Gay people is taking place in America. We now have the spectacle of people who last year were electrical engineers or bartenders, all of a sudden "finding religion" and becoming the pastor of a new Gay church, collecting fees for performing "marriage" ceremonies which are poor imitations of hetero marriage rites, not to mention a very subtle way of telling Gay people that they should be like heteros by aping their institutions – such as marriage, church-sponsored skin flick festivals, bingo, and collecting large sums for "missionary" work. Don't be misled ... there's big money in religion.

The form of exploitation of our people which upsets me most is when politicians solicit our votes with big promises; but when they get elected, they forget about us and their promises. The most outstanding example of this is US Rep. Bella Abzug (D-Manhattan) who, during her campaign for the House in 1970, appeared before Gay organizations in New York City promising to submit bills in Congress to guarantee to Gay people nationally equal opportunity in employment and housing. It is generally agreed in the Congressional District that the margin of her victory was attributed to her heavy support from Gay people. But, of course, since her election a year and a half ago, she has done nothing for Gay people that she promised.

At a Candidates Night meeting in Greenwich House shortly before the election, Bella was asked in front of 400 people if she would pledge to march with her Gay constituents in the June 1971 Christopher Street Liberation Day march. She stood, placed her hand over her heart and promised to do so. This promise elicited the only standing ovation received by any of the candidates that evening. And yet, when Christopher Street Liberation Day rolled around and 20,000 Gay people were marching, Congresswoman Abzug was sitting at home. She didn't even bother to make excuses or apologies – just silence. Needless to say, she will not receive the same wide support from Gay people in her re-election campaign.

The most offensive form of political exploitation of Gay Liberation recently has come from the so-called Socialist Workers Party (SWP). Until about a year ago, Gay people who were discovered in the SWP were unceremoniously kicked out of the party. But when Gay Liberation started to become a mass movement, all of a sudden, virtually overnight, SWP began to heavily exploit Gay Lib in New York, Houston, Washington, Los Angeles, Chicago and other cities. Almost every issue of their party newspaper, *The Militant,* contained articles on Gay Liberation and gave the impression that SWP not only supported the movement but was a founder of it.

Most of the mass peace marches in the past few years have been organized by SWP members and front groups such as the New York Peace Action Coalition. You may have seen some of their full-page ads in New York papers advertising these marches and listing names of people who supported them; and in the past year, those lists have included the same 4 or 5 individuals in the Gay Liberation movement who like to present themselves as the "leaders and spokesmen of the Homosexual Community." I should add here that I, too, was approached by SWP to have my name included in these ads; and to the best of my knowledge, I was the only person who declined and I told them why. Namely, by having these endorsements by the same 4 or 5 individuals as representing Gay Liberation, the movement tends to be defined nationally and locally by the views and personalities of these people; thus SWP is attempting to define the Gay Liberation movement. (Incidentally, SWP is controlled and run by honky hetero men.)

The Gay movement is a diverse and constantly evolving and changing organism; and we must resist attempts to by media or syndicates or clergy or political parties to pigeonhole us, to label us, to define us, or to tell us who our leaders are, if, indeed, we need "movement stars." John Kyper of Boston's Gay Male Liberation summed it up well in his recent article in *WIN Magazine,* on "Will Success Spoil Gay Lib?":

> To date, the movement's openness has been its greatest strength. No one voice can speak as *the* spokesman for gay liberation. There is a healthy, if at times trying, interplay of ideas; and a variety of organizations now exists to fulfill different needs. The purpose of gay liberation is to give homosexuals an outlet for the paranoia that society forces upon us. Not only do we want to create alternatives to the bars and the urban meat racks; we must also challenge the Social Lie through political action. We must encourage an atmosphere where gay people can trust each other.

And we will build this common trust in many ways, one of which is by becoming more sophisticated both socially and politically by being aware of the exploiters in our ranks and by judging our movement friends and not by what they say but by what they do. Actions *do* speak louder than words.

God & Gay Lib
June 1972

Who'd a thunk it? The most exciting religious phenomenon in America today is the growth of the homosexually oriented Metropolitan Community Church.

The first MCC was founded by Rev. Troy Perry in Los Angeles about three years ago, and since then, particularly in the last year, it has grown to approximately thirty churches and missions throughout the country from Hawaii to Florida; and in January of 1972, a New York MCC mission held its first meeting.

There are a number of other smaller Gay churches around the country, notably the Church of the Beloved Disciple in New York City and the United States Mission in Los Angeles. There's even a radical group called Gay Christian Revolutionaries in Berkeley, California (they publish a Gay Lib newspaper, *The Effeminist*).

A large part of the growth of the Gay churches in the past year has been the exposure given them by the news media. All the major news magazines and papers, TV, and radio have covered the phenomenon ... which could lead into another discussion of how the media define for us and, in some sense, create social movements such as "The Gay Church Thing." For example, a few years back, some guy held a press conference announcing the founding of a new organization, the purpose of which was to get people to clothe animals. If it is indecent for humans to go around naked, it was reasoned, then all God-fearing persons should see to it that their animals – from cows to pet cats – should at least wear garments covering their genitals.

Of course, the reporters jumped on the story and reported it as straight news. It was good copy; it was controversial; it was outrageous; it would help sell papers and increase TV ratings. A few months later, after the media orgy on the story had died down, the guy who held the original press conference announced that the whole thing was a hoax to demonstrate how the media, by what and how it reports stories, can and does define for most people what they think. I don't mean to imply that the Gay church movement and the clothes-for-animals movement are analogous in any way, or that the Gay churches are a hoax.

Organized religion has always been a sticky subject for Gay people. There's never been any research done on it, but I think it would be safe to say that the vast majority of Gay people leave the church or temple they are raised in – and for good reason. The ecclesiastical courts of the Middle Ages sentenced homosexuals to burning at the stake and most modern-day churches condemn us to a plot-in-purgatory hell-on-earth status.

While I'm sure that the Gay church movement can potentially bring through its doors thousands of Gay people, probably the majority of our people will not relate to it, but instead regard it as an aping of heterosexual institutions. It really turns me off to read that two men or two women were "married" in a Gay church with rings, best men/women vows, etc., the whole heterosexual thing. Homosexual love is strong and pure. The only thing holding lovers together is their love for each other – not because the church would regard them as sinners if they break up, or because they'd have legal hassles in divorce court, or because they don't want to fight over who's going to get the kids, or because their families and friends put various forms of pressure on them to stay together.

If two Gay people really want to have their relationship recognized and blessed for religious reasons, can't the Gay churches come up with something more creative, unique and indigenous to Gay life than what we've seen in the past year?

This leads to my main gripe about the Gay churches. At the moment, they differ from their heterosexual counterparts very little. Their activities run the gamut of the typical church scene – coffee hours, choir practices, hula dance classes, weddings, floral arrangement committees, drama groups, etc., which is all fine and dandy if that's your bag. I don't mean to demean these activities; they meet the needs and interest of the people involved. But you don't need a church for them and they have very little, if anything, to do with Christianity.

Whether consciously or sub-consciously, the Gay church movement today is saying to the power-establishment, "See, Gay people are no different from other people; we've got our own churches and they're just like yours." While, at the same time Gay Liberation is saying, "We're *not* just like you. We don't believe that white, heterosexual males should rule the world and inflict their sexism, racism, genocide and other forms of power-games on people. We want a decent world as exemplified by the radical from Nazareth, Jesus."

I hope that in the near future, the Gay church people will give some serious thought to really making the Gay church movement a creative, vital and inspiring force. Primitive Christianity, the Christianity of Jesus, bears little resemblance to so-called modern Christianity. You don't have to be a Christian to appreciate the life and example of Jesus. He was a simple, good man who was a visionary in his time; he saw that there was more to life than what we are, feel, hear or smell. And generally, without realizing it, Gay people have led "Christian" lives. For the most part, we go our own way, we don't try to impose our life-style on other people, we don't rape each other, we don't run around in gangs looking for heterosexuals to beat up, etc.

An example of the kind of things the Gay churches could be doing that would give them real validity to millions of Gay people has to do with what we call "coming out." When you stop and think about it, coming-out for a Gay person is a spiritual experience, a rebirth. More than one person has said to me that there were "ten years old," meaning that they came out ten years ago. Why not formally recognize coming-out as a religious or spiritual time in a Gay person's life? In my mind's eye, I can visualize a joyous and moving experience where hundreds of Gay people come out, similar to what it must have been like when Jesus baptized the multitudes in the Jordan River. It was a turning point in their lives, a joyous event, a rebirth of the spirit, not just another ritual with everyone sitting around in their Sunday best, fidgeting tin their seats and counting the minutes 'til they can get out and go home.

Religion in America is big business. In my way, I "pray" that the Gay churches will not become just another business – with a different clientele. Only time will tell.

Gay People and the Arts
September–October 1972

Since the blossoming of the Gay Liberation Movement in mid-1969 into a full-fledged political and social movement involving tens of thousands of Gay people, the one area where you would think, logically, that Gay people would assert themselves, would be "The Arts." After all, isn't it common knowledge and hasn't it always been so, that 99 per cent of male ballet dancers are Gay and at least 50 per cent of actors and hefty percentages of sculptors, artists, concert pianists, writers, set designers, producers, directors, stage managers, musicians, orchestra leaders, etc., are too?

But we have yet to see ads in the papers for Thomas Schippers conducting the premiere of Leonard Bernstein's "Homage to a Gay Brother – In Praise of Walt Whitman." Or Rudolf Nureyev and Erik Bruhn dancing a romantic pas de deux. Or Rock Hudson and Paul Newman starring in the film version of Gore Vidal's updated "The City and the Pillar." Or Van Cliburn playing Aaron Copland's heroic "Gay and Proud – Free at Last" concerto.

Instead we have "The Boys in the Band" with all of its cliches and stereotypes; we have dozens of so-called "male" movie houses around the country showing "skin-flicks" which supposedly have something to do with Gay Liberation; we have virtually all of the thousands of Gay people who are artists in different fields, producing, creating, and performing works for and primarily appealing to an exclusively heterosexual consciousness; and when Gay people or situations are portrayed, they are done in a manner and style so as to reinforce the audience's preconceived thinking.

The one outstanding exception to the preceding which I must mention is the movie of "Sunday Bloody Sunday," which, to the best of my knowledge, was written, produced, directed and starred in by heterosexual people; and yet, it is by far the most creative, human and honest film about Homosexual consciousness yet made.

As an example of how Gay people are oppressed in and by "The Arts," I offer my own personal experiences with the New York City Ballet Company when I was a student at the Company's School of American Ballet. It was common knowledge that George Balanchine, the director of the New York City Ballet, didn't like Homosexuals and that if you were Gay, much less Gay and proud, your chances of ever becoming a soloist were nil. That's why the worst dancers in the company who were usually heteros became the lead dancers. Balanchine's idea of a good male dancer was someone who filled the public's stereotype of what masculinity in the arts should be – in other words, that ballet is a "feminine" art and that male dancers should play the role of supporting the female and doing a two-minute solo which features aerobatic and athletic fetes in order for the audience to see the heterosexual role-playing of male/female recreated on stage – woman as passive, graceful, sensitive; man as supportive, strong, and clumsy.

The time is overdue for Gay people in the arts to come forward as creative people and to speak, write, create and perform about what they know best and to relate to the struggle of their Gay brothers and sisters by helping to break down the heterosexism of our culture. Already, there are stirrings towards this end.

I know a number of people in the New York City Ballet, for example, and in the not too distant future, they will take some action to change the situation in their company. It might come in the form of a strike or perhaps by "zapping" next year's opening. There is talk among some actors and actresses of forming a National Gay People's Theatre. In early May, a Gay Cultural Exposition was held at Rutgers University which featured Gay artists' sculpture, writings, songs, etc. Also in the past year, we have seen the publishing of two long-suppressed Gay novels – E.M. Forster's "Maurice," written in 1914, and Gertrude Stein's "Fernhurst & Q.E.D.," written in the early 1900s.

I remember about a year ago at a Gay People's Unity Rally at Columbia University (just prior to the march on Albany to demand Homosexual law reform), a woman came out, did a comedy sketch and then sang a heterosexual love song. Most of us in the audience (which number around 1,000) assumed that the entertainers at the rally were at least Gay themselves, or if they weren't they would certainly change the gender pronouns in any love songs to give them a Homosexual connotation. Needless to say, at the end of her "song," there were a lot of people who were very upset. But the surprising thing was that most people there weren't ruffled in the slightest. Can you imagine the reaction that would occur at Black People's Unity Rally if a white singer came out and sang a song celebrating the joys of being white, or a gentile singer came out at a Jewish Defense League Rally and sang "Onward, Christian Soldiers"?

Even here in New York City, which is supposedly "Gay-liberated," all of the Gay bars which feature entertainment either have Gay singers singing hetero love songs, or drag shows. I don't have anything, per se, against drag shows – I can enjoy a good drag show as well as anyone – but I can't help but wonder why that is the only form of entertainment allowed by the heterosexual bar owners of Gay bars. I've worked in a number of Gay bars over the years; so I have as good a knowledge as anyone of the mentality of the bar owners, the vast majority of whom are heterosexual. Most of them "hate fags" (as they put it) and I suppose by allowing only drag shows as entertainment in Gay bars they are able to show their contempt for our lifestyle by reinforcing the stereotype in front of us and actually getting us to think that we're being entertained. And to add insult to injury, the performers are paid next to nothing while the bar owner cleans up. (In case you didn't know it, Gay bars are a very lucrative business. In New York alone, Gay bars take in tens of millions of dollars yearly.)

To those of you reading this who are involved in any facet of "The Arts," stop for a moment and think whether or not your creativity is reflective of your whole being, taking into account equally your Gay consciousness along with your other feelings whether they be anti-war, bisexual, abstract or whatever. As an artist, you are a leader and molder of public opinion and attitudes and you also have the responsibility to be creative, innovative, thought-provoking and even at times, shocking.

If you're afraid to come out publicly in your art, look at the example of Merle Miller, who, up until the mid-50s, was one of this country's most promising up-and-coming young writers. From that point until 1970 he continued to write for a heterosexual audience about what they wanted to read and hear and his career went steadily downward. But in 1970, he "came out" by writing a piece for *The New York Times Magazine* about his Gayness, his pride, his oppression as a Gay Person, his hopes for the future generations of young Gay men and women; and overnight, his career blossomed and he again became a vital, creative and successful writer.

No doubt, before his public "coming out" he had many fears about how his colleagues would react, not to mention his family. But he survived it and is all the happier and more successful for it. You can be, too; try it, you'll like it!

Homosexual Law Reform
August 1972

While any thinking person, in good conscience, must support the idea of Homosexual Law Reform – the elimination of statutes in the various states which attempt to regulate consenting sexual behavior and the enactment of legislation at the municipal, state and federal levels of laws prohibiting discrimination based on sexual orientation – I think too much importance and energy is being attached to the idea of law reform. Let's face it; the cause of oppression of Gay people is not the sodomy laws or the lack of anti-discrimination legislation.

A case in point is the state of Illinois, where I was born and raised. Illinois was the first state, in 1961, to make consenting adult Homosexual behavior, in effect, legal. Yet, in the decade since, this first instance of Homosexual law reform has had virtually no effect on the lives of Gay people in Illinois. And why should it have any effect; such laws are unenforceable to begin with!

Support for Homosexual law reform in 1972 has become a safe political stance for most "good liberal" politicians. For example, among the dozen or so Democratic candidates for the presidential nomination, more than half of them have come out publicly for law reform in this area – not only for striking anti-Gay statutes from the law books, but also for legislation banning discrimination against Gay people in housing, employment, etc. And before the end of this decade, we will most likely see federal legislation passed amending the various Civil Rights Acts banning discrimination based on sexual orientation.

But then what? Is that the end of the Gay Liberation movement? Not by a long shot; our primary goals are so revolutionary that most people, including unfortunately most Gay people, don't realize the real impetus and vitality of the movement. As long as we allow the public, the media and the politicians the luxury of thinking that we are another minority group asking for equality and "law reform," things will progress calmly. But watch the you-know-what hit the fan when they suddenly realize that what we're calling for is the end to institutionalized sexism which raised boys to be fathers, soldiers, husbands and providers; and women to be mothers, wives, seamstresses and secretaries. When they realize that we're calling upon parents to raise their children to be free human beings with the capacity to love, physically and emotionally, all people, regardless of sex. When we call upon the public schools to use textbooks that portray equally same-sex relationships and opposite-sex relationships. When they come to the full realization that what we're asking is not change for us but change for them.

Aside from the relative unimportance I obviously attach to the idea of Homosexual law reform, there are also some very real dangers attached to it; for example:

1. The Homosexual Rights movement in England during the late fifties and sixties was based almost entirely on the law reform issue, namely, the enactment of the recommendations from the famous Wofenden [sic] Report. But when the Wofenden proposals were enacted by Parliament in the mid-sixties, the Gay movement in England virtually disbanded; and it wasn't until the past year that the movement has started to revive as Gay people came to realize that very little had changed and there was still a lot to be done. The same thing could happen in the US if we allow ourselves to think that law reform is our major goal.

2. As black people have learned that antidiscrimination legislation does not guarantee them equality, we, too, must realize that law will not guarantee any rights to us. If an employer or a union doesn't like Gay people, they'll find other reasons to fire us or refuse to hire us.

3. Homosexual law reform now provides many political office seekers with a banner to wave in front of Gay people to get out votes, and as has happened many times in the past year, we flock to their banner. But after they are elected, we generally hear nothing more from them.

4. In New York State alone during the past year, tens of thousands of dollars and much energy has been spent for Homosexual law reform while the substantive issues of Gay

Liberation, at best, get only lip service – such issues as building community, building group consciousness of our common oppression (the causes, not the effects) breaking the cycle of syndicate-police exploitation of our people in the bars, etc.

Homosexual law reform is obviously a good and just cause, but it is not an end in itself. And my major fear is that because of the time, money and publicity being given it today, we tend to lose sight of the truly inspiring message that Gay Liberation has to offer everyone, not only Gay people.

The following is a quote from Henry Hay, one of the first "Gay activists" in the early fifties, which I've used before but think it bears repeating as an expression of the basis of Gay Liberation:

"Homosexuals are and always have been through their oppression and in spite of brainwashing, a Free People ... a minority that shares each other's dream, that redirects the aggressive fighting instincts, competitiveness and inherited animal maleness and femaleness of the parent culture into appreciation of – nay, even a lifelong passion to call forth, the grace and tenderness ... the humility and compassion ... (of our) shared community of outlook.... Challenging us to break loose from the lockstep expectation of heterosexual life patterns so obliterating of our own natures. Our Homosexual liberation movement must consist of far-ranging communities of free spirits."

At the risk of being called a Pollyanna regarding my ideas about homosexual law reform, I think it is well on its way to fruition. And that Gay Liberation need only give it minor importance in allocation of money, time and people-power. In fact, a good argument could be made that law reform will come even quicker if we don't press for it at all. In the states that have reformed their consensual sodomy laws, for instance, there was little, if any, pressure from Gay people for law reform; and in the states where Gay organizations have lobbied and demonstrated for law reform, the State legislatures voted against it, notably New York and California.

Anyway, besides having little reality to the everyday problems that Gay people face, the law reform campaign is dull and uninspiring. Perhaps we should return in the spirit of one of the first Gay Liberation slogans which appeared shortly after the Christopher Street Uprising in 1969, "Homosexuals are Revolting – You Bet Your Sweet Ass We Are."

The Gay Vote 1972
September–October 1972

When I speak of the "Gay Vote 1972," I'm talking about an estimated 4,000,000 to 8,000,000 possible voters (depending on whose estimates you believe). The Gay vote has always been strong, but the difference is that in 1972, for the first time ever, Gay people are beginning to realize that through sheer numbers, we have the potential to influence the elections – not only for President, but right on down to Senators, Representatives, District Attorneys, Judges, Mayors, Governors, Assemblymen, State Senators, and even Dog Catchers.

However, since this is a presidential election year, the "brass ring" is the race to win the lease at 1600 Pennsylvania Avenue. And, for the first time in history – openly – Gay candidates are running in a number of states to win delegate positions at the Democratic National Convention to be held during July in Miami Beach. And there's a strong possibility that the issue of Gay rights will be raised on the convention floor in full view of millions of citizens watching on their TVs.

All of the announced candidates for the presidency in both major parties have been approached in the last few months by various Gay organizations around the country for their views on issues of concern to Gay people, particularly in the areas of employment, housing and public accommodations. The only major candidates who have not publicly responded have been Nixon, Ashbrook, Muskie, and Wallace. In capsule form, the responses of the other candidates are as follows:

Shirley Chisholm

She has publicly announced that if elected president, she would issue an executive order banning discrimination against Gay people by the Federal government in the areas of employment, armed forces, immigration, veterans' rights and that she would support an amendment to the Civil Rights Acts of 1964 and 1968 to ban discrimination against Gay people.

Hubert Humphrey

He has declined to say publicly what he would do, specifically, to help Gay people. However, he has said, "I see no reason why homosexual Americans should be excluded from equal protection under the law. I am against arbitrary discrimination against homosexuals, especially as it pertains to unfair occupational hiring practices. Homosexuals are citizens; let us treat them as such."

John Lindsay

"The Presidency ought to be more than a vehicle for cynical manipulation of power, as we unfortunately see it used today. It should be a source of inspiration and guidance to the American people, and especially on those issues where vigorous leadership alone can wrest changes in long held attitudes and can eliminate the fears that produce discrimination. Only when the tone of leadership in Washington has been changed ... will the grievances of homosexuals receive the attention and redress they have for so long warranted."

Eugene McCarthy

He has publicly announced that if elected president, he would issue an executive order banning discrimination against Gay people by the Federal government in the areas of employment, armed forces, immigration, veterans' rights and that he would support an amendment to the Civil Rights Acts of 1964 and 1968 to ban discrimination against Gay people.

Paul McCloskey

He has publicly announced that if elected president he would issue an executive order banning discrimination against Gay people by the Federal government in the areas of employment and immigration and that he would support an amendment to the Civil Rights Acts of 1964 and 1968 banning discrimination against Gay people. However, he has declined to support the end of discrimination against Gay people in the armed forces and in veterans' rights.

George McGovern

He "pledges the full moral and legal authority of his presidency towards restoring and guaranteeing first-class citizen rights for homosexually oriented individuals. We have found it necessary to spell out in legislation that there shall be no discrimination based on race, creed, national origin, or sex in housing, employment and public accommodations. Now we are recognizing that it is unfortunately also necessary to identify yet another group that has suffered harassment and deprivation. I hope for the day when we don't need to specify that 'Liberty and Justice for All' includes Blacks, Chicanos, American Indians, Women, Homosexuals, or any other group. *All* means *all.*" Senator McGovern has also promised to issue executive orders banning discrimination against Gay people in all fields and to support amendments to the Civil Rights Acts of 1964 and 1968.

As of this writing, the Democratic nomination has narrowed down to either Humphrey or McGovern; Nixon, of course, will be the Republican nominee; and George Wallace may or may not run as a third party candidate. The choice for Gay people between these four candidates should be very obvious. Nixon and Wallace have refused to say anything on Gay issues and Humphrey has refused to commit himself to anything specific. Only George McGovern has pledged "the full moral and legal authority of his presidency towards restoring and guaranteeing first-class citizen rights for homosexually oriented individuals." And further, if and when the issue of Gay rights is raised on the floor of the Democratic National Convention in Miami Beach, it will be raised by delegates pledged to McGovern.

For the past ten years in this country we have been approaching a crossroads in our history and this 1972 presidential election may prove to be the turning point. Since World War II, we have seen our government and our national policies dominated by big labor, big business, the military, special interests and secret deals between them; we have seen wars conducted without the consent of Congress, we have seen minority groups confined to a new ghetto called "welfare," we have seen the subtle manipulation of the American people through the media, we have seen national priorities given to moonshots, ABMS, corporate interests, and special interests; and we have seen the continued repression of Gay people through government-sanctioned discrimination in all fields.

For the first time in the history of any culture, we, as Gay People, have the opportunity to have a lasting impact on the history of our planet. It's still hard for me to believe it, but there actually is a major Presidential candidate who has come out publicly and unequivocally for the rights of Gay people everywhere.

George McGovern just may be OUR man!

Image Smashing
December 1972

We're all aware of the common stereotype of Gay people held by straight society – that of the exaggerated perfumed "fag" who caricatures society's definition of what a "real woman" is. Not only is his masquerade a put-down of what a "real woman" is, but he has also provided the media and the public with an easily recognizable 'model' of all Gay people. For decades, the stereotype of a black person was a watermelon-eating stupid loafer, thus enabling society to excuse itself for not relating and dealing with black people on an equal and human basis. In much the same way, the public's image of the "fag" has enabled it to refuse to deal with Gay people on an equal and human basis.

With all of the publicity and notoriety that Gay Liberation has received in the past few years, the "fag" stereotype has rapidly begun to be broken down. Millions of American citizens now realize that a Gay male or female may well be the boy or girl next door. But at the same time that we see this breaking down of old stereotypes, we see the establishment and promotion in the media of new Gay stereotypes.

There have been literally thousands of up-front gay-and-proud events and activities in the past year throughout the country; yet virtually the only ones we read about or see on television are the ones involving confrontation or disruptive tactics (such as the disruption of Mayor Lindsay's attendance at the season's opening of the Metropolitan Opera in New York, or reportage on the various demonstrations and pickets for Gay rights held around the country).

In earlier columns in *QQ*, I have spoken of the very real dangers the movement faces in allowing the media to define what Gay Liberation is and what its goals are. To date, we have been defined on TV and in the papers as either (a) a minority group seeking equal rights in housing, employment and public accommodations, or (b) a bunch of far-out, weirdo, bearded, male, unclean fanatics seeking to disrupt the entire system if we don't get our way. As you and I know, neither image of Gay people is true. Yet, large numbers of our people think of themselves as a new minority group and seek to mimic the aims and tactics of the Black Liberation Movement; and yes, there are thousands of far-out, bearded, male fanatics who will seek to disrupt everything if they don't get their way (much like a spoiled child will throw a temper tantrum in order to get what it wants, in the hopes that its parents, out of weariness, will give in).

But, as most of you already know, the vast majority of out of-the-closet, up-front Gay people do not fit either of the two above mentioned new stereotypes. Like our brothers and sisters in other sexual, ethnic, racial and cultural groups, all we desire is the freedom to live our lives peacefully, comfortably and with as little hassle as possible from the surrounding community. Not only do we not fit these new stereotypes, but, in reality, we are primarily no different in our likes, dislikes, hopes, aspirations, fears, etc., than other people. The only thing which binds us together as Gay people is our refusal to go along with society's dicta regarding how the sexes should relate with each other. As Gay people, we have said "No!" to the Battle of the Sexes and have opted instead to relate to people of our own sex and to emphasize our commonality with each other rather than to give in to our culture's idea that "opposites attract."

If you're like me, you've already asked yourself many times, "Why does the general public and the media insist on stereotyping Gay people? Granted, the new stereotypes are different, but they are still stereotypes." The only answer I've been able to come up with is that for some yet unexplained reason, people have a need to categorize and stereotype various minority groups, in order, I suppose, to give themselves a reason to refuse to listen to and relate to them as people much like themselves.

Another reason is that the press and TV since they are based on the profit motive of supply and demand, tend to emphasize stories and articles which tend to reinforce and meet the needs of their readers and viewers. And, let's face it, most people would rather read about or see on television a report of the latest "zap" by bearded, loud, militant "homos" than have to relate on an equal and loving basis with their Gay sons, daughters, nephews, nieces, uncles, aunts, etc.

If you've already informed your family and friends of your being Gay, you know of the layers of bullshit, guilts, fears and misconceptions, which have to be overcome by "straight" people before they can begin to relate to you as a human being. It's so much easier, in the short run, for people to dismiss us with some stereotyped image rather than to have to deal with us openly and honestly. But haven't you found, as I have, that once you get through those layers, a new relationship with family and friends emerges that gives both of you peace of mind and conscience.

In the Gay Liberation Movement, we have a term for those people who, like clockwork, send out press releases, and call up their favorite reporters on their local papers to get media coverage of their latest attention-grabbing gimmick. We call them "ego-trippers." Their primary raison d'etre is to call attention to themselves and to get their picture and/or names into the media and public eye. And, as you may have guessed, they are the people that the new Gay stereotypes are based on.

If the media didn't cater to these ego-trippers to spice up the evening news broadcasts and help sell newspapers, the Gay Liberation Movement today would be a much larger and effective force in our society. Gay people, like their counterparts in the general population, cannot identify with the stereotypes presented to us, which makes it all the more difficult for the thousands of concerned and committed Gay Liberationists to reach our millions of Gay brothers and sisters to confront their oppression and to consciously help in the fight against heterosexism which for centuries has kept 200,000,000 Americans brainwashed with the idea that men and women should behave, think, feel, act and love in a predetermined way.

Our Gay Liberation Movement is and must be a cause for all Gay people. To quote the Bible (Gospel of St. John, VIII, 32), "Ye shall know the truth; and the truth shall make you free." Know the truth; know that the new Gay stereotypes you read about and see on TV are not typical; know that there are thousands of your Gay brothers and sisters working every day throughout the world to make a better world; know that there are hundreds of Gay peoples' organizations which daily work quietly and without media attention to fight institutionalized heterosexism and to help you on a personal basis, if and when you need it, with various problems – job-wise, health-wise, legally and socially.

And above all, know yourself. Read, study, think – think of what a world would be like where men no longer had the need to prove their "manhood" by going to war and killing other men or by competing with other men for various forms of power!

Appendix D: *QQ Magazine*, 1973

The Lavender Syndicate – Part I
February 1973

When I "came out" at 13, one of the first things I learned about my new life was that most of the Gay bars were controlled by "the syndicate." So when I started going to them I didn't have to ask who those creepy straight guys in business suits were at the door.

It wasn't too many years ago – at least in New York State – when a Gay bar, per se, was illegal; the State Liquor Authority had a regulation which, in effect, made serving a drink to a Homosexual grounds for a bar losing its liquor license. In the mid-sixties, three of us who were active at that time with the Mattachine Society of New York conducted a "sip-in" at a Gay bar in Greenwich Village. We entered the bar with various reporters in tow, announced that we were Homosexuals and asked that we be served a drink. The bartender then refused to serve us – which enabled us to set up a case with the City Commission on Human Rights, and which a few months later led to the State Liquor Authority's changing its regulations, permitting Homosexual people to be served.

Aside from winning for Gay people the right to be served drinks in licensed premises, we had thought that this new legal status for Gay bars would help break the syndicate's stranglehold; we thought that Gay people themselves would step forward and open Gay bars; we thought that, at last, Gay people would begin to gain control over their own institutions. We had no illusions this would happen overnight, but we did think the corner had been turned.

We were wrong. Not only has the syndicate tightened its grip on Gay bars ... they have opened new so-called Gay establishments – movie houses, porno shops, baths, etc. The major difference between now and then is that now you rarely see any of the creepy straight guys in business suits. Most of the mob-run Gay establishments are run by "fronts." In other words, in a business where licensing is involved, such as bars, baths, movie houses, the only way to get a license is for someone with no previous criminal record to apply for it. Consequently, Gay people (with no previous criminal records) now appear as the owners – on paper – even though they didn't have a penny to invest in the operation.

In the past few years, many of us in the Gay Liberation Movement have been approached by mob figures offering us the ownership of record of one of their places. I was approached to be the "front" for one of their "male movie houses" here in New York City; and the only way I got out of it was by playing dumb. I kept saying I didn't understand and since I didn't have any money to put into the business, I couldn't see why they would want me to be the owner. After a month or so, they finally gave up on me. I won't say that I wasn't tempted; the idea of having a business, doing no work, and getting paid for it, is appealing. But I also realized that once I got in with them, that would be it. I would be known by law enforcement agencies as a "front for organized crime" for the rest of my life.

To give you some idea of the extent of syndicate operations in our Gay community:

1. Nationally, Gay syndicate operations run into the hundreds of millions of dollars bracket. There are thousands of mob-controlled Gay bars, movie houses, pornography shops, etc.
2. Thousands of Gay males have been and are today being blackmailed through contacts with syndicate-run "call boy" services or through contacts in mob-run Gay bars. One of these blackmail rings was broken temporarily a few years ago when the newspapers reported that an organized blackmail ring with mob connections had blackmailed Gay males, including a US Congressman, a prominent television entertainer and an Air Force General.
3. Thousands of Gay people have been turned into "pill-freaks" and worse through the easy accessibility of any kind of drug in mob-run Gay bars.
4. Syndicate-run Gay bars are a major outlet for other mob businesses – such as hijacked liquor and food, jukeboxes, vending machines – not to mention prostitution, blackmail and drug-pushing.
5. Certain Gay publications regularly give free space in the form of listings to the various syndicate Gay operations – the bars, baths, movie houses.
6. Even Gay Lib organizations have not been immune to the approaches of our "friends" in the underworld. A local mobster was quoted recently as saying, "I contribute to the (a Gay Lib organization's name) Legal Defense Fund so we won't be zapped." And to this day, the vast majority of Gay Lib organizations have virtually ignored the problem of syndicate/Mafia domination of Gay bars, which are, let's face it, the most important social institution that Gay people are allowed to have in this culture.

It is not secret among most Gay people that many of our major Gay institutions have long been controlled by the syndicate. If we are ever to gain control over our own lives, it must be clear that one of our major goals in the Gay Liberation movement is to rid our community of the parasites who have lured us into their closets. The closet of the Gay bar, where we are allowed to stand against the walls and stare at other Gay people while paying exorbitant prices for watered-down drinks. The closet of the porno shop, where we are allowed to spend $10 for a male-nudie magazine wrapped in cellophane and put quarters into vending machines to see a minute of two men making love. The closet of the drug-induced state, where we can attain a euphoric state of temporary bliss. The closet of the Gay movie house, where we have the "privilege" of spending $5 to see nude males for a couple hours.

There is going to be a long and difficult struggle on the part of thousands of Gay people before we can begin to tip the scales in this fight to wrest control of Gay institutions from the syndicate. But at the end of that struggle is the day when Gay people, particularly those who are just coming out, can go into a Gay bar or baths or movie house or bookshop and feel that they are a vital part of a Gay community where we interact on a free and loving basis.

In my next column, I will suggest ways that all of us can help in this struggle.

The Lavender Syndicate – Part II
April 1973

Last month I presented a brief outline of the extent of organized crime's domination over many of our Gay institutions, and I also recognized that before we could begin to gain control there would be a long and difficult struggle. When we talk about "syndicate" control, we're talking about a multi-million-dollar big business; and they're not going to just walk away because we say they should.

The first step in this fight is to somehow get our Gay brothers and sisters mad enough to want to do something about it. For too long and for whatever reasons, we have passively accepted the situation; but as our individual and group feelings of pride in our lifestyle and solidarity with our people grow, we find a new determination to assert control over our own lives.

Probably the major goal of the Gay Liberation Movement, but the least recognized, is that we are challenging Gay people to like themselves with a healthy self-respect and dignity; and when an historically downtrodden people begin to like themselves, they begin to get mad at institutions and groups which exploit and use them. That's why increasing numbers of Gay people are getting mad at governmental institutions which legislate against us; against religious institutions which condemn us; against business institutions which discriminate against us; and yes, against the crime crowd which controls our social institutions.

Just recently we have seen a few signs of this anger. In early September the Gay Revolution Network (a New York based group) set up an "Anti-Mafia War Council." The call for their first meeting read in part: "This monster, the Mafia, infects so much of Gay people's lives in New York's homosexual ghetto. Gay bars are one of their major sources of converting bad money (from heroin, bank robberies, hijacking, etc.) into good money. Practically every drink we buy, every meal we order, every drug we cop, every time we're robbed by a desperate junkie, we end up paying off this beast in some way. There are thousands of victims that have been twisted and torn up by these straight men who profit off us and are directly enhanced by the degree of oppression laid on us by the straight men in City Hall, Albany and in Washington."

The GRN further called on Gay people to boycott Mafia places and on Gay organizations to provide real alternatives and finally to "cut our movement and its members loose from Mafia influence now!"

And many Gay people here in New York City are now beginning to ask, "Why do some Gay publications give free space listings to all the syndicate-run places in town? Why do some of the Gay organizations accept large donations from syndicate operations and give them 'honorary homosexual' awards while maintaining a silence on the issue of mob control over our social institutions? Why did a former president of a Gay activists group, during Congresswoman Bella Abzug's recent primary campaign, take her on a well-publicized campaign tour to meet her Gay constituents in only syndicate-run establishments? Why does a former president of a Gay Liberation organization now work for a publicly identified 'soldier' in the syndicate?"

Questions like these are being asked because a lot of us are unwilling any longer to quietly sit back and see our Gay community exploited, and this anger must equally be directed towards so-called "leaders" in the movement who are "for sale." Also included in this group are the columnists in various Gay publications, local and national, who regularly glamorize and help to reinforce the syndicate Gay bar syndrome, while ignoring the negative control they exert over the minds and bodies of Gay people.

There are many ways that you can help in this struggle:

1. Express your anger to other Gay people. Let them know that we are going to have to run these parasites out of our lives; nobody is going to do it for us – not the police (of whom many are "on the take"), not the courts, not the media – only ourselves through our collective determination and pride.
2. If you're a member of a Gay organization which accepts payoffs from syndicate establishments, whether through

"advertising" in publications or "donations," get together with other up-front people in your group and put an end to it. And see to it that, publicly at least, your group takes a stand condemning the exploiters.
3. Beware of the people in our own community who seek to excuse and explain away the syndicate stranglehold on our social institutions. In particular, I'm referring to people who say, "Don't call anybody Mafia unless you can prove it." If it were that easy to prove, the problem would be well on its way to solution. Basically, you know if a place is mob-controlled – things like watered-down drinks, creepy straight guys at the entrance collecting "minimums," mysterious limousines that pull up around closing time and collect the money, easy availability of drugs on or near the premises, deliveries of hijacked liquor which come in unmarked trucks, etc.
4. And, in the not-too-distant future, when you see other Gay people picketing a place because of syndicate control, respect that picket line at the very least; and, if your anger is sufficient, join it.
5. And, finally, when you are personally convinced that a Gay establishment, whether it be a bar, a bathhouse, a publication, a bookshop, a movie house or an organization, is free of overt or covert syndicate control, support that establishment and get your friends to support it. Let the world know that as Gay people, we have the pride and determination to exert control over our own lives.

It is this kind of determination that the larger society respects. And if I have not yet managed to communicate my personal anger to YOU, I won't stop trying. I have been in this movement too long and am convinced that until we rid ourselves of outside control we will never even begin to be a free people.

Four More Years
April 1973

The 1972 Presidential campaign and the resultant landslide for Mr. Nixon on November 7th have great import for Gay people in general, and for the Gay Liberation Movement in particular.

For the first time ever, Gay Liberation became a national issue, although a muted one. For Mr. Nixon, McGovern's statement of support for equal rights for Gay people provided him with one more example to the American people of George McGovern's "radicalism." It was George Meany who stated publicly that – among other things, including George McGovern's ties with "those Gay Liberation people" – he could not support McGovern and thus declared the AFL-CIO's "neutrality." While there is great disagreement within our movement over McGovern's sincerity on the issue, the fact remains that it was the McGovern campaign which allowed some of the issues of concern to Gay people surface in a national election.

It was undoubtedly a political blunder of huge proportion for McGovern to even allow Gay issues to get a foot in the door of his campaign, much less to allow us to present our case on national television in front of the Democratic National Convention. It comes as no surprise to anyone that the national electorate is not ready to face Gay issues, and this is as it should be.

Change in national policies regarding Gay people cannot and will not come about until a majority of the people support such changes. These next four years of the Nixon administration will provide a real test for the Gay Liberation Movement. Will we turn our efforts to educating and winning the support of the people? Or will we turn our energies toward reacting to the "malign neglect" of the Washington administration?

I hope – and will do all I can to see to it – that the Movement will use these four years to build; to build and nurture a real *sense of community* among Gay people, particularly on the local level, and to build committed support among the people, in general, through a program of *outreach* to the larger community.

Building through Community

In the past eleven years, I have seen the Gay Liberation Movement grow from a few organizations and no more than a couple hundred of us to a national movement of close to one-thousand organizations and tens of thousands of activists. But this phenomenal growth of the past few years, particularly since the "Christopher Street Riots" of 1969, is meaningless until and unless we begin to relate more to the masses of Gay people and have a real impact on improving their daily lives. Appealing to Washington or the various state capitols for enactment of Gay Rights proposals has little meaning when related to the day-to-day lives of our people.

In such areas as Silver Lake in Los Angeles, Rogers Park in Chicago, Greenwich Village in Manhattan and Back Bay in Boston (to name a few), there are large concentrations of Gay people who live (and sometimes work) in the same community. And yet in these Gay communities, which exist in every major American city, very few of our people are active in their community – whether it be helping to formulate school policy in their local school boards, improving local private and public housing [to be] open to Gay people (not just families), and, in general, of building a viable feeling of community where people feel they have some control over what goes on in their local communities.

It is this feeling of powerlessness on the local level that I feel must be changed before we can begin to seriously think we can effect change on the national or state level. Somehow, in these Gay Ghettos, we must build and nurture a feeling amongst our people that they can create for themselves a real community of friends, neighbors and lovers – a real community where they have influence in their local schools, precincts and social institutions and that their local elected representatives are made answerable to their needs and feelings.

Outreach

At the same time that we are consolidating and giving permanence and meaning to millions of Gay people in their communities, we cannot neglect reaching out to the larger community through a program of education and open dialogue.

For example, we have tens of millions of potential allies in our efforts in the families of Gay people alone. At this time there are a number of "Parents of Gay People" organizations springing up around the country. And I think this is one of the most important trends in the Movement and something that every one of us can help to accelerate. For those of you who have taken the time and effort to re-educate your families on the subject of Homosexuality, you know of the great joy in having the love and support of your family. (For myself, I'll never forget the great surge of pride I felt when my mother told me she was proud of me when she heard me speak on Gay Liberation in public.)

Other programs of outreach in the next four years must include continued contacts with universities, unions, professional associations and other private and public institutions. In the past year, we have seen the establishment of Gay Centers on university campuses (notably Columbia); Gay caucuses in the National Education Association, the American Library Association and, most recently, the establishment of a Gay legal caucus.

To sum up, it would be easy for us to wring our hands over the fate of the first national candidate to support Gay rights issues and some of us probably will. But if we firmly believe that our case is just, we will use these four years to consolidate and strengthen our movement and begin to make it applicable to the day-to-day lives of the millions of Gay people. We will turn away from contrived protests for protest's sake; and we will work positively in our communities where we already have the potential for immediate and lasting change. We will reject the media freaks and ego-trippers in the movement and we will move out into our communities and relate directly to the people.

This is a time of testing and challenge to the Gay Liberation Movement. Will we meet that challenge?

Sex: How Important Is It?
June 1973

Sex is damned important to everyone, hetero or Gay. But the question we should be asking is, do we over-emphasize the sexual part of our being Gay males at the expense of developing social, cultural and group contacts between us?

In recent years, the larger American culture which we are a part of has "allowed" us to have Gay bars, baths, movie houses. The rationale being that since there are a lot of Homosexuals in the country, it is in the public interest to keep us isolated in bars, baths and movie houses where we are permitted to commit our "perverted" acts out of the view and minds of the general public. Did you ever wonder why the vast majority of Gay places are located in out-of-the-way areas within our major cities?

And like all oppressed peoples throughout history, we have until now accepted this isolation. We go to work every day – in the factories, offices, banks, department stores, construction sites, police and fire departments and even as elected members of local and federal legislatures – and to our co-workers we either represent ourselves as woman-chasers, at worst, or as virtual eunuchs, at best. But almost never are we known as Gay males. Only when we get off work and away from our families do we get dressed in the clothes we prefer, go to a Gay bar and "make out."

How many times have you gone to a Gay bar, stayed for hours, had too much to drink, and been depressed because you went home alone? How many of us go to a Gay bar for the simple and very human purpose of being with people like us and interacting with them on many levels – social, intellectual, cultural and yes, sexual?

Don't get me wrong, I'm not knocking sex; I've had more than my share of it over the years. But frankly, in recent years, I've become more than a little tired of making "conquests" in Gay bars. And, unless I'm deceiving myself, I perceive a general trend among our people away from the "one-night-stand" syndrome towards a real feeling of community and brotherhood based on more than a casual sexual basis.

This trend is part of something which is entirely new in historical terms and has its origins in the United States starting with the Great Depression–World War II era. It wasn't until that time that large numbers of Gay people began to gravitate into "ghetto" areas in every large city in this country. Not even in Europe, which we tend to think of as having a more tolerant attitude towards Homosexuals, have we seen the emergence of Gay ghettoes. Since World War II we have seen Gay ghettoes emerging in cities like Seattle, Portland, Salt Lake City, Houston, Dallas, New Orleans, Atlanta, Minneapolis–St. Paul, Milwaukee, Detroit, Cleveland, Cincinnati, Washington. And in the larger cities we find two or three Gay ghettoes in the same city: Los Angeles, San Francisco, Chicago, Philadelphia, New York, Boston.

My point in bringing this up in this context is that it wasn't until we began relating to each other on more than a sexual basis that we began to relate to each other culturally and socially; and this was due mostly to the emergence of these Gay ghettoes in the United States. It wasn't until we began to know each other as individuals in our community and interacting with each other on a day-to-day basis rather than nameless faces who made fleeting contacts in Gay bars.

If you, like thousands of your Gay brothers, want more out of Gay life than just anonymous sexual encounters, here are some suggestions:

1. When you go to a party or to a bar for an evening, *talk* with people, get to know them. Get over the idea that you have to go home with him that night and probably never see him again. How many times have you made passionate love with someone one night and then seen him on the street the next night and not even said hello?
2. Have Gay friends over for a casual social evening with dinner or dessert and coffee. And if you're part of a Gay couple, get to know other couples on a social basis.
3. Seek out other Gays where you work. Develop your natural feelings of group solidarity whether on your job or after work. And if you really want to be up-front, wear a Gay Lib button to work. (I'm reminded here of a regular customer in my bookshop who is a postman. And he wears a "Gay Revolution" button on his postman's hat every day.)
4. Develop social contacts with Gay women. It's surprising how few Gay males have Gay women as friends; and because of this, Gay males have, in general, many false stereotypes of Gay women. The stereotype of a Gay woman as a cigar-smoking, crude, garage mechanic is equally as false as the stereotype of Gay males.
5. Bring your family and Hetero friends into contact with your Gay life. Have your parents over for dinner at the same time as your Gay friends. And as far as your Hetero friends are concerned, if they react negatively to being socially with Gay people other than yourself, the odds are that they are your friends "in spite of your being Gay."

You'll find that by broadening your social and group contacts with other Gay people, *as Gay people,* your sex life will improve as well. And as we get to know each other on more than a purely sexual basis, we realize the great diversity and beauty of our Gay brothers. At the heart of the Gay Liberation Movement, which in the coming generations is going to do so much to change the basic structure of our society, is this feeling of group solidarity and purpose. Try it; you'll like it.

For All the Jack Staffords in the World
June 1973

Jack Stafford was recently murdered while cruising in a public park in Queens County, New York. Add his name to the rollcall of literally thousands of Gay males who have been murdered by hetero men in this country. Most murders of Gay males by "straight" men go unnoticed in the community and by the media. But the murder of Jack Stafford will receive some attention because he was active in the Gay Liberation Movement. He was an active member of the American Library Association's Gay Task Force.

I remember when I was in high school that one of the favorite pastimes of the boys who had to prove what "men" they were was to go down to the "queer" section of Chicago and beat one up. Then they would come back to school the next day and brag about it. The only other thing they ever bragged about was their conquests of girls; and if you don't think there's a connection between these two "sports," think about it!

When I was fourteen, I was arrested with a thirty-year-old male for Homosexual activity; and the only thing my stepfather had to say to me at the time was that "when I was your age, me and my buddies would go down to Clark and Division and beat up a few of 'em."

Many things have changed in these United States during the past decade; but one of the things that hasn't changed is the need of macho hetero men to prove their manhood to their buddies and their "girlfriends" by going out and beating up a queer and, in certain instances, killing a queer.

We'll have to leave it to the psychologists to delve into psyches of hetero men for the reasons behind their murder/rapes of Gay males. But as a people interested in self-preservation, we should take steps to protect our own.

Probably the most obvious way of self-protection would be to urge our brothers *not* to cruise in public places, especially at night. But that is not a realistic suggestion given the fact that many Gay males, almost ritualistically, cruise parks, johns, trucks, streets, etc. And this is inevitable, considering the limited avenues open to meet other Gay males.

But if you're in a period of your life where cruising in public places is your bag, at least take some rudimentary precautions. Like, if you see a gang of toughs in the park or area you're cruising, make a quick exit. And if your favorite cruising area is regularly harassed by hetero "men," do what some brothers in San Francisco did about six years ago.

In Golden Gate State Park, a gang of heteros were regularly beating on Gays. So a group of Gay males got together, hid in the bushes, and when they saw the gang, they overpowered them, made them strip and left them tied to the trees for the police to find. Needless to say, the park again became a peaceful cruising area. Vigilante action shouldn't be necessary; but as a final weapon to use, it can be effective.

Other ways you and your friends can protect yourselves are:

1. Carry a loud whistle and *use* it.
2. Take Karate lessons (a number of Gay groups now have Karate classes).
3. Get together with other Gay people in your community and demand that the local police crack down on neighborhood gangs that prey on Gay people.
4. If your city has an auxiliary civilian police unit, join and help patrol those areas that are unsafe for Gays.

While writing this article on the violence that "straight" men inflict on Gay males, a perfect example of this kind of thing has been reported in the media. You've probably read about it in your local papers.

It seems that three fraternity members of Chi Chi Chi Fraternity of Pierce College in Los Angeles, California, decided that Fred Bronner, another student at the college, was "obnoxious, and a mama's boy." So they decided to teach him a lesson by leaving him up in the mountains, whereupon Bronner, while trying to get back to civilization, fell off a cliff and died.

Whether Fred Bronner was Gay or not is beside the point. He was murdered for the same reasons our Gay brothers are murdered in this county. His lack of interest in girls, his disinterest in sports and his general passive nature were deemed a threat by his "brothers."

But the real tragedy of this kind of violence against Gay people is that it doesn't arouse indignation in the general community or even among Gay people themselves (yet). Even when the murderers have been apprehended, juries throughout the country have either acquitted the defendant or given him a light sentence if he used as his defense that the victim "made sexual advances toward him."

Can you imagine a Homosexual man or woman being acquitted or given a light sentence with a defense that the heterosexual made sexual advances? Of course not. And until heterosexual people are made to respect a Homosexual lifestyle as being just as good, just as valid, just as healthy and just as equal in the eyes of the law, the murders of Gay people by hets will continue and will continue to be excused by the system.

So rest in peace, Jack Stafford. If your death serves to dramatize to even one other Gay person the kind of anger and indignation that leads to a health demand for self-respect and self-preservation, it was not in vain.

Gray Is Good
August 1973

In the past couple of years, since passing my thirtieth birthday, I've become more conscious of how oppressive to all of our psyches is the fetish of Youth Cultism which permeates American culture – not to mention our Gay culture. The problem of ageism (like heterosexism and racism) is one that affects all of us – Gay and non-Gay, black and white, male and female, et al.

How many of us, in our before-thirty existence, dreaded the onset of "middle-age" signaled by our thirtieth birthdays? I think it's safe to say that the vast majority of us (myself included) regarded that thirtieth year as the crest in our lives; and that from then on, it was all downhill. I remember thinking, when I became twenty-five, that I only had five years left – almost as if my life would be over when I reached thirty – that no one would "want" me; that if I didn't have a lover by then, I never would; and that, in general, my value as a human being would be lessened.

Well, I've found out that was all a lot of BS. I'm more at peace now with myself than I ever was; I have perspective on relationships and ideas which gives me a degree of "calm"; I don't have the constant need anymore to "make out" all the time to prove to myself how desirable I am; I no longer have a need to "impress" others – they can either accept me as I am or not at all; and, most importantly, I no longer dread the coming of age. On the contrary, I actually welcome it, honestly.

Recently I received a phone call from a 24-year-old Gay male who was feeling "anxiety" because he had gone to a party over the weekend and hadn't met anyone; and he had to talk to someone in the hopes of relieving his anxiety feelings. We talked about how – as Gay people – we're psychologically conditioned by society to think of ourselves almost entirely in a sexual vein with the emphasis on youth being the key to desirability.

All of us want to be desirable to other people, both sexually and emotionally. But our culture places too much emphasis on youthfulness, which results in youth cultism. There is nothing innately better about being under-thirty than over-thirty, and vice versa. The needs, thoughts, ideas and feelings of every human being are of equal importance; but through societal conditioning, we give more importance to the under-thirties.

For example, in a recent Sunday edition of *The New York Times*, there was an article on Homosexual teachers. It told of a number of Gay teachers around the country who are fighting to end discrimination against Gay people in the teaching profession. At the end of the article, the author wrote, "There is concern that homosexual teachers are not appropriate models for children. And the ridicule with which such teachers are liable to be confronted, particularly from older boys, often makes for disciplinary problems. It is this difficulty that is the basis for the dismissals of homosexuals for 'unprofessional conduct.'"

Rather than disciplining the students (younger people) for their misbehavior vis-à-vis a Homosexual teacher, we find that the teachers (older people) are being fired or not hired for "unprofessional conduct." Think about it; this kind of pampering and catering to the prejudices of young people in our society is epidemic.

In terms of our Gay culture, look at the Gay bars with their emphasis on youth – go-go-boys, "Groovy Guy" contests in which all the contestants are usually under twenty-five. Look at the Gay publications – where the vast majority of pictures are under-thirty types subliminally telling us that youth and sexual desirability are synonymous. Look at the general news media reports that usually emphasize the activities and problems of young Gay people. And last if not least, look at the Gay Lib organizations themselves (with the exceptions of West Side Discussion Group in New York and SIR in San Francisco), whose social and political direction is geared to young people.

All of us have a great deal to learn from our older Gay brothers; it was an older Gay brother, Walt Whitman, who wrote some of the most beautiful Gay poetry in which he saw the future of democracy in "the love of comrades" and it was an older Gay brother, Oscar Wilde, who first stood up and predicted the emergence of "the love that dare not speak its name." It was an older Gay brother – Edward Carpenter – who first wrote of the political, economic and social implications of Gay Liberation.

And in my own personal experience, let me give tribute to the older Gay brothers who have enriched my life with their friendship:

Joe, 74, former college president, recently retired. Joe refuses to go along with the stereotype of Retired People. He takes gym class at the "Y" twice a week; he was actively involved as a volunteer worker in the McGovern campaign; he has an active and creative social life; his genuine warmth and enthusiasm is contagious; and he is enthusiastic and supportive of the emerging Gay Liberation movement.

Bernard, in his 60s, head of a major university library. Bernard refuses to give in to the idea that working people over 60 should be thinking of retiring soon and collecting Social Security. He puts in long hours and brings heartfelt devotion to his work. He helped pass out leaflets headed "Get The Mafia and the Cops out of Gay Bars" during the Christopher Street/Stonewall Riots; and he was active in the Gay Liberation Front.

Warren, in his 40s, a leader and worker in New York's West Side Discussion Group for over a decade. Warren's dedication over the years to the Gay movement is one of the keys to the continued growth of WSDG, which resulted recently in the opening of their Gay Community Center.

It is in our own self-interest, whatever our age, to work for an end to youth cultism. And, as Gay people, we have a particular self-interest because most of us do not create our own families with the attendant securities of having children and grandchildren.

If our Gay Liberation movement is to become a realistic and meaningful one, it must begin to consider the needs and problems of older Gay people. Like, is there discrimination against older Gay single people in the administration of Social Security? Do the various government-funded Senior Citizen programs discriminate against Gay people? Do we take into consideration the social and economic needs of our older brothers and sisters? And, in our own thinking, do we give more importance to the concerns of younger Gay people at the expense of older Gay people?

The past is prologue.

The Meaning of Obscenity
October 1973

The term *obscenity* is so loaded with personal value-judgments that it is virtually impossible to give it a universal definition. To Richard Nixon, Norman Vincent Peale, Billy Graham, Mao Tse Tung and others of like ilk, the mere sight of two men holding hands is "obscene." To many others like myself, "obscenity" best describes Richard Nixon's involvement in Watergate, or Mao Tse Tung's lieutenant saying "there are no homosexuals in China."

The obscenity issue is one which has more meaning for Gay people than for hets. In heterosexual literature, it is only the most extreme overt sexuality that is labeled *obscene*, but in Gay literature the standard is quite different. The mere sight of male genitals in a homosexual publication is enough to send the average anti-permissivist into a rage – but the same photographs presented in heterosexual publications are somehow acceptable. To illustrate this point, take for example the instant acceptance by the general public of the new "magazines for women" (*Playgirl* being the best known) which in no small way feature male nudes – when for years homosexual magazines have done the same thing with resultant oppression from the general public.

Some of you undoubtedly remember *One Magazine*, the first Gay publication in the USA. In the early 1950s, the US Post Office decided that *One* was obscene and banned it from the mails. *One* took the Post Office to court and after a protracted battle that went all the way to the Supreme Court, *One* won its case. But the most frightening aspect of that case was that the magazine was a rather literate journal of Gay poetry, fiction, letters, news, etc. In the more than 100 issues of *One* there were no pictures of nudes; and in only one issue was there a drawing of a male nude.

Even among some Gay liberationists the belief persists that all sexually oriented material is obscene. It is ironic and prophetic that the reactionaries among heterosexuals and many radicals among Gay people have this common bond. An example may be found in the radical Effeminists, a group of Gay radicals who have a patronizing attitude toward women, who refused sale of their publication to my bookshop because I carried *erotic* Gay magazines and books such as *QQ Magazine* and "Song of the Loon." I was only too pleased not to carry the Effeminists' publication and thereby reaffirm the idea that not only is Gay good, but also that Gay sex is good.

As Gay Liberation makes greater and greater strides and we begin to relate to one another on levels other than sexual, we will find that we Gay people really do like one another; sex then assumes its place as just another part of our Gay existence. By taking the emphasis off Gay sex we find that it is even more pleasurable, more open, more fulfilling – because as we move away from the image of ourselves that hets have forced us to assume we begin to define what our lives are really all about.

There is nothing good or bad, healthy or unhealthy, positive or negative about Gay sex *in itself* or any other life function – but heterosexual society judges it *obscene*. As Shakespeare said, "There is nothing good or bad; but thinking makes it so." We must think positively. Our Gay lifestyle *in itself* is neither good nor bad – but simply one of several possible choices. For those who have chosen it – it is good. It *is* beautiful.

We must never let those who would do us wrong convince us otherwise.

Notes

1. Early Out

1 Barbara Gittings and Kay Tobin Lahusen gay history papers and photographs, Manuscripts and Archives Division, New York Public Library, Astor, Lenox, and Tilden Foundations, Craig Rodwell Folder, 1966–70, interview with Craig Rodwell for *The Gay Crusaders*.
2 Craig Rodwell Papers, Manuscripts and Archives Division, New York Public Library, Astor, Lenox, and Tilden Foundations, Birth announcement, Box 5.
3 Michael Scherker, *The Reminiscences of Craig Rodwell*, New York, 1986, 1.
4 Unless otherwise noted, the account of Rodwell's early years and life here is drawn with appreciation from several sets of recorded interviews, including the 1970 interviews by Kay Tobin Lahusen for *The Gay Crusaders* (Paperback Library Edition, 1972), two oral history interviews by Michael Scherker for *The Reminiscences of Craig Rodwell* in 1986, and in hours of interviews two years before Rodwell's death by Martin Duberman for his book *Stonewall* (Plume/Penguin Random House, 1993), in the Martin B. Duberman Papers, Manuscripts and Archives Division, New York Public Library, Astor, Lenox, and Tilden Foundations.
5 Scherker, *The Reminiscences*, 1.
6 Ibid., 2.
7 "Scholarships to Be Aided by 'Sno-Ball,'" *Chicago Tribune*, December 28, 1952, 104, Newspapers.com.
8 *Bangor Daily News*, Bangor, ME, March 9, 1956, obituaries, 26, Newspapers.com.

9. Craig Rodwell Papers, Marion's family photo album, Box 5.
10. Scherker, *The Reminiscences*, 2.
11. Craig Rodwell Papers, Marion's family photo album, Box 5.
12. *Encyclopedia of Chicago*, "Rogers Park," http://www.encyclopedia.chicagohistory.org/pages/1086.html.
13. Craig Rodwell Papers, Sullivan High School progress reports, Box 13.
14. Craig Rodwell Papers, Marion Rodwell's family photo album, Box 14.
15. Baseball-Reference.com
16. Rodwell provided similar accounts on his Chicago cruising experiences to Kay Tobin Lahusen, Martin Duberman, Michael Scherker in the tape-recorded interviews.
17. Scherker, *The Reminiscences*, 4.
18. The account here of the police apprehension of Frank Bucalo and Craig Rodwell and the subsequent court actions is taken from the 1955 case records in the Criminal Court of Cook County. It is supplemented by Rodwell's own memory as told in taped interviews with Duberman and Scherker.
19. Marion Rodwell had remarried in 1951, while Craig was in Chicago Junior School, to Henry "Hank" Kastman.
20. Scherker, *The Reminiscences*, 5.
21. Criminal Court of Cook County case files, 1955.
22. "Kills Himself as Police Hunt Nude Photos," *Chicago Tribune*, March 7, 1957, 3, Newspapers.com.
23. *Transcript-Telegram*, Holyoke, MA, June 7, 1988, Obituaries, Newspapers.com.
24. Craig Rodwell Papers, Letter from Louis Rodwell to Craig Rodwell dated December 18, 1954, from Milwaukee, Box 13.
25. *ONE Magazine* out of Los Angeles and the *Mattachine Review* out of San Francisco began publication in 1953 and 1955, respectively. They and *The Ladder*, published first in 1956 by the Daughters of Bilitis and also out of San Francisco, were the earliest national publications of the homophile movement.
26. Jonathan Ned Katz, *Gay American History* (Meridian, [1976] 1992), 412. There are many published references to the origins of the word *Mattachine* as being Italian or Spanish. In his interview with Katz, Harry Hay said the origin was the French Société Mattachine, a secret fraternity of masked performers, which seemed to apply to the plight of homosexuals of the 1950s.
27. Craig Rodwell Papers, Chicago Public High Schools diploma, 1958, Box 13.
28. Craig Rodwell Papers, Boston Conservatory of Music letter of acceptance and report for first semester courses, Box 14.
29. Rodwell urged gay people in the arts to come out of the closet in the September–October 1972 issue of *QQ Magazine* in an article entitled "Gay People and the Arts."

30 Rodwell clarified in his interviews with Martin Duberman that the street queens did not go out in full drag, but they would wear eyeliner. He said he wasn't drawn to it, but that it was just something that was done and he fell in with it.

2. New York I – Harvey Milk, Light and Dark Days

1 David Carter, *Stonewall: The Riots That Sparked the Gay Revolution* (St. Martin's Press, 2004), 31, and Randy Shilts, *The Mayor of Castro Street* (St. Martin's Press, 1982).
2 Craig Rodwell Papers, Manuscripts and Archives Division, New York Public Library, Astor, Lenox, and Tilden Foundations, letter and memo to the New York Chief City Magistrate, October 2, 1959, Box 1.
3 Ibid., response from the Chief City Magistrate on October 8, 1959.
4 The date of the meeting between Rodwell and Milk has been variously referred to as 1960, 1961, and 1962 in published works. Considering other agreed-upon references in the timeline, 1961 appears to be correct. Lillian Faderman (*Harvey Milk*, Yale University Press, 2018, 249) notes that Harvey's lover Joe Campbell moved out in September 1961 and Faderman cites a letter from Milk to Joe Campbell with one last appeal to come back in December 1961. Meanwhile, Rodwell remembered a Christmas gift exchange with Milk (Duberman interview), and in his interview with Randy Shilts for *The Mayor of Castro Street*, Shilts' notes say that Milk had broken up with Campbell "2 or 3 weeks before [Milk] met Craig." Faderman also notes that Milk told Rodwell he was still grieving his relationship with Campbell. Rodwell remembers his age being "twenty," which would have been possible in 1961, having met Harvey prior to his birthday on October 31, when he would have turned twenty-one. That would have made him old enough to officially join Mattachine. Finally, the Riis Park incident was in September 1962, signaling the end of the relationship of about a year.
5 Unless otherwise noted, the details of the relationship between Craig Rodwell and Harvey Milk are based on Duberman's interviews with Rodwell for *Stonewall* and Shilts' description in *The Mayor of Castro Street*, and in Shilts' interview notes with Rodwell for the book.
6 Prior to AIDS, prior to computer dating, and Grindr, cruising was an almost necessary way for gay men to meet each other. Cruising locations in the US and around the world were passed along in the subculture and later published in various pocket guides.
7 Rodwell lays out the account of these circumstances and his regret over them in his taped interviews with Martin Duberman.
8 Rodwell provided a detailed account of his arrest at Riis Park to Michael Scherker for Scherker's oral history project in 1986. Rodwell provided a similar account in recorded interviews with Martin Duberman. This sequence relies on both interviews and attempts to reconcile differences

in Rodwell's memory of events that occurred more than two decades previous. Given that the Riis Park arrest occurred after he had met Harvey Milk and on Labor Day, the date of the incident would have to have been 1962. In an article he wrote for *QQ Magazine* in June 1971, he also referred to the Riis Park arrest as being nine years earlier. Similarly, David Carter, in *Stonewall*, also puts the Riis Park incident in 1962. In addition, a letter from a friend after Craig's attempt on his own life is postmarked 1962 (Craig Rodwell Papers, Box 1).
9 NYC LGBT Historic Sites Project website, Riis Park Beach.
10 Scherker, *The Reminiscences*, 32.
11 Craig remembered different amounts that he had to pay his fine in various interviews. In his *QQ Magazine* essay, Craig remembered that he had $21, but all amounts were less than the needed $25.
12 Randy Shilts, interview notes with Craig Rodwell, 1990. Rodwell recounted this portion of what happened in the House of Detention, specifically about his shaved head.
13 Shilts, *The Mayor of Castro Street*, 27.
14 Faderman, *Harvey Milk*, 47. After the arrest and conviction of Frank in Chicago and Craig's brush with the law himself, he ingested a handful of aspirin with a Coke, which he believed (incorrectly) would be fatal.
15 Dean Oswalt, interview with author, April 5, 2022. The short biographical account is based on Dean Oswalt's recollections of his older brother, who died in March 2022.
16 Faderman, *Harvey Milk*, 48–50.

3. New York II – Militants in Mattachine

1 Unless otherwise noted, the sequence of Rodwell's involvement in Mattachine in the 1960s and the series of pickets during those years reflects his memory in the three extensive interviews, the 1970 interview with Kay Tobin Lahusen, the 1986 interviews with Michael Scherker and the 1991 interviews with Martin Duberman. In some instances, dates and sequences have been reconciled where inconsistencies existed.
2 By 1964, the Mattachine Society of New York and other regional Mattachine groups were independent organizations, as the national society had dissolved in 1961.
3 Scherker, *The Reminiscences*, 12.
4 The date of this meeting and the beginning of a short affair is supported in Rodwell's interview with Martin Duberman, in which Rodwell remembers the meeting as January or February 1964. It also coincides with letters written by Leitsch to Rodwell from Fire Island in July 1964, indicating that the affair had run its course. Rodwell's memory was that the affair lasted less than a year. Meanwhile, Leitsch then showed up on the Mattachine Society of New York's committee lists in August 1964. All of that precedes the 1965 election in which Leitsch ran for "president elect" in May 1965.

5 "Historically Speaking," *New York Mattachine Times*, January–February 1973, Gale Archives of Sexuality and Gender, New York Public Library.
6 Craig Rodwell Papers, Manuscripts and Archives Division, New York Public Library, Astor, Lenox, and Tilden Foundations, undated letter from Dick Leitsch to Rodwell, Box 1.
7 Craig Rodwell Papers, letter from Dick Leitsch to Rodwell, July 1964, Box 1.
8 Barbara Gittings and Kay Tobin Lahusen gay history papers and photographs, New York Public Library, Craig Rodwell Folder 1966–70, notes for *The Gay Crusaders*.
9 *Eastern Mattachine Magazine*, May 1965, Gale Archives of Sexuality and Gender.
10 The subject of Julian Hodges' resignation has received differing interpretations. Rodwell told Martin Duberman there was a financial scandal that Hodges took the blame for; David Carter said that Leitsch told him that Hodges had admitted a misappropriation of funds; Jack Nichols, in his review of Duberman's book, said that Leitsch told him that it was a simple matter of reimbursement of Hodges' use of his personal credit card for ECHO conference accommodations; and in a letter to a Rutgers professor in November 1965, Leitsch said Hodges resigned due to a change in his job.
11 Randy Shilts, *Conduct Unbecoming* (St. Martin's Press, 1993), 17, 69, 164.
12 Rodwell summary of events of Whitehall demonstration, Duberman interviews, tape 6.
13 John Loughery, *The Other Side of Silence* (Henry Holt, 1998), 269.
14 Tracy Baim, *Barbara Gittings, Gay Pioneer* (Prairie Avenue Productions, 2015), 60–1.
15 Loughery, *The Other Side of Silence*, 269.
16 Baim, *Barbara Gittings, Gay Pioneer*, 60–1.
17 Michael G. Long, *Gay Is Good, The Life and Letters of Gay Rights Pioneer Franklin Kameny* (Syracuse University Press, 2014), 86.
18 Ibid., Note 11, 346.
19 John D'Emilio, *Sexual Politics, Sexual Communities* (University of Chicago Press, 1983), 164–5.
20 Baim, *Barbara Gittings, Gay Pioneer*, 60–1. This section relies on Barbara Gittings' list of protests, with dates, places, the number of picketers who attended, and known press coverage.
21 Duberman interviews, tape 8; Scherker, *The Reminiscences*, 16. Two and three decades later, Rodwell's memory of the sequence of the inspiration for the Annual Reminders has varied in published accounts. For the first Annual Reminder to occur on July 4, 1965, the inspiration for the reminder would have had to occur after the White House demonstrations in April and May. Some historians have placed the first reminder as being in 1966, but letters sent by Rodwell to Philadelphia refer, as do numerous other documents and a newspaper account, to 1965 as the first reminder, and the "fifth" reminder is well documented as being in 1969.
22 Baim, *Barbara Gittings, Gay Pioneer*, 61.
23 *The Philadelphia Inquirer*, July 5, 1965, 1, Newspapers.com.
24 Long, *Gay Is Good*, 97.

25. *New York Mattachine Newsletter*, 1965, Frank Kameny papers, The Deviant's Archive.
26. Barbara Gittings and Kay Tobin Lahusen gay history papers and photographs, New York Public Library, Craig Rodwell Folder 1966–70, notes for *The Gay Crusaders*.
27. Kameny letter to Rodwell, June 20, 1966, Gale Archives of Sexuality and Gender.
28. Craig Rodwell Papers, letter to John Marshall, June 1, 1966. Box 7, Folder 10.
29. Ibid., Annual Reminder Committee donation and reservation checklist and contract with the Allied Bus Corp.
30. Craig Rodwell Papers, "Rough Draft" of remarks to Mattachine Midwest.
31. Scherker, *The Reminiscences*, 29.
32. Scherker, *The Reminiscences*, 25.
33. A sit-in had occurred the previous year at Dewey's coffee shop in Philadelphia, when several LGBT teenagers refused to leave after being denied service because of their sexual orientation, which, while not publicized widely, would have been known about by the sip-in protesters.
34. The details of the planned sip-in have been recounted numerous times. I have relied on Craig Rodwell's accounts to Michael Scherker and Martin Duberman, the research by David Carter in *Stonewall*, and the contemporaneous reporting by Thomas A. Johnson, "3 Deviates Invite Exclusion by Bars," *New York Times*, April 22, 1966, 43.
35. This is the direct quote Johnson used in the *Times* story.
36. Julius' was actually in support of the sip-in. As reported by Philip Crawford Jr. in *The Mafia and the Gays* (Philip Crawford Jr., North Haven, CT, [2015] 2023), Julius' had received an order on April 1, 1966, which suspended its liquor license on the grounds it was disorderly for permitting homosexuals as customers around midnight on November 12, 1965. Julius' was appealing the suspension and wanted the State Liquor Authority to end the policy of not serving gay customers. 68–70.
37. Craig Rodwell Papers, press release, "Homosexuals Challenge SLA," dated April 22, 1966, Box 1.
38. "SLA Won't Act Against Bars Refusing Service to Deviates," *New York Times*, April 26, 1966, 55.
39. "Policemen Forbidden to Entrap Homosexuals to Make Arrests," *New York Times*, May 11, 1966, 36, TimesMachine.
40. Scherker, *The Reminiscences*, 27.
41. The account of this relationship and related experiences was described in an author interview with David Stienecker on January 16, 2022.

4. Inside the Oscar Wilde – Mercer Street

1. Scherker, *The Reminiscences*, 20.
2. Craig Rodwell Papers, Manuscripts and Archives Division, New York Public Library, Astor, Lenox, and Tilden Foundations, Correspondence with Richard Leitsch, November 2, 1966, Box 1.

3 These dates are confirmed in the press release announcing the opening of the Oscar Wilde (Frank Kameny Papers, The Deviant's Archive, Library of Congress, OWMB folder) and in correspondence with Dick Leitsch in a letter from Rodwell to the Board of Directors of Mattachine Society of New York (Gale Archives of Sexuality and Gender, Correspondence Dick Leitsch, letter from Rodwell to the Board of Directors of MSNY, January 1966–February 1967).
4 Duberman interviews with Rodwell, 1991, Tape 6.
5 "John B. Whyte, 75, Model and Fire Island Developer," *New York Times*, April 12, 2004, Section B, 7, TimesMachine.
6 Karl Grossman, "The Fire Island Trials: The Stonewall Before Stonewall," *Fire Island News*, June 21, 2019. Grossman was a police beat reporter for the Long Island Press and covered Suffolk County.
7 Description of the area in the 1960s from author interview with Fred Sargeant, January 28, 2008.
8 The account of the opening of the bookshop is drawn from Rodwell's interviews with Michael Scherker and Kay Tobin Lahusen's *The Gay Crusaders*.
9 Advertisement, *Village Voice*, November 16, 1967, 6, Google archive.
10 Various publications have listed the opening of the Oscar Wilde on Thanksgiving, which may have arisen through a shorthand for Thanksgiving week. Both the grand opening announcement and the press release put the opening at November 18–19. The 19th being a Sunday would qualify as "Thanksgiving week."
11 Press release announcing bookshop opening, Frank Kameny Papers, OWMB folder, The Deviant's Archive, Library of Congress.
12 Ibid.
13 Ibid.
14 Duberman, *Stonewall*, 202.
15 *An Introduction to the Homophile Movement* (Institute of Social Ethics, Hartford, CT, 1967), Foster Gunnison Jr. Papers, University of Connecticut, Christopher Street Liberation Day Committee, Archives and Special Collections.
16 Ibid., 7.
17 Ibid., 29.
18 The Oscar Wilde was the first bookstore in the United States to open that was dedicated solely to gay and lesbian literature. Hal Call had opened his Adonis bookstore in San Francisco earlier in 1967, but it focused mostly on erotica. (See Lucas Hilderbrand, "The Uncut Version: The Mattachine Society's Pornographic Epilogue," *Sexualities*, University of California, 2015; and Dr. Bill Lipsky, "Hal Call: Homophiles and the Struggle for Social Acceptance," *San Francisco Bay Times*, August 11, 2022; and Lillian Faderman, *The Gay Revolution*," 669, n.6.) However, the distinction of being the first to open and under what qualifications is almost beside the point. The Oscar Wilde became an immediate community center. It was the heartbeat of the movement for many activists, who

would board a bus to the Annual Reminders. It also was the communication center during the Stonewall riots, and the center of the action for the first Christopher Street Liberation Day march. The Adonis, meanwhile, leaned into the successful business of gay erotica. (See Joe Bourdage, "Hal Call, Pan-Graphic Press, and the Adonis Bookstore, Historical Essay," FoundSF.org.)
19 Tobin, *The Gay Crusaders*, 71.
20 Duberman interviews, Tape 6.
21 Duberman interviews, Tape 1.
22 Richard Ellman, *Oscar Wilde* (Alfred A. Knopf, 1988), 186, 206.
23 MSNY Newsletter, August 1964, Archives of Gender and Sexuality.
24 Fred Sargeant, interview with author, January 28, 2008.
25 Mail Order Catalog, 1968, Craig Rodwell Papers.
26 Ellman, *Oscar Wilde*, 386.
27 Letter from Clark Polak to Craig Rodwell from Trojan Book Service, Craig Rodwell Papers, Box 6. The reference to Mary Renault refers to the British author who wrote serious fiction about male couples.
28 Unless otherwise noted in this chapter, the behind-the-scenes account of Rodwell and Sargeant's relationship and their work together at the Oscar Wilde is taken from the author's interviews with Sargeant in January–February 2008
29 Randy Wicker, interview with author, September 2022.
30 Oscar Wilde Mail Order Catalog, 1968, Craig Rodwell Papers.
31 Ibid.
32 Ibid.
33 Correspondence between Rodwell and Ed Fancher of *The Village Voice*, March 1968, Craig Rodwell Papers, Box 6.
34 Dudley Clendinen and Adam Nagourney, *Out for Good, The Struggle to Build A Gay Rights Movement in America* (Touchstone, 1990). 45.
35 Oscar Wilde Mail Order Catalog, 1968, Craig Rodwell Papers.
36 Correspondence between Craig Rodwell and the DOB, June 1970, Craig Rodwell Papers, Box 1.
37 Duberman interviews with Rodwell, Tape 6.
38 *The New York Hymnal*, February 1968, Vol. I, No.1.
39 The letters to the Post and to Dear Abby in this section are found in Craig Rodwell Papers, Box 2.
40 Betsy Kalin, interview with Kay Lahusen, March 2018, Outwords Archive, https://theoutwordsarchive.org/interview/lahusen-kay/.
41 Ora McCreary, "A Witness to Gay History: Some Memories of 1968–72," 2008, and interview with the author on May 5, 2022.
42 This sequence regarding Ellen Broidy's involvement with the Oscar Wilde was provided during an author interview on June 6, 2022.
43 Margaret Talbot and David Talbot, *By the Light of Burning Dreams* (David and Margaret Talbot/HarperCollins, 2021), 217–18.
44 Jonathan Ned Katz, interview with the author, May 7, 2023.
45 Sargeant interview, January–February 2008.

46 The section on violence at the Oscar Wilde is drawn from Rodwell's reminiscences with Michael Scherker (21) and interviews with Fred Sargeant.
47 Letter from FBI, 1970, Craig Rodwell Papers, Box 1.
48 "1969, A Year of Bombings," *New York Times*, City Room blog, August 27, 2009, TimesMachine.
49 Rodger Streitmatter, *Unspeakable: The Rise of the Gay and Lesbian Press in America* (Faber and Faber, 1995). 86.
50 Craig Rodwell Papers, Draft letter to "Gay Brothers & Sisters," February 1972, Box 2.

5. *The New York Hymnal*

1 Rodwell used several different forms of capitalization for *The New York Hymnal*, sometimes all upper case, sometimes all lower case, or a combination. For consistency, this text uses uppers and lowers.
2 Prior to the digital age, the light table was invaluable asset to getting copy and headlines straight. Composition and paste-up on top of a template seen through a light table made it possible to get a professional look.
3 Encyclopedia of Lesbian, Gay, Bisexual, and Transgender History in America, Vol. 2 (Charles Scribner's Sons, 2004), 341.
4 *The New York Hymnal*, Vol. I, no 1, February 1968, 1–2.
5 Ibid., 2.
6 Additional references to *The New York Hymnal* in this section are from issues in Volume I, Nos. 1–6 and Volume II, No. 1.
7 This historical synopsis relies on Carter's *Stonewall* (St. Martin's Press, 2004).
8 It was something of a contradiction to use pseudonyms in *The Hymnal* after Rodwell's decision at the Mattachine Newsletter to use his own name, but he wanted the impression of a larger staff.
9 According to the NYC Historic Sites project (https://www.nyclgbtsites.org/site/corduroy-club/), the Corduroy Club was a private social club started in 1966 that offered the largely older lesbian and gay community an alternative to the bar scene, holding such events as dances, card parties, plays, movies, and dinners. By 1968 it had a membership of more than 1,000. The club was founded by members of the West Side Discussion Group. *Gay Scene Guide* in 1969 listed it as "a bottle club – bring your own drinks for set-ups. Nice cleanly-run establishment…. It's a quiet and reserved club, crowded weekends." Rodwell described it in *The Hymnal* as "probably the only legitimate private club in New York City." In 1970 the Mattachine Society's *Guidebook* called it the "oldest and finest legitimately private gay club in the city," noting that an existing member must sponsor another's membership. The Corduroy Club was a significant effort by the pre-Stonewall LGBT community in New York to have a social space that was outside of the control of the Mafia, New York State Liquor Authority regulations, and police arrests and entrapment.

10 Craig Rodwell Papers, Manuscripts and Archives Division, New York Public Library, Astor, Lenox, and Tilden Foundations, Professional and Political Correspondence 1963–1970, Box 1.
11 By comparison, Lilli Vincenz, who was the editor of Washington Mattachine's *The Homosexual Citizen*, resigned in 1967 after an article she had accepted on astrology was rejected by Frank Kameny (an astronomer). With Vincenz gone, there were no further issues of *The Homosexual Citizen* after May 1967. (See Streitmatter's *Unspeakable* for this and other editorial disputes in the lesbian and gay press.)
12 A comprehensive history of the lesbian and gay press is available in Streitmatter's *Unspeakable* and in Tracy Baim's *Gay Press, Gay Power: The Growth of LGBT Community Newspapers in America* (Prairie Avenue Productions and Windy City Media Group, 2012).

6. Stonewall and Gay Power

1 Michael Denneny, *On Christopher Street* (University of Chicago Press, 2023), 291.
2 Various published reports refer to the card game as poker or bridge. It was neither; Sargeant says it was canasta.
3 The description of the events at Stonewall and the sequence of Craig Rodwell's and Fred Sargeant's involvement is taken from two author interviews with Fred Sargeant in 2001 and 2008 as well as Rodwell's oral history with Michael Scherker and recorded interviews Martin Duberman conducted for his book *Stonewall*.
4 It is helpful to realize that the first "night" of the riots was in the very early hours of Saturday morning (July 28, 1969) but sometimes referred to as Friday night. The second "night" of the riots was truly Saturday night.
5 Carter, *The Stonewall Riots*, 131.
6 Author interview with Fred Sargeant, 2008. Sargeant clearly recalls their position as being directly across the street from the entrance to the Stonewall. He was positioned opposite the door and could see into the bar when the door opened. He and Rodwell had been separated from time to time during the night and they moved with the crowd. At one point, Rodwell climbed a "stoop," often mentioned in accounts of the riot. There is only one set of stairs near the Stonewall, and it's at 55 Christopher Street, just west of the Stonewall, where Rodwell could view the crowd. Christopher Park in 1969 was overgrown, and not maintained as it is today. At night, you couldn't see through the park due to vegetation and tree growth.
7 The sequence of the police action follows the timeline set out by Carter in *The Stonewall Riots*.
8 Sargeant had never been interviewed about this, although Rodwell had related his version in various accounts, sometimes saying that Sargeant told him to shut up. Rodwell was known to enhance his story from time to time, as he had when he wrote an entire letter in Sargeant's name to Frank Kameny after the last Annual Reminder, even though Sargeant had not

attended the reminder to keep the Oscar Wilde open after the Stonewall riots. The enhancements were a source of tension in their relationship.
9 Dennis Altman, *Homosexual Oppression & Liberation* (New York University Press, 1971), 116.
10 Author interview with Edmund White (March 10, 2024), in which he references his letter to Ann and Alfred Corn shortly after the riots broke out.
11 Sargeant remembered this in detail. While he didn't know DeLarverie, he was convinced when he saw photos of her later that she was the lesbian he had seen just feet away who had uttered the plea for help that became a turning point of the riot. Dick Leitsch of New York Mattachine also reported that it was a lesbian who threw the first punch during the riots in his story for *The Advocate* (See Streitmatter, *Unspeakable*, 120, n.8.) The lore that developed around Marsha P. Johnson and Sylvia Rivera as having been the spark for the riots was colorful but false. Neither was there at the start of the riots, by their own accounts.
12 Charles Kaiser, *The Gay Metropolis* (Houghton-Mifflin, 1997), 198. Historian David Carter questions whether the "unidentified lesbian" was DeLarverie as she had minimized her role in a public symposium and was not taken into custody. Carter's theory is that people would have seen her and known her, but as was noted she did not come out of the door of the Stonewall, there was great confusion, and it was nighttime. The fact that Sargeant didn't know DeLarverie counters Carter's theory that everyone would have known her. Rodwell and Sargeant both lived and worked in the Village, and Carter did not interview Sargeant.
13 "Stormé DeLarverie, Early Leader in the Gay Rights Movement, Is Dead," *New York Times*, May 30, 2014, B-16, TimesMachine.
14 *Newsweek* did not cover the Stonewall riots until October 1969, while *Time* magazine did not cover the riots at all until ten years later. *Time* did publish its controversial report on homosexuality in America in October 1969, which prompted a protest at their offices in New York.
15 Fred Sargeant, interview with author, 2008.
16 Timeline and sequence summarized from David Carter's exhaustive research into the riot in *The Stonewall Riots* chapter, "Lancing the Festering Wound of Anger."
17 David Carter suggested that Rodwell was the person that Edmund White saw, but Sargeant says it was likely him, since Craig had gone home to get some sleep before whatever was going to happen Saturday night.
18 "Village Raid Stirs Melee," *New York Post*, Sunday, June 29, 1969, 14.
19 Scherker, *The Reminiscences*, 45–6.
20 Carter, *The Stonewall Riots*, 183. He estimated the crowd at "a couple of thousand."
21 Carter, *The Stonewall Riots*, 194.
22 Fred Sargeant is clear on his memory of this point. There were so many people, cars could not get through. But the two of them had not set up a checkpoint of who was gay and who was not in vehicles. It was the kind of story Rodwell liked to embellish.

23 Leaflet – "Get the Mafia and the Cops out of Gay Bars," Craig Rodwell, New York, June 28, 1969. Various sources have suggested different times for the writing and distribution of the leaflet, because it references both Friday and Saturday nights. There's also the confusion about perceiving "Friday night" as the early hours of Saturday morning. Sargeant clarifies this issue. There were two leaflets. The first was to let people know what was going on. The second one – the one that survives – focused on the Mafia and the police.
24 The full text of the flyer is at the end of this chapter.
25 An additional printing of this flyer from the original 5,000 may have occurred. Sargeant remembers a print run of 5,000, Rodwell remembered in his interviews with Duberman, thousands. An exhibit of "Great Moments in Gay/Lesbian History, 1969–1971," indicates that 10,000 copies were distributed through the course of the riots. Craig Rodwell Papers, New York Public Library, Undated exhibit program, Box 6.
26 *New York Daily News*, June 29, 1969, 30. Newspapers.com.
27 *New York Times*, June 29, 1969, 33, TimesMachine.
28 *New York Times*, June 30, 1969, 22, TimesMachine.
29 *Village Voice*, July 3, 1969, 1. While the issue date is July 3, the protest of Lucian Truscott's language, which referred to the "forces of faggotry," occurred on Wednesday when the issue first became available. Google archive.
30 That he anticipated something like this happening is related in the Scherker and Duberman interviews and is corroborated by the Sargeant interviews.
31 The lost audio of this moment was revealed in 2004 when David Carter played it at a panel discussion for his new book that broke down the Stonewall riots into moment-by-moment historical facts. The author was in attendance for the panel discussion for the launch of Carter's book, New York Historical Society, New York, June 2, 2004. It is also documented in Lincoln Anderson's article in *The Villager*, "'I'm Sorry,' Says Inspector Who Led Stonewall Raid," posted online on June 22, 2004.
32 Scherker, *The Reminiscences*, 46.
33 Ibid.
34 Fred Sargeant, "Anger Management," *New York Times*, 2009.
35 The documentation of The Snake Pit raid is widespread. This account is summarized from Craig Rodwell's oral history with Michael Scherker, interviews with Fred Sargeant, newspaper accounts, the Mattachine Society of New York Newsletter from April 1970, and Arthur Bell's *Dancing the Gay Lib Blues* (Simon and Schuster, 1971).
36 Bell, *Dancing the Gay Lib Blues*, 8.
37 Panel of the New York Historical Society, June 2, 2004. The author was in attendance for the panel discussion for the launch of David Carter's book. The panel was also reported in *The Villager*, posted online on June 22, 2004. Seymour Pine died in 2010 at the age of ninety-one.

7. Dear Craig

1. Correspondence, August 29, 1969, Craig Rodwell Papers, Manuscripts and Archives Division, New York Public Library, Astor, Lenox, and Tilden Foundations, Box 1.
2. Correspondence, August 16, 1972, Craig Rodwell Papers, Box 1.
3. Correspondence, June 19, 1969, Craig Rodwell Papers, Box 1.
4. Correspondence, October 1972, Craig Rodwell Papers, Box 1.
5. Correspondence, March 26, 1972, Craig Rodwell Papers, Box 1.
6. Letter from an Army private to Rodwell, July 14, 1969, Craig Rodwell Papers, Box 1.
7. Letters to the Homophile Youth Movement and reply from Alfred Gross on May 22, 1969. Alfred A. Gross had been in regular communication in the late 1960s with Rodwell's friend, Foster Gunnison. *The New York Times*, in its obituary for Alfred Gross on June 2, 1987, reported that he had been the founder of the George W. Henry Foundation and served as its executive director from 1937 to 1974.
8. Letter from Louis, January 22, 1970, Craig Rodwell Papers, Box 1.
9. "Slain Youth Found Here NY Viet Vet," *San Francisco Examiner*, October 16, 1970, 51. There were several other similar accounts in newspapers, including one from UPI. None of the accounts mentioned that Louis could have been slain because of his sexual orientation, although that was certainly possible.

8. Let's March

1. Scherker, *The Reminiscences*, 1986; author interview with Fred Sargeant, June 2022. Sargeant recalled the circumstances of the departure, as he was going to keep the Oscar Wilde open while Rodwell traveled to Philadelphia for the Annual Reminder.
2. The inclusion of this short list is indicative of the impact of this aspect of the movement. Ernest Hole, for example, had been visiting New York from London in 1968–9 and had become friends with Craig and Fred at the Oscar Wilde. Hole was inspired by his visit to open the first LGBT bookshop in London in 1979. Kay Tobin would later write *The Gay Crusaders*. Don Teal would write *The Gay Militants*. Charles Pitts was already known for his programs on WBAI, and he had interviewed Sargeant for The New Symposium shortly after the Stonewall riots. Martha Shelley would co-found the Gay Liberation Front, becoming a successful author and lesbian activist. Terry Rohnke, who helped with the music in the Oscar Wilde, would later work for *David Letterman* and *Saturday Night Live*. Barbara Gittings had organized the Daughters of Bilitis New York chapter and had been editor of the DOB's journal, *The Ladder*. Kameny had already founded the Washington chapter of Mattachine and had led numerous gay rights efforts.
3. "5th Annual Reminder – July 4, 1969," Frank Kameny Papers, The Deviant's Archive, Library of Congress.

4 Ibid.
5 This incident and the following sequence of events at the Annual Reminder are as told to Michael Scherker in *The Reminiscences* in 1986.
6 Ibid.
7 Letter from Kameny to Rodwell, July 11, 1969, Box 7, 5th Annual Reminder folder, Box 7. Craig Rodwell Papers, Manuscripts and Archives Division, New York Public Library, Astor, Lenox, and Tilden Foundations.
8 Homophile Youth Movement, 105–1, Frank Kameny Papers, The Deviant's Archive, Library of Congress, thedeviantsarchive.org.
9 It was not beyond Rodwell to orchestrate events for effect, and he did this with Kameny before the fall ERCHO meeting by writing a letter to Kameny questioning his behavior during the 1969 Annual Reminder. Wanting to have more impact than another communication from Rodwell himself, he had signed Sargeant's name to the letter as vice-chair of HYMN. The letter from "Sargeant" and Kameny's lengthy response are in the Kameny papers at the LOC and at thedeviantsarchive.org. Sargeant, in fact, did not attend the last reminder in order to keep the Oscar Wilde open in the critical days after the riots.
10 The timeline of when Rodwell began to conceive of a march instead of an annual reminder is based on discussions Rodwell had with his lover, Fred Sargeant. While other accounts imagine the genesis of the march occurring later in 1969, in fact the two discussed it well before the fifth Annual Reminder. For example, in *The New York Hymnal* of August–September 1968, Rodwell reported on the fourth Annual Reminder and concluded by saying that the fifth reminder "will have a different format than previous demonstrations." Years later, Rodwell told Martin Duberman that he came up with the name – Christopher Street Liberation Day – and the committee just weeks after the Stonewall riots.
11 Author interview via Zoom with Ellen Broidy, June 2022.
12 Tape-recorded interview with Craig Rodwell, Barbara Gittings and Kay Tobin Lahusen gay history papers and photographs, New York Public Library, Box 123.
13 Ibid.
14 The details of the ERCHO meeting are contained in Susan Day's detailed minutes. The Deviant's Archive, Library of Congress, Frank Kameny Papers, Minutes of the Eastern Regional Conference of Homophile Organizations, November 1–2, 1969, 67–3.
15 *Gay Power* was criticized for being exploitive and perpetuating homosexual stereotypes, and the resolution encouraged all gay employees at *Gay Power* to quit. See Susan Day's notes from the ERCHO meeting in the Frank Kameny Papers, 67–3, Library of Congress, The Deviant's Archive, thedeviantsarchive.org, and the "Homophile Action League's coverage of the ERCHO meeting in its newsletter of January–February, 1970 Vol. II Issue. 2" in the Gale Archives of Sexuality and Gender.
16 ERCHO meeting minutes, The Deviant's Archive, Library of Congress, Frank Kameny Papers, 67–3.

17 ERCHO Conference, Informational Sheet from Robert Angell, Frank Kameny Papers, Library of Congress, The Deviant's Archive, thedeviantsarchive.org, 67–3.
18 While Christopher Street Liberation Day on June 28, 1970, is considered the first planned public march, a gay power rally and vigil of about 300 to 400 homosexuals was held in Washington Square Park on July 27, 1969. It was run by Martha Shelley and Marty Robinson. They then led a crowd to the Stonewall Inn, which is described by Eric Cervini in *The Deviant's War* (Picador – Farrar, Straus and Giroux, 2020), 310. Cervini quotes Shelley as saying, "welcome to this city's first gay power vigil." The action is also described in *The Gay Militants* (St. Martin's Press, 1971) by Donn Teal, who attended the event and stated that "[t]he Vigil then moved to Sheridan Square opposite the Stonewall Inn" (21). It ended with singing and hugging, and a planned walk to the 6th Precinct was canceled. Toby Marotta, in *The Politics of Homosexuality* (Houghton Mifflin Company, 1981, 82), also describes the event as a vigil planned by Mattachine and the Daughters of Bilitis to oppose police harassment, with a subsequent march to the Stonewall.
19 "The Homosexual in America," *Time*, October 31, 1969, 56–67.
20 Sargeant described this reaction and the protest in his remarks at the start of the 2014 Pride march in New York City, where he was honored and led the march as a "first organizer."
21 Ellen Broidy, interview with the author, June 2022.
22 Carl Lee, "It's What's Happening," *The New York Hymnal*, January 1970, 2.
23 Rodwell's account in these paragraphs of the meetings in his and Sargeant's apartment that led up to the first march can be found in Scherker's *The Reminiscences*, 64–7.
24 Foster Gunnison saved voluminous documentation of the formation of the Christopher Street Liberation Day Committee and related activities and financial accounts. This section relies on his bulletins, agendas, press releases, financial statements, and flyers in the Foster Gunnison Jr. Papers, University of Connecticut, Archives and Special Collections, University of Connecticut Library; Christopher Street Liberation Day Committee, Bulletins and Reports, 1970, 1972.
25 Marotta, *The Politics of Homosexuality*, 166–7.
26 Letter from Foster Gunnison to Craig Rodwell, May 13, 1970, Craig Rodwell Papers, Box 4.
27 GLF was in existence from 1969 to 1971, and GAA was in existence from 1969 to 1973. Jim Owles was GAA's first president.
28 Fred Sargeant, interview with author, 2024. Sargeant was manager of the shop at the time GLF expressed an interest in being involved with the shop. He and Rodwell were concerned that the idea would be to absorb the business.
29 Tape-recorded interview with Craig Rodwell, December 1970, Barbara Gittings and Kay Tobin Lahusen gay history papers and photographs, New York Public Library, Box 123.

30 Application for Parade Permit, Craig Rodwell Papers, Box 4.
31 Scherker, *The Reminiscences*, 68.
32 Permit for Gay Be-In (Happening), June 24, 1970, Department of Parks, City of New York, Manhattan Burrough.
33 Gay Pride Week activities listing, Craig Rodwell Papers, Box 4.
34 Marotta, *The Politics of Homosexuality*, 167–9.
35 CSLD arm band, Craig Rodwell Papers, Box 4.
36 Fred Sargeant, interview with author, 2008.
37 Perhaps because the permit was hand-delivered or for some other reason, and unlike the permit for the gay-in at Sheep Meadow, the parade permit is not among the records of the New York City Police Department per a Freedom of Information Law request by the author and response on September 8, 2023.
38 Scherker, *The Reminiscences*.
39 CSLD March "Welcome," Craig Rodwell Papers, Box 4.
40 Fred Sargeant, interview with author, 2008.
41 While the meeting place for the march was advertised as Sheridan Square, there were people gathering at the Waverly Street staging area, which, due to its northerly location, became the stepping off point. Fred Sargeant, interview with author, 2008; Sargeant was one of the CSLD marshals and was photographed by George Desantis at the head of the march with the only bullhorn.
42 "Gay and Proud," video, 1970, Lilli Vincenz papers, Library of Congress.
43 Some accounts of the first march suggest that the pace was so fast that the walk to Central Park was more like a run; Lilli Vincenz's documentation of the march shows otherwise. Some strode briskly, some walked, some stopped to talk, but it was not a run. Rodwell did tell Kay Tobin in his interview for *The Gay Crusaders* that the police were responsible for setting the pace of the march and that they had set the pace too fast. Sargeant also confirms that the march was not a gallop up Sixth Avenue.
44 Charles Pitts, WBAI recording, Christopher Street Liberation Day march, June 28, 1970, Collection 168, Audio Tape 19, LGBT Community Center National History Archive.
45 Scherker, *The Reminiscences*, 69.
46 Ibid.
47 *Gay Freedom 1970, QQ Magazine*, New York, 1970.
48 Duberman interview with Rodwell, 1991.
49 Duberman interview with Rodwell, 1991.
50 Lacey Fosburgh, "Thousands of Homosexuals Hold a Protest Rally in Central Park," *New York Times*, June 29, 1970, 1, TimesMachine.
51 Jonathan Black "A Happy Birthday for Gay Liberation," *Village Voice*, July 3–9, 1. Google archive.
52 CSLDUC bulletins and accounts, Craig Rodwell Papers, Box 4.
53 Scherker, *The Reminiscences*, 70.

9. QQ Magazine

1. Articles and editorials written by Craig Rodwell for *QQ Magazine* between 1970 and 1973 are included in appendices, with appreciation for the magazine's creator, George Desantis.
2. *Queen's Quarterly*, Spring 1969, 34.
3. Ibid., Summer 1969, 5.
4. Homosexual Information Center, *Tangents Magazine*, May–July 1969, 28.
5. *Queen's Quarterly*, Summer 1969, 38–9, 51–2.
6. William Parker, "Employment Discrimination Is Being Confronted," *Vector Magazine*, Society for Individual Rights, San Francisco, 1971, 38–9. Rodwell also mentioned the same incident in a guest editorial in *QQ Magazine* in February 1971.
7. "Mr. Fire Island," *QQ Magazine*, Fall 1970, 24–5.
8. Donn Teal in *The Gay Militants* agreed with the designation of *QQ* as the "first continuing national magazine for homosexual men," and cited a circulation of 95,000 as of November 1970. 66.
9. Lucas Hilderbrand, "A Suitcase Full of Vaseline, or Travels in the 1970s Gay World," *Journal of the History of Sexuality*, 2013, 376–8. https://www.jstor.org/stable/24616541.
10. *QQ Magazine*, December 1971, 39, 45. Dick Michaels, the editor of *The Advocate*, told Kay Tobin for *The Gay Crusaders* that *The Advocate* (which had changed its name from *The Los Angeles Advocate* to *The Advocate* in 1970) had a press run of 39,000 in 1971, which would comport with a pass-along readership in the vicinity of the QQ advertisement of 120,000, or four readers for each copy.
11. Baim, *Gay Press, Gay Power*, 94.
12. *Encyclopedia of Lesbian, Gay, Bisexual and Transgender History in America*, 341.
13. *QQ Magazine*, Spring 1970, 19.
14. Sargeant remembers his mother taking him to a tennis court when he was about six years old, where he was photographed with his arm extended, pointing to an imaginary plane in the sky, in a modeling session for the Dick and Jane children's book series. The series was published by Scott, Foresman and Company of Chicago in the 1930s and was updated through the 1960s. In the 1956 edition of *We Come and Go*, "Dick" points to an airplane in the sky in the *See It Go* story.
15. *QQ Magazine*, Fall 1970, 9, 52.
16. *QQ Magazine*, April 1971, 5, 45. An editorial comment accompanying Rodwell's guest editorial indicated that Rodwell was chosen for the piece because he was a leader in the movement, but not strongly affiliated with any one group.
17. *QQ Magazine*, June 1971, 25; August 1971, 54.
18. Rodwell addressed the issue throughout his professional life and from the beginning at the Oscar Wilde, attempting to balance his stock with gay and lesbian titles. He prided himself on the diversity of his bookshop staff from the very start.

19 Rodwell did not consider Dick Leitsch to have been a lover, but a brief affair.
20 Supplementary interview with Craig Rodwell, Barbara Gittings and Kay Tobin Lahusen Gay History Papers and Photographs, Box 123.
21 Author interview with Ellen Broidy, June 2022.
22 Author interviews with Fred Sargeant, January and February 2008.
23 *QQ Magazine*, February 1972, 27.
24 *QQ Magazine*, April 1972, 5.
25 Rep. Abzug did introduce the Equality Act in 1974 (on the fifth anniversary of the Stonewall riots) in the 93rd Congress. Rep. Edward Koch was a co-sponsor. Congress.gov, HR14752. It has been reintroduced several times in recent years but has not been passed by Congress.
26 *QQ Magazine*, June 1972, 54.
27 *QQ Magazine*, October 1972, 54.
28 Supreme Court.gov, *Bostock v. Clayton County, Georgia*, June 15, 2020. But as noted above, Congress had not approved the Equality Act as of 2024.
29 *QQ Magazine*, August 1972, 5.
30 *QQ Magazine*, September–October 1972, 5. It is unknown why the results were not published in an earlier issue as the conventions had been held in July and the results were known by the time the September issue was published.
31 *QQ Magazine*, December 1972, 5.
32 Both the Mercer Street and Christopher Street locations of the Oscar Wilde were listed in *QQ*'s published store locator from October 1973 to June 1974. The NYC LGBT Historic Sites Project, nyclgbtsites.org/site/oscar-wilde-memorial-bookshop/, lists the closing of Mercer Street as May 1974.
33 *QQ Magazine*, February 1973, 47.
34 *QQ Magazine*, April 1973, 54.
35 Ibid., 5.
36 *New York Daily News*, December 12, 1972, 311. The story appeared in both the Queens and Brooklyn pages of the newspaper, in which the *Daily News* also reported on the indictment of suspect David J. Speights. Neither the *Daily News* nor *The New York Times* reported anything about the murders being hate motivated. In fact, both newspapers referred to the fact that both suspects' wallets were missing. The *Times* referred to Oxenhorn as a bachelor. The *Daily News* identified Stafford, but the *Times* reported Stafford as a second man who was unidentified. Newspapers.com.
37 *QQ Magazine*, June 1973, 54.
38 *QQ Magazine*, August 1973, 54.

10. Christian Science

1 Duberman interviews for *Stonewall*. Tape 1.
2 Fred Sargeant, interview with author, 2008.
3 Tobin, *The Gay Crusaders*, 66.
4 Bob McCullough, interview and correspondence with the author, November 2022.

5 Robert Peel's three-volume biography of Mary Baker Eddy was considered to be the first scholarly examination of the founder of Christian Science. Rodwell would have placed either the first volume, *The Years of Discovery* (pub. 1966), or the second volume, *The Years of Trial* (pub. 1971), in his bookshop. Both had photographs of Mary Baker Eddy on the cover, which would have caught the attention of someone interested in Christian Science, as was the case with Ray Spitale, according to the author's interview with Bob McCullough. The last of the three volumes, *The Years of Authority*, was published in 1977. Peel died in 1992 in Boston at the age of eighty-two, and according to his obituary in the *Boston Globe*, he was taken to the hospital against his will. He was single his entire life.
6 Bruce Stores, *Christian Science: Its Encounter with Lesbian/Gay America* (iUniverse Inc., 2004). The discussion of the placement of the Mary Baker Eddy biography and the subsequent discovery of the book by Ray Spitale is referenced on pages 68–70.
7 "Signs of the Times" bulletin, May 1973, Gale Archives of Sexuality and Gender, Lesbian Herstory House Archives, Bookstores: Gay: Oscar Wilde, 1970 – November 15, 1988.
8 *Christian Science Sentinel* website, sentinel.christianscience.com.
9 Carl J. Welz, "Homosexuality Can Be Healed," *Christian Science Sentinel*, April 22, 1967. sentinel.christianscience.com.
10 Naomi Price, "The Bible and Homosexuality," *Christian Science Sentinel*, November 18, 1972. sentinel.christianscience.com.
11 Steven Lee Fair, "Healing Homosexuality," *Christian Science Sentinel*, March 5, 1979. sentinel.christianscience.com.
12 The account of the development of Gay People in Christian Science and the subsequent publication of the pamphlet *Gay People in Christian Science?* is summarized from the author's interview with Bob McCullough, Bruce Stores' *Christian Science: Its Encounter with Lesbian/Gay America*, and Craig Rodwell's interviews with Martin Duberman for his book *Stonewall*.
13 Stores, *Christian Science: Its Encounter with Lesbian/Gay America*, 42–4; and James Franklin, "A Rift Among Christian Scientists," *Boston Globe*, March 12, 1978. Newspapers.com.
14 Scherker, *The Reminiscences*. Rodwell explained what he meant by *heterosexism* when he said: "It's very similar to the term *racism* or *sexism*. It's the erroneous belief that people of the heterosexual persuasion are in some way or manner are superior to the people of the homosexual persuasion, in a nutshell."
15 *Gay People in Christian Science?* pamphlet, 1979, New York, courtesy of Bruce Stores.
16 Stores, *Christian Science: Its Encounter with Lesbian/Gay America*. This account is based on the chapter "The Beginning of Lesbian/Gay Christian Science Groups." It is also supported by the recollections in the author interview with Bob McCullough.
17 A flotilla of tall ships sailed into Boston Harbor at the end of May 1980 to commemorate Boston's 350th anniversary. The parade of ships included

the billowed sails of eight big square-riggers and dozens of other ships in a visual display seen by hundreds of thousands of visitors.
18 Duberman interviews with Rodwell, Tape 1.
19 Stores, *Christian Science: Its Encounter with Lesbian/Gay America*, 83.
20 Ibid., 92.
21 Ibid., 99.
22 The gay community reclaimed the pink triangle as a symbol of strength in the mid-1970s after it was used in the 1930s and '40s to identify homosexual men in Nazi concentration camps. The Nazi regime persecuted homosexual men because sex between men was illegal, and they were considered to be a threat to the family structure and the procreation of a master race. Lesbians were also persecuted and imprisoned for anti-social or political reasons since there was no law forbidding sex between women, and they were forced to wear a black triangle badge. The triangle patches with the point down were sewn to the left breast and right pant leg. It was considered the lowest symbol in the prison hierarchy. See also: Heinz Herger, *The Men with the Pink Triangle*, London, Gay Men's Press, 1980, 31. The inverted pink triangle with the point up was prominently adopted during the AIDS crisis and the "Silence = Death" campaign starting in 1987.
23 Rodwell interview with Duberman; and Stores, *Christian Science*.
24 "Court in Massachusetts Upholds Christian Science Monitor's Dismissal of A Lesbian," *New York Times*, August 22, 1985, 16, TimesMachine.
25 Stores, *Christian Science*, 117.

11. Inside the Oscar Wilde – Christopher Street

1 Foster Gunnison Jr. Papers, Archives and Special Collections, University of Connecticut Library, CSLD, Bulletins and Reports, 1970, 1972.
2 Ibid.
3 Ibid.
4 Ibid.
5 Ibid.
6 Arthur Bell, "Hostility Comes Out of the Closet," *Village Voice*, June 28, 1973, 1. Google Archive.
7 Ibid.
8 Ibid.
9 It is documented among a variety of sources that Kay Tobin Lahusen was the main author of *The Gay Crusaders*, in spite of the fact that the cover lists Randy Wicker as a co-author. Further, Wicker was not present for the interviews Lahusen had with Rodwell for the book.
10 Betsy Kalin, interview with Kay Tobin Lahusen, March 2018, Outwords Archive, theoutwordsarchive.org.
11 Craig Rodwell Papers, Manuscripts and Archives Division, New York Public Library, Astor, Lenox, and Tilden Foundations. In correspondence with his landlord, Rodwell states in February 1974 that he will close the

Mercer Street location. In another letter in April 1974, he provides official notice per a verbal agreement on March 8 that he would continue to rent the shop for two months.

12 Letter from Kay Tobin Lahusen to Craig Rodwell, July 28, Box 6.
13 "Signs of the Times" bulletin, May 1973, Gale Archives of Sexuality and Gender, Lesbian Herstory House Archives, Bookstores: Gay: Oscar Wilde, 1970 – November 15, 1988,
14 Author interview with Tom Wilson Weinberg, December 2024.
15 Ethan Geto interview with the author, June 2024.
16 Philip Ryan, "Pink Triangle History," Letters, *The New York Blade*, January 7, 2000. Ryan says in his letter that he was the person who suggested using the triangle as a symbol in this New York campaign, having learned of its significance the previous year (1974) when historian Jim Steakley published a history of homosexuals in German concentration camps in *The Body Politic*, a gay publication in Toronto. It was one of the earliest uses of the triangle for the purpose of gay advocacy.
17 "Memo to Select Members of the Study Group," from Ethan M. Geto, Pink Triangle Campaign, July 28, 1975, Philip G. Ryan Papers, Manuscripts and Archives Division, New York Public Library, Astor, Lenox, and Tilden Foundations.
18 Ira Glasser, "The Yellow Star and the Pink Triangle," *New York Times*, September 10, 1975, 45, TimesMachine.
19 Ryan, "Pink Triangle History."
20 A listing of T-shirts offered by the Oscar Wilde notes that the triangle in the Silence=Death T-shirt is pointed up. It is likely the bookshop noted this design because previous uses on buttons and banners depicted the triangle with the flat side up. When the Silence=Death poster was designed, though, the triangle was inverted by mistake. Once the flip was realized, the collective that designed the originators decided to own the new design as a symbol against victimhood, later adopted by ACT UP. See also: Avram Finkelstein, *After Silence* (University of California Press, 2018), 45.
21 Jonathan Ned Katz, interview with the author, May 7, 2023.
22 Letter to the West Side Discussion Group Board of Directors, October 10, 1977, Craig Rodwell Papers, OWMB business correspondence, Box 6.
23 "Gay Journalist-Activist Slain," *Gay* Magazine, Houstonlgbthistory.org, October 1972. Ralph Schaffer was a journalist and activist and the co-founder the Los Angeles Gay Liberation Front, who had been shot and killed in the Gaywill Funky Shop in Hollywood in August 1972.
24 Correspondence with the Christopher Street West Association, June 1978, Craig Rodwell Papers, Box 6.
25 Correspondence, September 1, 1971, Craig Rodwell Papers, Box 6.
26 Larry Kramer, *Faggots* (Penguin Books, 1978), 335.
27 John Lahr, "Camp Tales," *New York Times*, January 14, 1979, Section SM, 24, TimesMachine.

28 Craig Rodwell Papers, personal and professional correspondence, 1971–1980, Box 1. This account is based on correspondence between two of the shop's patrons from Brooklyn and Rodwell.
29 Vito Russo, *Our Time*, Episode 6, "Writers," WNYC-TV, March 16, 1983, https://www.youtube.com/watch?v=bbb9jfunymw.
30 Craig Rodwell Papers, personal and professional correspondence, 1971–1980, Box 1.
31 "Book Shipment from New York Seized by Customs," April 1978, *Gay Community News*, 3. *The Body Politic* was the newspaper that inspired the use of the pink triangle in the New York Intro 554 campaign through its coverage of the treatment of homosexuals in German concentration camps.
32 "Milk, First Gay to Be Supervisor," *San Francisco Examiner*, Extra, November 27, 1978, 17. Newspapers.com.
33 "Harvey Milk Leaves San Francisco a Legacy of Love," *San Francisco Examiner*, December 1, 1978, 3. Newspapers.com.
34 Craig Rodwell Papers, Notes on the death of Harvey Milk and notice of candlelight vigil. It is most likely the remarks were prepared for delivery at the Sheridan Square vigil, since Rodwell mentions in the notes that Harvey Milk's ashes had been scattered over San Francisco Bay "yesterday," which would have been Saturday, December 2, 1978, Box 6.
35 Ibid.
36 Bookshop catalog from 1968, Craig Rodwell Papers.
37 Catalogs from the Oscar Wilde Memorial Bookshop, Jesús Lebrón Papers, Box 1, The Bronx County Archives at the Bronx County Historical Society Research Library, Box 1.
38 The lambda symbol was used as the symbol of the Gay Activists Alliance in its early days. As Arthur Bell described in his book *Dancing the Gay Lib Blues* (31), "The organization needed a quick identification symbol. After weeks of designing eagle and cock heads and such, one of our people cleverly came up with the lambda, the eleventh letter of the Greek lower-case alphabet, a sort of upside-down two-pronged check mark. The lambda design is clean, it's meaning was right for our group. In chemistry and physics the lambda symbolizes a complete exchange of energy – the movement or span of time that's witness to absolute activity."
39 Author interview with Tom Wilson Weinberg, December 2024.
40 Letter and press release from NAMBLA, August 1980, Craig Rodwell Papers, Box 6.
41 WBAI panel program, September 27, 1980, Pacifica Radio Archives.
42 Notes in the 1985 OWMB catalog, Jesús Lebrón Papers, Box 1.
43 Ibid.
44 Barbara Grier's (1933–2011) Naiad Press was a publishing house founded in 1973 for books authored by lesbians. Her company published *Lesbian Nuns: Breaking Silence*, by editors Rosemary Curb and Nancy Manahan. About the book, the OWMB catalog for 1985 said: "This title has

already received more national publicity than any other Gay or Lesbian book ever."
45 The account in this section is based on Fred Carl's interview with the author, December 2022.
46 Fred Carl went on to a successful career in the arts; in 2022, he was working as an associate arts professor in the NYU/Tisch School of the Arts Graduate Musical Theatre Writing Program and was one of the associate deans of faculty at the Tisch School of the Arts.
47 The account in this section of Nan Buzard's time in New York and at the Oscar Wilde is based on an interview with the author in December 2022.
48 Brendan Fay's arrival in New York and his early experiences are described in a *Huffington Post* essay "Finding Jesús on Christopher Street" in 2012. The discovery of the Oscar Wilde by Brendan Fay and the related stories in this section are recounted from an interview with the author in December 2022.
49 Ibid.
50 *The Black Diaries of Roger Casement* details the intimate homosexual experiences of Irish revolutionary Roger Casement. The authenticity of the diaries has been debated. Casement was hanged for treason in London in 1916 after the Easter Rising, which was aimed at establishing an independent Irish republic.
51 Author correspondence with Jesús Lebrón, January 19, 2023.
52 Jesús Lebrón was hired to be the manager of the bookshop in 1987 and worked there for eight years. His leadership and contributions to gay activism are documented in his papers, which reside at the Bronx County Historical Society.
53 Gay and lesbian organizations continued to be barred from the St. Patrick's Day Parade until 2016, when the Ancient Order of Hibernians was forced to reverse itself after years of political and legal pressure.
54 Author correspondence with Brendan Fay, October 2022.
55 Author interview with Brendan Fay, September 2022.
56 Letter from Craig Rodwell to John McNeill, July 30, 1980, courtesy of Brendan Fay.
57 Letter to the reporter from *The New York Times*, November 21, 1979, Craig Rodwell Papers, Box 2.
58 This account relies on the reporting of Arthur Bell in *The Village Voice* as well as contemporaneous reporting in *The New York Times*, the *Daily News*, *Newsday*, and live reporting on WBAI.
59 Letter to Mayor Ed Koch, July 24, 1979, Craig Rodwell Papers, Box 3.
60 Ibid.
61 "Protesters Call the Film 'Cruising' Antihomosexual," *New York Times*, July 26, 1979, B-7, TimesMachine.
62 Correspondence, November 1976, Craig Rodwell Papers, Box 2.

12. Monuments, Myths, and Memorials

1. The details of the origination of the idea and funding of the Gay Liberation sculpture, mentioned in a number of published articles, are summarized here from the NYC Department of Parks & Recreation public description of the sculpture and the glbtq.com encyclopedia entry by Claude J. Summers in 2003.
2. The Kent State sculpture, "Abraham and Isaac," donated in 1978, was never installed at the university, because it was considered to be inappropriate. It was installed instead at Princeton University.
3. "George Segal's Gay Liberation," Claude J. Summers, Glbtq.com encyclopedia, 2003.
4. "Homosexual-Liberation Statue Is Planned for Sheridan Square," *New York Times*, July 21, 1979, 10, TimesMachine.
5. "Some Objections to the Segal 'Gay Liberation' Statue," September 5, 1980, Craig Rodwell Papers, Manuscripts and Archives Division, New York Public Library, Astor, Lenox, and Tilden Foundations, Box 4.
6. Carol Vogel, "The Art Market," George Segal Sculpture, *New York Times*, June 1992, 16, TimesMachine.
7. Letter to Rodwell from "Bruce," Craig Rodwell Papers, Box 4.
8. Scherker, *The Reminiscences*, 78.
9. *New York Mattachine Newsletter*, April 1970, Gale Archives of Sexuality and Gender, New York Public Library.
10. Letter from Foster Gunnison to Dick Leitsch, November 23, 1970, Craig Rodwell Papers, Box 1.
11. *Stonewall Uprising*, interview with Dick Leitsch, American Experience, American Archive of Public Broadcasting, Boston, MA, and Washington, DC, americanarchive.org/catalog/cpb-aacip-15-pr7mp4wr01.
12. Ibid.
13. Bruce Weber, "Sam Ciccone, a Champion of Gay Police Officers, Dies at 71," *New York Times*, May 17, 2015, TimesMachine.
14. Letter from Sam Ciccone, Craig Rodwell Papers, personal and professional correspondence, 1971–1980, Box 1.
15. Remarks by Deacon Maccubbin. The 1992 Lambda Literary Award for Publisher's Service was presented at its fifth annual Lambda Literary Awards Banquet at the Intercontinental Hotel in Miami on Friday, May 28, 1993. Maccubbin's written remarks are the foundation of this section. Craig Rodwell Papers, Box 1.
16. Ibid.
17. Author interview with Bob McCullough, November 2022.
18. Martin Duberman Papers, Manuscripts and Archives Division, New York Public Library, Astor, Lenox, and Tilden Foundations, tape-recorded interviews with Rodwell for "Stonewall, The Definitive Story of the LGBTQ Rights Uprising That Changed America," Tape 1.
19. Letter from Julia Noël Goldman, March 3, 1993, Craig Rodwell Papers, Box 1.

20 Letter from Mayor David Dinkins to Rodwell, April 16, 1993, Craig Rodwell Papers, Box 1.
21 Letter from Nancy Garden to Rodwell, June 4, 1993, Craig Rodwell Papers, Box 1.
22 Memorial service at the LGBT Center in New York, July 1993, remarks by Craig's brother, Jack Rodwell, Videotape 800–02–006, Center Records, LGBT Community Center National History Archive.
23 Ibid. The account of the service is based on the videotape unless otherwise noted. Both Randy Wicker and Julia Noël Goldman were involved in taping the service using Goldman's camera.
24 The location at Christopher and Gay streets, near the Oscar Wilde, was one of the locations used in the 1993 film "Carlito's Way," with Al Pacino and Sean Penn.
25 The location of Rodwell's remains appears to be unknown. As of the date of this publication, no memorial to his life's work has been constructed.

13. Transitions

1 Business certificates for transfer of the Oscar Wilde Memorial Bookshop to William Offenbaker, 1993, LGBT Community Center National History Archive, Collection 86, Box 10.
2 Time Out, Lobo Bookshop and Café, Ann Walton Sieber, *Outsmart Magazine*, December 1999, outsmartmagazine.com.
3 Kevin Howell, "The Oscar Doesn't Go To ..." *Publisher's Weekly*, Vol. 250, Issue 3, January 20, 2003.
4 Author interview with Deacon Maccubbin, September 21, 2022.
5 Ibid.
6 Author correspondence with Kim Brinster, October 2022.

Epilogue

1 Arthur Bell, "Skull Murphy, The Gay Double Agent, *Village Voice*, May 8, 1978, 1. Google archive.
2 Crawford Jr., *The Mafia and the Gays*, 99.
3 Bell, "Skull Murphy."
4 Letter from the Stonewall Foundation to the Oscar Wilde, March 2, 1983, and Rodwell's response on March 15, 1983, Craig Rodwell Papers, Box 3.
5 This account is drawn from contemporaneous gay press accounts of the time in the *New York City News, New York Native,* and *The Connection.* LGBT Community Center National History Archive, New York, Christopher Street Liberation Day Committee, Box 11.
6 Candida Scott Piel interview with the author, May 6, 2023.
7 Minutes of June 11, 1984, Christopher Street Liberation Day Committee meeting, LGBT Community Center National History Archive, Collection 86, Box 4,

8 Heritage of Pride certificate of incorporation, LGBT Community Center National History Archive, Collection 86, Box 1.
9 Candida Scott Piel interview with the author.
10 "Homosexuals Parade in the Face of Death," June 29, 1987, *New York Times*, TimesMachine.
11 Coverage of Annual Pride March, June 27, 1988, *New York Times*.
12 Lou Chibbaro Jr., "Our History of Marching on Washington," *Washington Blade*, June 11, 2017.
13 Christopher Street Liberation Day Committee, amendment to the certificate of incorporation, December 1989, LGBT Community Center National History Archive, Collection 86, Box 1, Folder 3.
14 IRS Form 990, Year 2022, Heritage of Pride, New York.
15 Clifford Levy, "Thousands March in a Celebration of Gay Pride," *New York Times*, June 28, 1993, TimesMachine.
16 Letter from Kay Tobin Lahusen to Rodwell, April 8, 1983, Craig Rodwell Papers, Box 1.
17 Candida Scott Piel, interview with the author, May 6, 2023.
18 For an analysis as to why the Stonewall riots made a historical mark, see: "Movements and Memory: The Making of the Stonewall Myth," Elizabeth Armstrong and Suzanna Crage, *American Sociological Review* 71 (October 2006): 724–51. Armstrong and Crage lay out a thorough and compelling study of the factors that contributed to the Stonewall riots as an "achievement" of gay liberation "rather than an account of its origins." Their analysis shows how and why activists found the event commemorable as opposed to other events of homosexual oppression and how activists had the capacity to create "a commemorative vehicle" – that is, the first march.
19 Scherker, *The Reminiscences*. This section relies upon Rodwell's concluding statements in his 1986 oral history interview.
20 Gay Pride Week schedule, 1971, Foster Gunnison Jr. Papers, Archives and Special Collections, University of Connecticut Library, Chirstopher Street Liberation Day Committee, Bulletins and Reports, 1970, 1972.
21 Scherker, *The Reminiscences*, 85.

Bibliography

Altman, Dennis. *Homosexual Oppression & Liberation*. New York University Press, 1971.

Anderson, Lincoln. "'I'm Sorry,' Says Inspector Who Led Stonewall Raid." *The Villager*, June 16–22, 2004. thevillager.com.

Angelou, Maya. *The Complete Poems of Maya Angelou*. Random House, 1994.

Ardery, Breck. *Gay & Proud* [LP], 1970. https://www.queermusicheritage.com.

Armstrong, Elizabeth, and Suzanna Crage. "Movements and Memory: The Making of the Stonewall Myth," *American Sociological Review* 71 (2006).

Baim, Tracy. *Barbara Gittings, Gay Pioneer*. Prairie Avenue Productions, 2015.

– *Gay Press, Gay Power: The Growth of LGBT Community Newspapers in America*. Prairie Avenue Productions/Windy City Media Group, 2012.

Barbara Gittings and Kay Tobin Lahusen Gay History Papers and Photographs. Manuscripts and Archives Division, New York Public Library, Astor, Lenox, and Tilden Foundations.

Bell, Arthur. *Dancing the Gay Lib Blues*. Simon & Schuster, 1971.

– "Hostility Comes Out of the Closet." *Village Voice*, June 28, 1973. Google Archive.

- "Skull Murphy, The Gay Double Agent." *Village Voice*, May 8, 1978. Google Archive.
Bettye Lane Gay Rights Movement Photographs. Manuscripts and Archives Division, New York Public Library, Astor, Lenox, and Tilden Foundations.
Black, Jonathan. "A Happy Birthday for Gay Liberation." *Village Voice*, July 2, 1970. Google Archive.
Bourdage, Joe. "Hal Call, Pan-Graphic Press, and the Adonis Bookstore, Historical Essay." Accessed February 8, 2025. https://www.foundsf.org/index.php?title=Hal_Call,_Pan-Graphic_Press,_and_the_Adonis_Bookstore.
Carter, David. *Stonewall: The Riots That Sparked the Gay Revolution.* St. Martin's Press, 2004.
Cervini, Eric. *The Deviant's War*. Picador/Farrar, Straus and Giroux, 2020.
Chibbaro Jr., Lou. "Our History of Marching on Washington." *Washington Blade*, June 11, 2017.
Chicago Tribune. "Kills Himself as Police Hunt Nude Photos." March 7, 1957. Newspapers.com.
- "Scholarships to Be Aided by 'Sno-Ball.'" December 28, 1952, 104, Newspapers.com.
Clendinen, Dudley, and Adam Nagourney. *Out for Good: The Struggle to Build a Gay Rights Movement in America*. Simon & Schuster, 1999.
Craig Rodwell Memorial Service at the LGBT Center in New York [Videotape], July 1993, LGBT Community Center National History Archive.
Craig Rodwell Papers. Manuscripts and Archives Division, New York Public Library, Astor, Lenox, and Tilden Foundations.
Crawford Jr., Philip. *The Mafia and the Gays*. CreateSpace, [2015] 2023.
Criminal Court of Cook County, Case Records, 1955.
Curb, Rosemary, and Nancy Manahan. *Lesbian Nuns: Breaking Silence*. Naiad Press, 1985.
Danyluk, Harry, and Jesse Brodey. "Murder of Cantor and 2d Man Charged to a Prisoner in NJ." *New York Daily News*, December 12, 1972. Newspapers.com.
Davis, Kate, and David Heilbroner. *Stonewall Uprising*. Q-Ball Productions (2010), PBS American Experience, 2011.
D'Emilio, John. *Sexual Politics, Sexual Communities, The Making of a Homosexual Minority in the United States, 1940–1970*. University of Chicago Press, 1983.

Denneny, Michael. *On Christopher Street*. University of Chicago Press, 2023.
Deviant's Archive, Frank Kameny Papers, Library of Congress.
Diana Davies Photographs. Manuscripts and Archives Division, New York Public Library, Astor, Lenox, and Tilden Foundations.
Duberman, Martin. *Stonewall, The Definitive Story of the LGBTQ Rights Uprising That Changed America*. St. Martin's Press, 1993.
Eastern Mattachine Magazine, May 1965. Gale Archives of Sexuality and Gender.
Eastern Regional Conference of Homophile Organizations. Minutes of Philadelphia Conference, November 1–2, 1969. Frank Kameny Papers, Deviant's Archive, 67–3. thedeviantsarchive.org.
Ellman, Richard. *Oscar Wilde*. Alfred A. Knopf, 1988.
Encyclopedia of Chicago. "Rogers Park." http://www.encyclopedia.chicagohistory.org/pages/1086.html.
Encyclopedia of Lesbian, Gay, Bisexual, and Transgender History in America. Charles Scribner's Sons, 2004.
Eskow, Dennis. "3 Cops Hurt, As Bar Raid Riles Crowd." *New York Daily News*, June 29, 1969. Newspapers.com.
Faderman, Lillian. *The Gay Revolution*. Simon & Schuster, 2015.
– *Harvey Milk*. Yale University Press, 2018.
Fair, Steven Lee. "Healing Homosexuality." March 5, 1979, *Christian Science Sentinel*. sentinel.christianscience.com.
Fay, Brendan. "Finding Jesús on Christopher Street." *Huffington Post*, June 8, 2012.
Finkelstein, Avram. *After Silence*. University of California Press, 2018.
Fosburgh, Lacey. "Thousands of Homosexuals Hold a Protest Rally in Central Park." *New York Times*, June 29, 1970. TimesMachine.
Foster Gunnison Jr. Papers. Archives and Special Collections, University of Connecticut Library.
Franklin, James. "A Rift Among Christian Scientists." *Boston Globe*, March 12, 1978. Newspapers.com.
Fred W. McDarrah Gay Pride Photographs Collection. Fales Library and Special Collections, New York University Libraries.
Gay Freedom. QQ Publishing, 1970.
Gay Magazine. "Gay Journalist-Activist Slain." Houstonlgbthistory.org, October 1972.
Gay People in Christian Science? [Pamphlet] 1979.
Glasser, Ira. "The Yellow Star and the Pink Triangle." *New York Times*, September 10, 1975. TimesMachine.

Grossman, Karl. "The Fire Island Trials: The Stonewall Before Stonewall," *Fire Island News,* June 21, 2019.

Herger, Heinz. *The Men with the Pink Triangle.* Gay Men's Press, 1980.

Hilderbrand, Lucas. "A Suitcase Full of Vaseline, or Travels in the 1970s Gay World." *Journal of the History of Sexuality* 22, no. 3 (2013).

– "The Uncut Version: The Mattachine Society's Pornographic Epilogue." *Sexualities.* University of California, 2015.

Hoffman, Martin. *The Gay World.* Basic Books, 1968.

Homophile Action League. Newsletter of January–February 1970 (I: 2). Gale Archives of Sexuality and Gender.

Howell, Kevin. "The Oscar Doesn't Go To …" *Publisher's Weekly,* January 20, 2003.

IRS Form 990. "Year 2020." Heritage of Pride, New York.

Jesús Lebrón Papers. Bronx County Archives at Bronx County Historical Society Research Library.

Johnson, Thomas A. "3 Deviates Invite Exclusion by Bars." *New York Times,* April 22, 1963. TimesMachine.

Kaiser, Charles. *The Gay Metropolis.* Houghton-Mifflin Company, 1997.

Kalin, Betsy. Interview with Kay Lahusen. *Outwords Archive,* 2018. theoutwordsarchive.org.

Katz, Jonathan Ned. *Gay American History: Lesbians and Gay Men in the USA.* Meridian [1976] 1992.

Kramer, Larry. *Faggots.* Penguin Books, 1978.

Lahr, John. "Camp Tales." *New York Times,* January 14, 1979. TimesMachine.

Lee, Carl. "It's What's Happening." *The New York Hymnal.* January 1970.

Levy, Clifford. "Thousands March in a Celebration of Gay Pride." *New York Times,* June 28, 1993. TimesMachine.

LGBT Community Center National History Archive. Business Certificates for Transfer of the Oscar Wilde Memorial Bookshop to William Offenbaker, 1993. Collection 86, Box 10.

– "Charles Pitts on The New Symposium." July 1969 Interview with Fred Sargeant at the Oscar Wilde Memorial Bookshop. WBAI, Collection 168, Audio Tape 70.

– "Charles Pitts Recording, Christopher Street Liberation Day March." June 28, 1970. WBAI, Collection 168, Audio Tape 19.

– Christopher Street Liberation Day Committee. Amendment to the Certificate of Incorporation, December 1989. Collection 86, Box 1, Folder 3.

- Christopher Street Liberation Day Committee. Minutes of June 11, 1984, Meeting. Collection 86, Box 4.
- Demonstration of Cruising Film, 1979. Rudy Grillo Collection, Collection 3, Box 10, Cassette 76.

Lipsky, Bill. "Hal Call: Homophiles and the Struggle for Social Acceptance." *San Francisco Bay Times*, August 11, 2022.

Long, Michael G. *Gay Is Good, The Life and Letters of Gay Rights Pioneer Franklin Kameny*. Syracuse University Press, 2014.

Loughery, John. *The Other Side of Silence*. Henry Holt, 1998.

Marotta, Toby. *The Politics of Homosexuality*. Houghton Mifflin, 1981.

Martin Duberman Papers, Recorded Interviews with Craig Rodwell, 1991. New York Public Library, Manuscripts and Archives Division, Astor, Lenox, and Tilden Foundations.

McCreary, Ora. "A Witness to Gay History: Some Memories of 1968–72." Unpublished essay shared with author, 2008.

McDarrah, Fred W., and Timothy S. McDarrah. *Gay Pride: Photographs from Stonewall to Today*. Chicago Review Press, 1994.

McNeill, John J. *The Church and the Homosexual*. Beacon Press, 1976.

New York Historical Society. Panel with Seymour Pine. New York, June 2, 2004.

New York Mattachine Newsletter. April 1964. Frank Kameny Papers, The Deviant's Archive, Library of Congress.
- April 1970. Gale Archives of Sexuality and Gender.
- July 1965. Frank Kameny Papers, The Deviant's Archive, Library of Congress.
- March 1970. Gale Archives of Sexuality and Gender.
- November 1965. Frank Kameny Papers, The Deviant's Archive, Library of Congress.

New York Mattachine Times. "Historically Speaking." January–February 1973, 15. Gale Archives of Sexuality and Gender.

New York Post. "Village Raid Stirs Melee." June 29, 1969.

New York Times. "Court in Massachusetts Upholds Christian Science Monitor's Dismissal of A Lesbian." August 22, 1985, 16. TimesMachine.
- "Homosexual-Liberation Statue Is Planned for Sheridan Square." July 21, 1979. TimesMachine.
- "Homosexuals Parade in the Face of Death." June 29, 1987. TimesMachine.

- "John B. Whyte, 75, Model and Fire Island Developer." April 12, 2004. TimesMachine.
- "1969, A Year of Bombings." City Room Blog, August 27, 2009. TimesMachine.
- "Policemen Forbidden to Entrap Homosexuals to Make Arrests." May 11, 1966. TimesMachine.
- "Protesters Call the Film 'Cruising' Antihomosexual." July 26, 1979. TimesMachine.
- "SLA Won't Act Against Bars Refusing Service to Deviates." April 26, 1965. TimesMachine.
- Stonewall coverage. Various articles, June 29, 1969, 33; June 30, 1969. TimesMachine.
- "Stormé DeLarverie, Early Leader in the Gay Rights Movement, Is Dead." May 30, 2014. TimesMachine.

NYC LGBT Historic Sites Project. "Corduroy Club." Accessed February 8, 2025. https://www.nyclgbtsites.org/site/corduroy-club/.
- "Riis Park Beach." Accessed February 8, 2025. https://www.nyclgbtsites.org/site/beach-at-jacob-riis-park/.

Oscar Wilde Memorial Bookshop Mail Order Catalog, 1968. Craig Rodwell Papers, Manuscripts and Archives Division, New York Public Library, Box 4.

Pacifica Radio Archives. WBAI panel, September 27, 1980.

Parker, William. "Employment Discrimination Is Being Confronted." *Vector Magazine*, 1971. Society for Individual Rights, San Francisco.

Philadelphia Inquirer, July 5, 1965. Newspapers.com.

Philip G. Ryan Papers. Manuscripts and Archives Division, New York Public Library, Astor, Lenox, and Tilden Foundations.

Price, Naomi. "The Bible and Homosexuality." *Christian Science Sentinel*, November 18, 1972. sentinel.christianscience.com.

QQ Magazine. "Mr. Fire Island." Fall 1970, 24–5.
- "Gay Is Good." Summer 1969, 38–9, 51–2.

Queen's Quarterly Collection. LGBT Community Center National History Archive.

Randy Shilts Papers. Interview Notes with Craig Rodwell for *The Mayor of Castro Street*, 1990. James C. Hormel LGBTQIA Center, San Francisco Public Library.

Robert Giard Papers. Yale Collection of American Literature, Beinecke Rare Book and Manuscript Library.

Rodwell, Craig. "Exploitation and Gay Lib." *QQ Magazine*, April 1972.
- "For All the Jack Staffords." *QQ Magazine*, June 1973.
- "Four More Years." Editorial, *QQ Magazine*, April 1973.
- "Gay and Free." *QQ Magazine*, December 1971.
- "Gay People and the Arts." *QQ Magazine*, September–October 1972.
- "Gay Power Gains." *The New York Hymnal* I, no. 6.
- "The Gay Vote." *QQ Magazine*, September 1972.
- "Get the Mafia and the Cops out of Gay Bars." Stonewall Riots Leaflet, New York, June 28, 1969.
- "God & Gay Lib." *QQ Magazine*, June 1972.
- "Gray Is Good," *QQ Magazine*, August 1973.
- "Hanging In Together." *QQ Magazine*, April 1971.
- "How It Is Gay Liberation." *QQ Magazine*, Fall 1970.
- "HYMNAL Makes Bow." *The New York Hymnal* I, no. 1.
- "Image Smashing." *QQ Magazine*, November–December 1972.
- "Johnny Cop Wants You." *QQ Magazine*, June 1971.
- "The Lavender Syndicate." *QQ Magazine*, February 1973.
- "The Lavender Syndicate – Part II." *QQ Magazine*, April 1973.
- "Mafia Control of Gay Bars." *The New York Hymnal* I, no. 2.
- "Mafia on the Spot: Mafia Control of Gay Bars Comes to Public's Attention." *The New York Hymnal* I, no. 1.
- "Martin Luther King Jr." *The New York Hymnal* I, no. 3.
- "McCarthy Wins Poll." *The New York Hymnal* I, no. 4.
- "The Meaning of Obscenity." *QQ Magazine*, October 1973.
- "Random Thoughts." *QQ Magazine*, October 1971.
- "Reflections on Ten Years of Gay Lib." *QQ Magazine*, February 1972.
- "Robert F. Kennedy." Editorial, *The New York Hymnal* I, no. 5.
- "Sex – How Important Is It?" *QQ Magazine*, June 1973.
- "The Tarnished Golden Rule." *QQ Magazine*, February 1971.
- "What to Do When You're Arrested." *QQ Magazine*, August 1971.

Russo, Vito. *Our Time*. Episode 6, March 16, 1983. https://www.youtube.com/watch?v=bbb9jfunymw.

Ryan, Philip. "Pink Triangle History." Letter in *The New York Blade*, January 7, 2000.

San Francisco Examiner. "Harvey Milk Leaves San Francisco a Legacy of Love." December 1, 1978. Newspapers.com.
- "Milk, First Gay to Be Supervisor." November 27, 1978. Newspapers.com.
- "Slain Youth Found Here NY Viet Vet." October 16, 1970.

Sargeant, Fred. "Anger Management." *New York Times*, June 25, 2009.
Scherker, Michael. *The Reminiscences of Craig Rodwell*. Oral history transcript, 1986.
Shilts, Randy. *Conduct Unbecoming*. St. Martin's Press, 1993.
– *The Mayor of Castro Street*. St. Martin's Press, 1982.
Sieber, Ann Walton. "Time Out: Lobo Bookshop and Café." *Outsmart Magazine*, December 1999.
Smith, Howard "View from Inside, Full Moon over the Stonewall." *Village Voice*, July 3, 1969. Google archive.
Stores, Bruce. *Christian Science: Its Encounter with Lesbian/Gay America*. iUniverse, 2004.
Streitmatter, Rodger. *Unspeakable: The Rise of the Gay and Lesbian Press in America*. Faber and Faber, 1995.
Summers, Claude J. "George Segal's Gay Liberation." *Glbtq.com Encyclopedia*, 2003.
Talbot, Margaret, and David Talbot. *By the Light of Burning Dreams*. Harper Collins, 2021.
Tangents Magazine. May–July 1969. Homosexual Information Center, West Hollywood, CA.
Teal, Donn. *The Gay Militants*. St. Martin's Press, 1971.
Time. "The Homosexual in America." October 31, 1969.
Tobin, Kay, and Randy Wicker. *The Gay Crusaders*. Paperback Library, 1972.
Truscott, Lucian IV. "View from Outside: Gay Power Comes to Sheridan Square." *Village Voice*, July 3, 1969. Google archive.
Vincenz, Lilli. "Gay and Proud." Video, 1970. Library of Congress.
Vogel, Carol. "The Art Market." *New York Times*, June 19, 1992, TimesMachine.
Weber, Bruce. "Sam Ciccone, a Champion of Gay Police Officers, Dies at 71." *New York Times*, May 17, 2015. TimesMachine.
Welz, Carl J. "Homosexuality Can Be Healed." *Christian Science Sentinel*, April 22, 1967. sentinel.christianscience.com.
White, Edmund. Letter to Ann and Alfred Corn. https://outhistory.org/exhibits/show/stonewall-riot-police-reports/contents/edmund-white-letter.

Index

Abzug, Bella, 378n25; Rodwell's criticisms of, 165, 200, 318–19, 344
ACT UP: demonstrations/events, 217–18, 227; pink triangle merchandise, 205, 381n20
Advocate, The, 96, 154, 240, 371n11; name modification, 84, 377n10; readership, 154
AIDS epidemic, 380n22; ACT UP actions in, 205, 227; gay men's life expectancy and, 175, 219, 246, 261; OWMB resources on, 216–18; support/recognition efforts in, 220, 229, 247, 262–3
Angelou, Maya ("When Great Trees Fall"), 251
Annual Reminders, 284, 370–1n8; breaking routine of, 127–8; bus boarding at OWMB for, 48–50, 125–7, 267, 367n18; changes after, 128–31, 143, 265; ending of, 50–1, 81, 111, 125, 128–30; inspiration from, 240, 267–8; launching and conservative rules of, 47–9, 125–6, 186, 365n21; planning/promotion of, 79, 86, 90, 92, 125–6, 152–3; Rodwell's presence in, 47–9, 127–8, 161, 228, 240, 373n1
armed forces. *See* military service
arts, gay people in the, 35, 164–7, 236–8, 324–7, 383n46

Balanchine, George, 26, 166, 325
ballet, 24–6, 30, 34, 166–7, 324–6
Bawer, Bruce, 256
Bechdel, Alison (*More Dykes to Watch Out For*), 218–19, 223
Bell, Arthur (*Dancing the Gay Lib Blues*), 200–1, 382n38
Bennett, Michael (*A Chorus Line*), 218
Bible, the: anti-homosexual citing of, 182; boarding school study of, 10, 179; (re)interpretation of, 184–5, 190–1, 229, 337

Black authors/writing, 160, 213, 219–20
Blackheart Collective journal, 219–20
Black liberation organizing, 168, 285, 295–6, 326, 335. *See also* civil rights movement
Bleecker Street apartment: event organizing at, 81, 104–5, 129–36, 148, 198; *Hymnal*/pamphlet writing at, 83, 184; moving into/living at, 65–7, 75, 77–9, 100, 161–2
boarding school. *See* Chicago Junior School
Body Politic, The, 210, 381n16, 382n31
Boston, 316, 379n5; ballet study in, 24–5; Christian Science protests in, 180–4, 186–9, 379n17; Gay communities in, 347, 350; *Gay Community News*, 188, 210; Pride celebrations/organizing in, 147, 265, 289, 296, 308
Bourcheron, Robert (*Epitaphs for the Plague Dead*), 217
Bowie, David, 163
Boys in the Band (play), 68, 93; gay stereotypes and, 146, 157, 166, 294, 324
Briggs, Kenneth A., 229
Brinster, Kim, 254–5
Broidy, Ellen: Christopher Street Liberation Day organizing, 76–7, 81, 129–32, 147; friendship with Rodwell, 4, 77, 161; NYU Student Homophile League, 76, 130, 148; OWMB volunteering, 76–7; picketing Time-Life Building, 1–2, 134–5; Weinstein Hall protest, 148
Brown, Michael, 139

Bucalo, Frank (Francis), 19, 21, 55, 362n18; arrest and court case, 16–18, 20
Buzard, Nan, 221–3

Cafiero, Renée, 44
Call, Hal, 367–8n18
Campbell, Joe, 30, 36, 363n4
Canada, 21, 228; customs seizure of books, 210; legislation on homosexuality, 90–1
Carl, Fred, 218–23, 383n46
Carter, David (*Stonewall*), 114, 365n10, 371n12, 372n31
Casement, Roger, 225–6, 383n50
Castro, Fidel, 46, 298
Castro Camera, 29, 267
Catholicism, homosexuality and, 227–9
Chicago, 56, 289, 316, 319; anti-homosexual violence in, 19, 173, 352; cruising in, 14–20, 28; Gay communities in, 347, 350; Mattachine Society in, 22–3; police in, 14–20, 55; Pride events/organizing in, 147, 257, 265–6, 285, 296, 308; Rodwell's childhood/high school years in, 2, 7–8, 24, 30, 83, 249; Rodwell's later visits/stays in, 36, 55
Chicago Cubs, 10–11, 14, 23, 244
Chicago Junior School, 9, 22, 25, 29; Rodwell's time in, 2, 10–13, 18, 63, 179
Chisholm, Shirley, 168, 332
Christianity, Primitive, 166, 179–80, 323
Christian Science: auditing of, 183–4; Board of Directors of, 181–4, 186–7, 189; boarding school instruction (*see* Chicago Junior School); connections

formed based on, 180–2, 202; Gay People in (group), 183–90, 244; Golden Rule and, 157, 185, 190–3, 291–5; Jesus's teachings and,179–80, 192–3; Mother Church confrontation, 180–4, 186–91; racism, shifting views on, 194; Rodwell's critiques of, 179–80, 184–6, 189–95, 244, 291–5; views on homosexuality, 180, 182, 186, 189–91, 244. *See also* Eddy, Mary Baker

Christian Science Journal, 183, 186, 189–90

Christian Science Monitor, 181, 187–9

Christian Science Sentinel articles, 182, 184, 189–90

Christopher Street Liberation Day march, 99, 222, 241; approval at ERCHO meeting, 132–3; changes to subsequent versions of, 197–201, 260–2; committee for, 129, 135–9, 144–8, 157–8, 197–200, 258–63; floats in, 135–6, 198–9, 258, 260; fundraising/ revenue for, 136–7, 140, 148, 198, 263; Gay Be-In and, 140, 144–5; lavender line origin in New York, 261; marshals for, 141–4, 250, 259–60, 311, 376n41; parade permits for, 139–40, 142, 149, 130; participation in, 56, 131–3, 135–40, 142–6, 153, 224; planning, 2, 61, 76–8, 129–32, 135–40, 197–9, 240; Rodwell's role in, 96, 129–30, 136–40, 175, 200–1, 247, 265–8; route changes, 200–1, 257–61. *See also* Heritage of Pride; Pride marches

Ciccone, Sam, 240–1

Civil Marriage Trail, 228

Civil Rights Act amendments, 167, 328, 332–3

civil rights movement, 50–2, 67, 92, 281; homosexual struggle similarities with, 25, 91, 157, 262

Clarke, Lige, 45, 81, 96, 154

Clinton, Kate, 242

Coalition of Conscience, 204

Colt, Zebedy, 68–9

Cook, Blanche (*Eleanor Roosevelt*), 242

Cory, Donald Webster (*The Lesbian in America/The Homosexual in America*), 68, 70, 95

court case(s), 179, 294, 331; anti-discrimination, 167, 358; anti-homosexual judgments in, 28–9, 32–4, 53–4, 90, 188, 322; Bucalo trial, 16–18, 20; harassment in, 28–9, 55–6, 59, 159, 300–1, 306

cruising, 152, 214, 363n6; Pacino film, 231–3; police surveillance of, 16–17, 26–7, 30; Rodwell's experiences, 14–20, 22–4, 27–9, 40; violence/safety concerns with, 172–3, 305, 352–3

Cuba, treatment of homosexuals in, 46, 298

Daily News, 103; coverage of homosexuality, 109, 172, 247, 378n36

Daughters of Bilitis, 141; protest involvement/organizing, 134, 264, 296, 309, 375n18; publications from, 70–1, 85, 181, 362n25, 373n2

Davies, Diana, 205

Day, Susan, 131

"Dear Abby" column, 73, 91

DeLarverie, Stormé, 102–3, 371nn11–12

398 | Index

Denneny, Michael, 99
Desantis, George (*QQ Magazine*), 96, 145, 152–6, 294, 376n41
Dinkins, David, 227, 245, 262
discrimination: by bars, 53–4, 268, 343; based on sex, 89–90, 55, 333; against Black people, 160, 191, 219, 329, 354; court cases to address, 93, 167, 188, 358; employment, 42, 47–8, 94, 165–7, 203, 219; legal measures to counter, 167–8, 203–4, 285, 328–9; by police/courts, 28–9, 55–6, 59, 159, 300–1, 306; politician promises to end, 165, 176, 211, 318, 332–4; protesting homosexual, 46–8, 219, 236–7, 343, 355–7; Rodwell's work to counter, 95, 118, 159, 334
drag shows, 167, 326
DRUM magazine, 64, 84–5
Duberman, Martin (*Stonewall*), 244, 248, 363n30

East Coast Homophile Organizations (ECHO), 45, 47, 50–1, 365n10. *See also* Eastern Regional Conference of Homophile Organizations
Eastern Regional Conference of Homophile Organizations (ERCHO), 148, 239; Annual Reminder pickets by, 50, 81, 90, 125, 128; Christopher Street Liberation Day march proposal, 77, 81, 129–33, 137, 147; post-march reports to, 147
Eddy, Mary Baker, 185, 191, 244; publications by/about, 181–2, 379n5; Rodwell quoting, 159, 191–2, 307–8; writings/lessons of, 179–80, 191–4
Edel, Deborah, 263
ego-trippers, 169, 172, 337, 349
elderly gay people, 176, 357

Fair, Steven Lee, 182
families: creating Gay, 75, 357; homosexual inhibition with, 67, 101, 291, 314; photos/memories of, 12, 14; Rodwell's push for openness with, 7, 156, 163, 175, 327, 347–51; support from, 202, 227, 269, 337
Fay, Brendan (*Taking A Chance on God*), 224–30
Fierstein, Harvey (*Torch Song Trilogy*), 214, 219, 224
Fire Island, 41, 58–9, 208, 364n4; Body Beautiful Contest, 153, 155
Foreman, Matt, 261
Fosburgh, Lacey, 146
foster homes, Rodwell's time in, 2, 8, 12
Fouratt, Jim, 134

Gambino, Anthony, 258–60
Garden, Nancy (*Annie on My Mind*), 215, 246
GAY (lesbian and gay newspaper), 96, 154
Gay Activists Alliance (GAA), 382n38; involvement with, 78, 120, 139, 181, 258, 375n27; protest involvement, 113, 141, 200, 216; strategies/aims of, 138, 264, 296, 298, 309
gay bars, 58, 317; creating alternatives to, 174, 320, 344–5, 349–50, 356; discrimination by, 53–4, 268, 343; in films, 232, 294; Mafia exploitation of, 88–9, 164, 170–1, 265, 278–81, 340–5; police entrapment in/around, 26, 51, 54, 302, 304–5; police raids of, 100–2, 112–13, 231, 308–11; Pride march involvement by, 199–201, 258; Rodwell writing about Mafia control of, 86–7, 94, 97, 107,

126, 326–30; underage seeking of, 24, 339. *See also* Liquor Authority; Stonewall riots
gay churches, 165–6, 318, 321–4
Gay Community News (Boston), 188, 210
Gay Crusaders, The (Tobin Lahusen) 73, 118, 130, 180, 202, 213
Gay Freedom 1970 (Desantis/*QQ Magazine*), 145, 153, 162, 241
Gay Is Good messaging, 119, 285; at OWMB, 5, 61, 66, 206; Rodwell's writing with, 92, 152
gay liberation, 203, 215, 233; creating community in, 174, 320, 344–5, 356–9; exploitation of movement for, 62, 164–7, 207–10, 316–20, 337–45; need for, 291–2, 298, 302, 327–31; organizations/publications, 131, 198, 210, 289–90, 295–6, 356; protests/marches for, 113, 130, 146, 239–40, 260–1; reflections on, 156–8, 162–3, 175–7, 313–15, 346–52; Rodwell's leadership in, 3–5, 63, 118, 131, 170–2, 264–9; sculpture, 235–8; Stonewall riots as pivotal in, 96, 156, 287–8, 308; writing about God and, 179–80, 184, 321–4
Gay Liberation Front (GLF), 375n27; involvement with, 77, 122, 309, 357, 373n2; protest involvement, 69, 113, 134, 148, 264; strategies/aims of, 4, 96, 138, 141, 295–6, 298
gay marriages, 88, 165–6, 318
"Gay People and The Arts" (*QQ Magazine*), 164–7, 324–7
Gay Power: newspaper, 96, 131; promotion of, 92, 94, 110, 239, 284–5, 287–8; as Stonewall rallying cry, 2, 5, 86, 101–2, 106, 143, 268

Gay Pride Week(s), 137, 140–1, 265–6
gay rights movement: activists, 143, 373n2; politician discussion/support of, 172, 331, 334–5, 348; protesting for, 46, 347; Rodwell's contribution to, 2, 201–4, 228, 247, 268; sculpture for, 236–7; Stonewall riots as pivotal for, 112, 228
gay sex, 15–16, 349–51, 358–9
Gay's The Word, 267
gay voters, 168, 316, 331
Geto, Ethan, 203–4
Gittings, Barbara, 176, 264, 373n2; friendship with Rodwell, 71, 75, 203, 224; pickets of 1965: 365n20; protest participation, 45, 47–8, 126; relationship with Kay Tobin Lahusen, 180–1
Glasser, Ira, 204
"God & Gay Lib" (*QQ Magazine*), 179–80, 184, 321–4
Goldman, Julia Noël, 229–30, 244–5, 249, 253, 385n23
Greenwich Village, 57, 63, 231–2, 237, 316; bar raids/protests in, 100–1, 105–7, 211, 288, 308, 339; cruising in, 27–8, 40; Mafia-controlled bars in, 86–8, 278–9; marching from/to, 81, 143, 200, 257–8; OWMB presence in, 170, 198, 201, 226, 231, 255; "queer" community in, 22, 67, 120, 163, 297, 313, 347
Grier, Barbara, 71, 218, 382n44
Grillo, Rudy, 215
Gunnison Jr., Foster, 239; "An Introduction to the Homophile Movement," 61–2; CSLDUC involvement, 136–7, 146–8, 197–9, 375n24; friendship with Rodwell, 61–2, 373n7

"Hanging In Together" (*QQ Magazine*), 158, 295–9
Hanlon, Emily (*The Wing and the Flame*), 214
Happy Prince, The (Wilde) 10, 63
Hart, Lois, 134
Hay, Harry, 23
Hay, Louise (AIDS: *A Positive Approach/You Can Heal Your Life*), 217
Heritage of Pride, 257, 261–3
heterosexism, 166, 354; organizing to counter, 160, 169–70, 212, 233; Rodwell's coining of, 2, 157, 184, 379n14; Rodwell writing about, 186, 194, 291–2, 325, 337–8
heterosexuality: discriminatory norms of, 40, 157, 159, 231; gay church movement and, 165–6, 322–3; gay sex versus, 358–9; homosexuality as equal with, 11, 45, 185, 190–2, 290–1; law reform and, 167, 299, 330–1, 354; privileging of, 236, 290, 299–306, 315, 325
heterosexuals, 26, 91; arts/cultural representations, 96, 236, 325–7, 358; attempts to persuade/educate, 23, 48, 86; harassment and violence by, 159, 173; picketing/protest support by, 44, 50, 127–8, 284; solidarity with homosexuals, 62, 108, 315
Hodges, Julian, 40–2, 58, 365n10
Hoffman, Martin (The Gay World), 68
Hole, Ernest, 126, 267, 373n2
homophile, definition and use of, 3, 61–2, 157, 292
homophile movement: actions to support, 94; growth of, 281; heterosexual ignorance of, 135; history/roots of, 61, 91, 136, 199, 308; OWMB presence in, 61–2, 70, 152–3, 156, 292; publications/writing on, 61, 65, 68, 84–6, 151, 154–5, 362n25; Rodwell's leadership in, 4, 29, 39, 80, 103, 245, 264
homophile organizations, 60, 76; formation/categories of, 289–90, 296; lack of support for New York, 277, 280, 285; seeking help from, 91, 303; support for Christopher Street Liberation Day march, 130–2, 136–7, 147. *See also* East Coast Homophile Organizations
Homophile Youth Movement in Neighborhoods (HYMN), 152, 285; establishment/naming of, 71–2, 77; involvement with, 2, 96, 111, 119, 374n9; political opinion polls, 91–2, 282–3; protest involvement, 80, 105, 108, 113, 126, 265; support for Christopher Street Liberation Day march, 130–1, 141, 199; *The Hymnal* (see *New York Hymnal*)
homosexuality: Christian Science/religion and, 40, 180–6, 189–93, 229, 244; coming out to family about, 88, 348; discrimination against, 293, 302; as equal to heterosexuality, 62, 193, 229, 287; history of, 61, 63, 94, 191; legislation (reforms) on, 91; media coverage of, 163, 313–14, 371n14; Oscar Wilde and, 61, 63; psychiatric/psychological analyses of, 25, 40, 61, 68, 147, 176; resources about, 68, 70; as sickness, 45, 72–3, 92, 284, 264; stereotypes about, 1–2, 72, 119, 284

Hudson, Rock, 166, 216, 324
Humm, Andy, 114
Humphrey, Hubert, 168, 282, 332–4

Irish Lesbian & Gay Organization, 225–8
"It's What's Happening" *Hymnal* column, 89, 135

Jackson, Isaac, 219–20
Julius' Bar, sip-in at, 53–5, 66, 88, 248, 268, 366n36

Kameny, Frank, 143, 239, 370n11; "Gay Is Good" slogan, 92, 175; as homophile movement pioneer, 176, 264; Mattachine involvement, 45, 373n2; organizing Annual Reminders, 45–9, 125–6; as Regional Conference chair, 45, 47, 92, 126, 130–1; relations with Rodwell, 45, 48, 75, 127–8, 374n9
Katz, Jonathan Ned (*Gay American History*), 77–8, 205–6, 213
Kerry, Reginald, 183, 186
Kilburn, George, 9–12
King Jr., Martin Luther, 91, 281–2
Koch, Edward, 232–3, 262, 378n25
Koten, Bernard, 75, 176, 357
Kozachenko, Kathy, 163
Kramer, Larry (*Faggots*/*The Normal Heart*), 208–10, 216–18

Ladder, The (lesbian journal), 85, 362n25; Barbara Gittings as editor of, 45, 181, 373n2; bookshop carrying of, 70–1, 84
Lahr, John (*The Orton Diaries*), 208–9, 218
Lahusen, Kay Tobin, 71, 176; protest/march involvement, 126, 224; Rodwell's friendship/work with, 75, 138, 161, 181, 201, 263; *The Gay Crusaders*, 73, 118, 130, 180, 202, 213
Lambda Literary Award, 242–3, 254, 384n15
Lambda Rising (bookshop), 242, 254
lambda symbol merchandise, 205, 214, 382n38
language usage, 3–4, 158, 231, 289; bigoted, 110, 372n29
Larkin, Clay (*A Different Love*), 214
Lavender and Green Alliance, 228
law reform, homosexual, 164, 291; demonstrations for, 141, 302, 326; OWMB material on, 60–1; Rodwell's commentary on, 167, 299, 327–31, 354
leaflets/flyers, 138; Annual Reminder, 49, 51, 126; anti-Mafia/cop, 80, 88, 201, 265–8, 357, 372n23; Christian Science protest, 187; Christopher Street Liberation Day march, 140, 142; homosexual pride-focused, 23, 40, 83; production and distribution of, 105–6, 111, 129, 134, 372n25; Stonewall riots, 97–9, 105–8, 112–15, 176, 241, 357
Lebrón, Jesús, 226–8, 383n52
Leitsch, Dick: Annual Reminder involvement, 47; Mattachine involvement, 40, 42, 57, 240; Rodwell's relationship with, 40–2, 57, 239–40, 364n4; sip-in leadership, 52–3, 268
lesbian community, 3, 102, 148, 229–30; in Christopher Street Liberation Day march, 141–3, 145, 198–9; discrimination

lesbian community (*continued*)
facing, 89, 187–8, 210;
Mattachine involvement,
44; organizations, 134, 200,
263, 296; OWMB literature
for, 2, 62–3, 68, 84–5, 213–15;
politicians, 163; Rodwell's
respect/support for, 70–1, 76–7,
198–9, 218. See also *Ladder, The*
Lesbian, Gay, Bisexual &
Transgender Community
Center, 223–4, 230, 247
Lesbian Herstory Archives, 263
Lindsay, John, 92, 108, 310, 335;
election polling on, 168, 282–3, 332
Lingle, Larry (Lobo Bookshop),
254–5
Liquor Authority: challenging
regulations of, 51–4, 317,
339–40, 366n36; licensing issues
with, 86, 89, 100–1, 109, 279;
regulations on serving gay
people, 51–3, 86–9
liquor hijacking, 317, 341, 345
Lorde, Audre (*The Black
Unicorn/A Burst of Light/Zami/
Undersong*), 213, 218–19, 242
Louis (Army private), 121–3, 267
Lowery, Calvin, 214–15

Maccubbin, Deacon, 242–4, 254–5
Mackenroth, Bob, 180–2
Madsen, Chris, 187–8
Mafia: exploitation of gay bars,
115, 164, 170–1, 265, 278–81,
340–5; influence on Christopher
Street Liberation Day march,
258–60; leaflets against, 80, 88,
201, 265–8, 357, 372n23; police
connections with, 80, 87, 115,
288, 310, 317, 330; porn, control
of, 170–1, 340–2; Rodwell's
complaints about, 86–90, 94, 97,
107, 126, 326–30; Stonewall Inn
and, 86, 89, 101, 106–8, 258–60

"Mafia on the Spot" *Hymnal*
column, 86–9, 97, 170, 278–80
Marotta, Toby (*The Politics of
Homosexuality*), 4, 375n18
Marshall, John, 49, 136
Mattachine Review, 22, 84, 362n25
Mattachine Society, 2, 61, 84,
153, 296, 309; conservatism/
reformism of, 4, 57–8, 71–4,
78, 133; founding of, 23, 45;
Midwest, 23, 50, 55; newsletters/
magazines, 29, 39–42, 55–6,
63, 184; of New York, 39–41,
46–51, 66, 106, 136, 145, 239–40;
protest involvement, 44–6,
48, 106, 145; Rodwell's search
for, 22–3, 25; sip-in, 52–5, 66,
88, 339; volunteering with, 29,
39–44, 57, 67, 239–40, 246–8; of
Washington, 44–6, 49, 85, 136;
West Side Discussion Group
(*see* West Side Discussion
Group); young adults group,
50–1, 118
Maupin, Armistead (*Tales of the
City*), 214
McCarthy, Eugene, 92, 168, 282–3,
332–3
McCloskey, Paul, 168, 333
McCreary, Ora, 74–5
McCullough, Bob, 180–2, 244
McGovern, George, 168–72,
333–4, 346, 357
McNeill, John (*The Church and the
Homosexual*), 213, 228–9
military service, 103, 283;
discharge from, 16, 43, 48, 94,
307, 332; draft examination
banning homosexuals, 43–5, 48,
91, 94; gay people in, 16, 120–3,
241, 267; Rodwell's criticisms
of, 169, 241, 307, 334
Milk, Harvey, 36–7, 64, 84, 163,
267; killing of, 210–11, 263,
382n34; memorial services

in California and New York, 211–12; Rodwell's relationship with, 28–31, 34, 160–1, 211–12, 363n4
Mohr, Richard (*Gay Ideas*), 242
Monette, Paul (*Becoming a Man*), 242
Murphy, Ed, 250, 258, 385n1

name-calling, homophobic, 2, 26, 32, 80, 283; violence and, 158, 173, 300, 352
Navratilova, Martina, 163
Nazis, oppression of homosexuality, 188, 214, 229; pink triangles and, 191, 203–5, 212, 380n22
newspapers, 248, 341; coverage of homosexuality, 46, 49, 54, 91, 106, 163, 319; gay, 96, 131, 154, 210, 212, 297; Rodwell's interest in, 14, 72, 106, 231, 264, 313
Newsweek, 103, 371n14
New Symposium (II), 93, 111, 285, 373n2
New York Hymnal, 121; advertising and publication of, 69, 72, 83–6, 95–6, 155–7; columns, 89–95, 135, 181; coverage of Mafia in, 86–9, 97, 101, 170, 201, 278–81; as extension of HYMN, 84; politics, commentary on, 200, 282–5; Rodwell's devotion to, 79, 83–8, 96, 152, 184, 268
New York Post: notification of protests, 52, 103; Rodwell's complaints to, 72–3; Stonewall, coverage of, 106, 109
New York Times, 80, 204, 278; book reviews in, 208, 229; coverage of marches, 146, 199, 261–2; homosexual representations in, 58, 102, 236–7, 327, 355–6; language use in, 231, 249;
notification of protests, 52, 103; on OWMB closure, 255–6; politics coverage, 90, 160; sip-in coverage, 53–4; Stonewall, coverage of, 109–10
Nichols, Jack, 45–7, 81, 96, 154, 365n10
Nixon, Richard, 92, 171–2, 282, 331–4, 346, 358
Noble, Elaine, 163
North American Conference of Homophile Organizations (NACHO), 239, 285
North American Man/Boy Love Association (NAMBLA), 215–16, 249

O'Dell, Brian, 260–1
Offenbaker, Bill, 250–1, 253–4
ONE magazine, 22, 85, 362n25
Oscar Wilde Memorial Bookshop (OWMB): activism through, 221, 230–1, 267–8; Bookazine, stock from, 66–7, 203; community space, 105–6, 123, 221–3, 231, 248, 266; financial precarity of, 79, 202–3, 230; as ground-breaking, 2, 61–2, 74–8, 84–5, 202, 228; homophile movement presence, 61–2, 70, 152–3, 156, 292; mailing list, 95, 137, 140, 266; mail order catalogs, 63–4, 67–70, 212–14, 218, 267; name choice, 60–1; opening of (Mercer Street), 2–3, 59–61, 65–7, 245, 255; ownership changes and closure of, 253–6; porn, prohibition on, 61, 64–5, 81, 208; second (Christopher Street) location, 170, 201–2; slogans, 66, 70, 213; Stonewall riots, role in/after, 80, 105–6, 111, 266; store stock, 2, 60–4, 68–71, 95, 206, 213–18; threats facing, 79–80, 255–6

Oswalt, Collin, 25, 28, 31, 34–6
Owles, Jim, 200, 258, 375n27
Oxenhorn, Wallace, 173, 378n36

Pacino, Al, 231–2, 249
parents: education for/dialogue with, 172, 314–15, 329; gay people as good, 164, 316; Rodwell's early relationships with, 10, 12, 18–19; supportive, 24–5, 35–6, 226–7, 247–8, 255, 348; struggles coming out to, 118–19, 134, 213, 289
Philadelphia, 145, 147, 224, 296; Annual Reminder picketing, 47–51, 111, 125–31, 267–8, 284, 373n1; Gay communities in, 350; gay publications from, 64, 84; Giovanni's Room, 203, 209; Pride marches in, 265–7; protests in, 44, 92, 228, 366n33
picketing, homosexual, 43; ERCHO involvement in, 50, 81, 90, 125, 128; heterosexual support in, 44, 50, 127–8, 284; Independence Hall (Philadelphia) (*see* Annual Reminders); Pentagon, 48; Whitehall Street Induction Center, 44, 66, 248, 268; White House, 45–8, 365n21
Piel, Candida Scott, 260–1, 264
Pine, Seymour, 112–14, 372n37; Stonewall riots involvement, 100–4, 109–10
pink triangle, 191, 381n16; merchandise, 203–5, 212, 217, 381n20; reclaiming of, 203–5, 380n22, 382n31
Pitts, Charles, 93, 111, 126, 144, 373n2
Polak, Clark, 64, 81
police, 353; Chicago, 14–20, 55; cruising, surveillance of, 16–17, 26–7, 30; discrimination by, 28–9, 55–6, 59, 159, 300–3, 306; entrapment in/around bars, 26, 51, 54, 302, 304–5; gay people as, 162, 240–2; harassment by, 30–3, 34, 158, 179, 363n8; instructions in case of arrest by, 304–8; Mafia connections, 80, 87, 107, 115, 310, 317, 330; raids, 100–4, 109–10, 112–13, 231, 288, 308–11; resentment toward, 32–3, 302, 344; Rodwell's articles critiquing, 158–9, 310, 310, 314, 317
porn, gay, 151; distribution of, 64, 170; Mafia control of, 170–1, 340–2; OWMB prohibition on, 61, 64–5, 81, 208; stereotypes about, 166, 171, 208
Price, Naomi, 182, 184–5
Pride Guide, 258–9
Pride marches, 188, 205, 265–7; New York (*see* Christopher Street Liberation Day march)
psychiatry/psychology, 231, 355; treatment via, 19, 36, 180, 314; views of homosexuality, 40, 61, 68, 73, 147, 176, 264

QQ Magazine: Gay Freedom 1970 publication, 145, 153, 162, 241; George Desantis's role in, 96, 145, 152–6, 294, 376n41; purpose, content, distribution of, 151–4, 177; Rodwell's writing/ collaboration with, 3, 152–7, 164–7, 179–80, 184, 291–9, 321–7

raids: gay establishment, 112–13, 231, 288, 308–11; legal prohibitions on, 58–9; protests against, 100–1, 105–7, 211, 288, 308, 339; Stonewall Inn, 100–4, 109–10

Ralph Schaffer Memorial Award, 207
Rechy, John (*Numbers/City of Night*), 95, 210
Rhodes, Linda, 129; as Ellen Broidy's partner, 2, 76, 81
rights, homosexual, 44, 94, 329. *See also* gay rights movement
Riis Park, 300, 363n4; police harassment at, 30–2, 34, 158, 179, 363n8
Roberts, Joe, 249–50, 258
Roberts, Michele (*A Piece of the Night*), 214
Rodwell, Craig: activism impacts of, 3–5, 63, 73–4, 95–6, 118, 131, 170–2, 238–40; attempt to take own life, 34–5; boarding school experiences, 2, 10–13, 18, 63, 179; cancer, 243, 246, 253; childhood independence, 8, 10–13, 18, 24–5; Christian Science, critiques, 179–80, 184–6, 189–95, 244, 291–5; Christopher Street Liberation Day march role, 129–30, 136–40, 175, 200–1, 247, 265–8; court case in Chicago, 16–19; as crotchety, 220–2, 230, 244, 248, 253; cruising experiences, 14–20, 22–4, 27–9, 40; death and memorial, 246–50; as an employer, 3–4, 220–4, 229–31; as feminist, 3–4, 71, 248; friendships, 4, 61–2, 71, 75, 77, 161, 201–3, 224; on future of gay liberation, 156–8, 162–3, 175–7, 313–15, 346–52; high school years, 2, 7–8, 24, 30, 83, 249; Homophile Youth Movement (*see* Homophile Youth Movement in Neighborhoods); *Hymnal*, work on, 79, 83–8, 96, 152, 184, 268; letters of support to/from, 117–21, 243–6, 263; picketing Time-Life Building, 1, 134–5; as revolutionary/pioneer, 4–5, 242–3, 247–9, 264–9; Riis Park arrest (*see* Riis Park); serious relationships of, 2, 28–31, 65–8, 148, 160–2, 201, 211–12; signature analysis, 207–8; at sip-in, 52–5
Rodwell, Jack, 36, 246, 249, 385n22
Rodwell, Louis, 7–8, 19, 21–2, 36
Rodwell, Marion, 15, 20, 60, 250, 255; documentation of Rodwell's childhood, 9–10, 12, 14; marriages of, 7–8, 18–19, 362n19; support for Rodwell, 17–19, 24–5, 35–6, 172, 247–8, 255
Rogers Park, 12, 24
Rohnke, Terry, 68, 75, 126
Russo, Vito (*Our Time/Celluloid Closet*), 209, 218

Sargeant, Fred: author involvement with, 3; as bookshop manager, 2, 66–7, 70, 78–80; in Christopher Street Liberation Day march, 81, 129–30, 142–6, 153; Eastern Regional Conference involvement, 131, 133, 148; friendships at bookshop, 74–6; HYMN involvement, 2, 72, 111, 113; as model in *QQ* and *Dick and Jane* book, 155; picketing Time-Life Building, 1–2, 134–5; policing career, 162, 241; relationship with Rodwell, 2, 65–8, 148, 160–2, 201; Stonewall riots, participation in, 93, 99–108, 111–12, 268, 370n6
Scherker, Michael, 269, 363n8

SCREW magazine, 81, 96
sculpture, Gay Liberation, 235–8
Segal, George, 235–6
sex: discrimination based on, 89–90, 55, 333; laws forbidding consensual homosexual, 94, 287, 299, 380n22; Rodwell writing about, 62, 174–5, 349–51, 359; youthful exploration of, 15, 20
sexism: fight against, 249, 317, 323, 328–9; institutionalized, 167–8, 314, 328–9; Rodwell's use of term, 72, 159–60, 379n14. *See also* heterosexism
Shelley, Martha, 131–3, 199, 373n2, 375n18
Sherman, Martin (*Bent*), 205, 214
Shilts, Randy (*And the Band Played On*), 217, 262n4
"Signs of the Times," *Hymnal* column, 90–1, 181
sip-in, 88, 339, 248, 366nn32–5; involvement in, 66, 239–40, 268; planning and execution of, 52–5, 339
Smith, Howard, 103, 110
Smoleff, Samuel, 27–8
Snake Pit raid, 112–13, 372n35
Socialist Workers Party, 165, 250, 319–20
Society for Individual Rights (SIR), 85, 94, 277–8, 356
Spitale, Ray, 181–2, 379n5
Springfield, Dusty, 163
Stafford, Jack, 172–3, 352, 354, 378n36
Stein, Gertrude, 213, 326
stereotyping, gay, 1–2, 72, 119, 284, 374n15; *Boys in the Band* play, 146, 157, 166, 294, 324; porn and, 166, 171, 208; Rodwell's commentary on, 169, 279, 325, 334–8, 351

Stienecker, David, 55–6
Stonewall Inn: Mafia connections with, 86, 89, 101, 106–8, 258–60; police raids of, 100–4, 109–10; Rodwell's complaints about, 86–7, 94, 97, 107, 126, 326–30
Stonewall riots: accounts/testimonies of, 74, 93, 99–108, 268, 288, 370n6; gay liberation impacts, 96, 111–12, 156, 228, 287–8, 308; Gay Power rallying cry, 2, 5, 86, 101–2, 106, 143, 268; folklore about, 107, 238–9, 371n22; HYMN/leafletting work around, 72, 97–9, 105–8, 241, 357; Mafia-cops leaflet, 107–8, 115; news coverage of, 103, 106, 109–10, 146; organizing after, 112–15, 176, 240, 308; OWMB role in/after, 80, 105–6, 111–12, 266; paddy wagons in, 101–3, 109, 111, 113
Sullivan High School: graduation from, 24, 30; Rodwell's time in, 14–16, 19, 23, 173, 352, 403; typing class skills, 13, 25, 29, 84

Tangents, 85, 152
"Tarnished Golden Rule, The" (*QQ Magazine*), 157, 291–5
Teal, Don (*The Gay Militants*), 126, 373n2, 375n18, 377n8
Thorstad, David, 216
Time magazine: coverage of homosexuality, 1–2, 77, 93–4, 133–5, 247, 371n14; notification of protests, 103; picketing building of, 1, 134–5
Timmons, John, 52–3, 268
Toklas, Alice B. 68, 213
Truscott IV, Lucian, 103, 110, 372n29
Turner, Ellen, 223–4, 249

Vector magazine, 84–5
Vietnam War, 47; critiques of US involvement in, 67, 92, 129, 160; draft for, 43, 91; gay soldiers in, 120–2; protests against, 129, 140, 229, 235
Village Voice, 212, 248; coverage of Stonewall riots, 103, 110, 146; notification of protests, 52, 126; OWMB advertising/conflicts with, 60, 62, 65, 69–70, 157, 292; Pride celebration ads/coverage, 140, 146–7, 200
Viñales, Diego, 113
Vincenz, Lilli (*Gay and Proud*), 45, 143, 370n11, 376n43
violence, 72; acceptance of homophobic, 19, 153, 283, 293, 298; activist use of, 158, 287, 296; against Gay people, 33, 172–4, 231–2, 352–4; political, 283; Stonewall riots, 265, 288
Voeller, Bruce, 235, 238

Walker, Alice (*The Color Purple*), 214
Wall Street Journal, 93, 284–5
Washington, DC, 71, 129, 168; gay communities in, 319, 350; gay and lesbian marches on, 227, 231, 262; Mattachine Society in, 44–6, 49, 85, 136, 296, 370n11; picketing White House in, 44–8, 84, 365n21; Pride marches in, 205, 265–6. *See also* Lambda Rising
WBAI radio station, 93, 111, 144, 215
Weinberg, Tom Wilson ("Gay Name Game"), 203, 214, 264, 267
Welz, Carl, 182, 184
West Side Discussion Group, 258, 296, 356–7, 369n9; Rodwell's relationship with, 25, 31, 85, 206–7
WGAY radio station, 68, 75
White, Dan, 210, 262
White, Edmund (*The Beautiful Room Is Empty/A Boy's Own Story*), 102, 105, 218, 223, 371n17
Whitehall Street Induction Center picket, 44, 248, 365n12
Whyte, John, 58
Wicker, Randy, 39, 247–8, 380n9; activism of, 44–6, 53, 66
Wilde, Oscar, 63; Lord Alfred Douglas as lover, 63–4; writings of, 64
Williams, Tennessee, 206
Williamson, Cris ("Portrait"), 214, 226

youth cultism, 175, 355–7